POVERTY AND THE ADEQUACY OF SOCIAL SECURITY IN THE EC

Poverty and the Adequacy of Social Security in the EC

A comparative analysis

Edited by

HERMAN DELEECK
KAREL VAN DEN BOSCH
LIEVE DE LATHOUWER
Centre for Social Policy, University of Antwerp

EUROPASS Research Consortium

Avebury

Aldershot · Brookfield USA · Hong Kong · Singapore · Sydney

Published by
Avebury
Ashgate Publishing Limited
Gower House
Croft Road
Aldershot
Hampshire GU11 3HR
England

Ashgate Publishing Company
Old Post Road
Brookfield
Vermont 05036
USA

A CIP catalogue record for this book is available from the British Library and the US Library of Congress.

Reprinted 1995

ISBN 1 85628 395 X

Printed and bound in Great Britain by Antony Rowe Ltd, Chippenham, Wiltshire

Contents

List of tables

ix

List of figures

Europass collaborators

Belgium: Prof. dr. H. Deleeck (project leader and overall coordinator)
                   B. Cantillon
                   L. De Lathouwer
                   B. Meulemans
                   B. Storms
                   R. Van Dam
                   K. Van Den Bosch
                   Centrum voor Sociaal Beleid, Universiteit Antwerpen (UFSIA)

The Netherlands: R. Muffels (project leader)
                   Prof. dr. J. Berghman (project leader)
                   Prof. dr. ir. A. Kapteyn (project leader)
                   A. Alessie
                   A. De Vries
                   P. Kolkhuis Tanke
                   B. Melenberg
                   H. Vermeulen
                   Instituut voor Sociaal Wetenschappelijk Onderzoek, I.V.A.
                   Subfaculteit Sociale Zekerheidswetenschappen
                   Katholieke Universiteit Brabant, Tilburg

Luxembourg: Prof. dr. G. Schaber (project leader)
                   Prof. dr. P. Dickes
                   Dr. P. Hausman
                   Centre d'Etudes de Populations, de Pauvreté et de Politiques
                   Socio-Economiques, Walferdange

Ireland: Prof. dr. B. Whelan (project leader)
                   Prof. dr. B. Nolan
                   T. Callan
                   D. Hannan
                   Economic and Social Research Institute, Dublin

Lorraine: (France)	Prof. dr. J.-C. Ray (project leader) B. Jeandidier Equipe de recherche pour l'Analyse Dynamique des Effets des Politiques Sociales, Université Nancy II and CNRS
Greece:	Prof. dr. J. Yfantopoulos (project leader) D. Batourdos E. Fagadaki C. Kappi A. Kostaki O. Papaliou C. Papatheodorou National Center of Social Research, Athene
Catalonia: (Spain)	Prof. dr. J. Estivill (project leader) J. Aiguabella J. De la Hoz Gabinet d'Estudis Socials, Barcelona

Foreword

O. Quintin

This work is the result of an international study, conducted between 1985 and 1989 by a working group which united research centres from seven European countries: Belgium, Greece, Spain, France, Ireland, Luxembourg and The Netherlands. The study aimed at contributing to the knowledge about poverty in Europe, and it is for this reason that the Commission of the European Communities, Directorate General V - Employment, Industrial Relations and Social Affairs - has provided financial support, within the framework of its second programme to combat poverty (1985-1989).

Measuring poverty is not only of interest to scientist and statisticians: it is also of political importance for decision-makers and social actors in the Member States and the Community. Statistical research provides them with useful indicators of the extent of certain situations, the trends in their development, and the effects of actual policies.

Undoubtedly the improvement of knowledge concerning the fight against poverty cannot be limited to the production of statistical series, and even less to statistical series based on a monetary definition of poverty only. The Commission has taken note of the fact that each definition and each measure of poverty are as much political as they are scientific, and it it aware of the precision and the carefulness of the analyses that have been proposed, particularly when the sources of the data that are utilised are not of the same quality in each country. Also, the Commission is trying to promote studies in which the multidimensional nature of social exclusion is recognized.

In view of the above, the importance of the present study is threefold.

In the first place, the authors have utilised and evaluated five different approaches to the definition of the poverty line, and their analyses make it possible to specify the advantages and drawbacks, even if the methods that have been studied have all in common that they take only the financial aspect of poverty into account.

In the second place, the authors have tried to carry out a dynamic analysis of poverty, by using the panel method of reinterviewing the same sample of households at regular intervals. This dynamic analysis could not be done for all countries, but the results suggest that the way insecurity of subsistence develops over time is an important characteristic of our societies: one part of the population experiences fluctuations in its financial situation, and finds itself, at certain moments, in income poverty; this implies that the poor are neither a homogeneous entity, nor a social group that is completely marginalised with respect to the rest of the population.

Finally, the authors have studied the transfers that provide social protection, with the aim of evaluating their effectiveness in solving the problem of income poverty. The results vary by country, and sometimes they need to be refined, in particular in those instances where the quality of the survey data is weak. Nevertheless, they contribute to the knowledge about the effects of social protection.

We are aware of the difficulties of all international research, and we owe our gratitude to the authors for their collaborative effort.

Within the limits of its resources, the Commission intends to develop similar collaborations, which presuppose the active support of national authorities and researchers: the building of Europe and the fight against poverty come about also through the encouragement of such partnerships for the improvement of knowledge.

O. QUINTIN
Head of Division
Commission of the
European Communities
Directorate General V

Preface

This report is the result of a collaborative research project started in 1985 by seven research groups in as many countries of the European Community. It was financed for one half by the Commission of the E.C. (D.G.V), within the framework of the second Community Action Programme to Combat Poverty; the other half was provided by national governments. In this age of abbreviations we have christened the research consortium and the project 'EUROPASS': European Research On Poverty And Social Security. From the start, the study aimed at both methodological and substantive results.

Substantive research issues were the number of poor ([1]) in each country, the social groups at high risk of poverty and the impact of social security transfers. Not the financial resources available for social protection (welfare effort) were studied, but rather the social results that are in fact achieved (welfare outcomes). The goal was an evaluation of the adequacy of the social security system, using social subsistence minima by type of household as standards.

Methodologically, five different methods to derive poverty lines were applied and evaluated. By using panel surveys of households (in which the same sample of households is re-interviewed at regular intervals), duration and change of poverty status could be measured, providing an important new perspective on the extent of poverty.

The project was comparative. Despite the diverse institutional structures of social security in the countries concerned, we worked with standardized concepts and questionnaires, with the same methods and within the same analytical framework. On the basis of these common instruments, each research group has collected its data (using sample surveys of households) and has analysed them. The results were then compiled into comparative tables. Besides this comparative report there are also national reports for each country (see bibliography).

The national research groups are responsible for the results of their own country. The Centre for Social Policy (University of Antwerp) designed the analytical framework, compiled the comparative tables, and drafted the comparative report. This report is approved by all partners in the research project.

What are the most important results of this study?
- several estimates of the number of poor, by strict and by more generous standards;
- an evaluation of the adequacy of social security transfers, with the following result: Greece and Catalonia: limited resources and/or low efficiency (large share of transfers to non-poor), therefore low effectiveness (many are left in poverty); Ireland: more resources, but very high needs, high efficiency, high effectiveness; Benelux and Lorraine: ample resources, high effectiveness;
- it has been shown that it is possible to set up an internationally comparative system of social (result) indicators;
- an evaluation of poverty lines, i.c. two subjective ones (socially realistic, but unstable) and a statistical or relative poverty line (stable, but arbitrary, and with an equivalence scale that is problematic (2);
- some longitudinal results on poverty, which show the importance, but also the difficulty of panel analysis;
- an empirical perspective on the domain of European social policy, esp. social security transfers: it appears that, besides legal and institutional differences, there is also great diversity as regards social and socio-demographic circumstances, as well as regards the adequacy of social security.

These results have important implications for European social policy. To advance the convergence of social protection schemes, more mutual exchange of information is needed, not only of the legal forms, but certainly also of their actual operation and results. Comparative analysis could provide better knowledge on the determinants of the adequacy of social security. It would be a significant step forward for social policy analysis (and practice) if the Commission of the E.C. would in all member countries initiate a survey with a standardized questionnaire, designed to provide a system of social indicators, enabling the Commission (and others) to monitor the evolution of social protection in Europe.

A side effect of this study, but an important one, is that at several locations in Europe profound and concrete research activities have been started, which are undoubtedly a lasting achievement. Furthermore, strong social as well as scientific ties have been established between researchers across Europe. This, too, is a step towards European integration. The coordinator wants to express his gratitude to all participants for the spirit of cooperation and scholarly dedication in which this project has been conducted.

H. DELEECK
Coordinator

Acknowledgements

The research project which is reported in this book has been realised with financial support from the Commission of the European Communities, Directorate General V, within the framework of the second Community Action Programme to Combat Poverty. Additional finance was provided by the governments of the Member States involved.

Only the authors are responsible for the views and opinions expressed in this book, which do not necessarily reflect those of the Commission or the national governments.

We gratefully acknowledge the help, in word and deed, provided by O. Quintin (DG-V) and by L. Barreiros (Eurostat) and their collaborators. We also thank those persons whose efforts made this project possible, the late Prof. G. Veldkamp, L. Lamers, L. Cryns and R. Draperie.

The publication of this book was made possible by a generous subsidy from the University of Antwerp (UFSIA).

Many thanks are due to the secretarial staff of the Department of Sociology and Social Policy, in particular to I. Van Zele, who has typed many earlier versions of this work. She is also to be credited for efficiently editing the final manuscript into camera-ready-copy.

Notes

(1) The concept of poverty is politically and emotionally charged, and therefore in many senses ambiguous; here it has a precise meaning, referring to households with an income below a certain (high or low) minimum level. Instead of poverty, the term insecurity of the means of subsistence is sometimes used, to indicate situations that are less harsh.

(2) Cf. the comment by R. Haveman in Eurostat, *Analysing Poverty in the European Community*, Eurostat News, nr. 1, 1990, p. 459-467.

1 Introduction: Concepts, methods and data

1.1. Context and aims of the project

In its report on the first Community Programme to Combat Poverty, the Commission of the EC (1981) concluded that an effort was needed "to collect adequate and comparable statistics on each dimension of poverty so that progress in combatting can be monitored on a regular basis." (p. 41). It had six more specific recommendations:
- collection of more and better data on net income of the low income groups, including the composition of net income according to sources (including types of public and private transfer payments);
- data should refer to the same year, should be collected at regular intervals and should become available in a short time span;
- data should contain the main characteristics of households so that breakdowns to identify groups with high poverty risk can be made;
- data should be roughly consistent with the aggregate income figures of the national accounts;
- data should be based on the same definition of net income, the same year and the same definition of household (income unit);
- data should also contain some information on assets, consumer durables and debts of household (see also Roche, 1984, p. 98).

For the second poverty programme it was suggested that it should comprise, among others, a special study into "the development of indicators to measure income poverty and poverty of living conditions on a common European base" (Roche, 1984, p. 128).

The research project which is reported here was part of the Second European Action Programme to Combat Poverty. It constituted an effort to work towards the goal, set by the Commission, of adequate and comparable statistics on poverty in the EC. Although not all specific recommendations are realized to the same degree, in other respects (notably the panel approach) it goes beyond these.

More specifically, the aims of this research project are the following:
1) to establish in a comparative way the number of poor households in each country/region and to identify social groups at high risk of poverty;
2) to assess the adequacy of social security, in the sense of guaranteeing a minimum income;
3) to incorporate all results in a standardized system of social indicators;
4) to develop and evaluate methods of measurement of poverty;
5) to distinguish between temporary and longer-term poverty by means of the panel method.

The comparative set of social indicators would enable policymakers to monitor changes in the domains of poverty and social security. It aims at providing reliable and systematic information to policy-makers and to the broad public, on the European level as well as in the member states, to stimulate political debate on these topics and to help formulating better policies in these domains.

The report has the following contents. The remainder of this introduction is devoted to some methodological issues and to a description of the data. Next, the first part presents descriptive indicators of the distribution of income and social transfers over deciles of disposable income as well as over deciles of standardized income. Although this part is not directly concerned with poverty, it is very relevant for what follows, because an overall picture of the distribution of income and social security is necessary for an understanding of poverty and the adequacy of social security. Nevertheless, attention is somewhat focused on the bottom parts of the distributions. The second part of the report deals with the poverty lines, the numbers of households in poverty and the social distribution of poverty. This part also contains some rather limited results on deprivation. The third part is concerned with the adequacy of social security, understood as a minimum income protection. Results of panel-analyses for five countries are presented in the fourth part. The final part summarizes and concludes.

1.2. Definition and measurement of poverty

Poverty, an ambiguous notion

Essentially poverty is an ambiguous notion. It is relative, gradual, multi-dimensional and thus difficult to define and to register.

Poverty is relative in time and space. What kinds of living situations are described as poverty, depends on the social and economic circumstances and the level of prosperity of a society at a certain moment. Thus, it is not possible to describe poverty in a concrete way, once and for all, in an absolute sense. However, emphasizing the relative character of poverty has a threefold danger: (a) inflation of the number of poor due to a very generous concept, (b) confusion between poverty and inequality; (c) reduction of poverty to a macro-statistical phenomenon.

Poverty seems to be gradual. One cannot say that a household is either poor or not-poor ([1]). One can at least make a distinction between households that find themselves in financial insecurity, but are not (yet) excluded from the standard way of life, the very poor who live in a permanent state of need, and the people on, or outside, the margins of society, such as the homeless.

Poverty is multi-dimensional. Poverty is not restricted to one dimension, e.g. income, but it manifests itself in all domains of life, such as housing, education, health. Poverty can be seen as a general (threat of) non-participation in the important values of society. Nevertheless income plays a crucial role in this, and perhaps is the single most valid indicator of poverty.

Finally there is the duration of poverty: being poor for a few months is less serious than being poor for a several years. One can distinguish between short-term poverty (due to a sudden loss of income) and long-term or more structural poverty (due to a permanently weak social and economic position of the household). The introduction of the longitudinal perspective in this research project by means of the panel method therefore enables us to get a better understanding of the nature, the causes and the persistence of poverty.

Because of these characteristics of poverty, it is not possible to define one unique and valid poverty line, below which all households are undeniably poor. Each possible level of a poverty line represents a more or less arbitrary choice, as to where, in the gradual continuum from getting along easily to a state of dire need, one wants to draw the line.

From a scientific point of view, different poverty lines can be applied and evaluated. The number of poor depends on the definition used and the method of measurement applied. From a policy point of view, research is not able to produce one single valid criterion for judgement. Nevertheless, policymakers need to have a poverty line as a guiding instrument in the political debate. It should be clear that an operational poverty line in a national or international perspective always presupposes a consensus or political (reasonable) convention on the level of minimum income.

Types of poverty lines

A poverty line is a criterion or standard by which a researcher can decide in empirical research whether a certain household is poor or not. But because the concept of poverty is ambiguous, a poverty line can be drawn in several ways and at several levels. Various methods have been proposed to derive the poverty line. Five different types can be distinguished.

a) *The budget method.* By this method the researcher or other expert selects a basket of goods and services deemed necessary, the total cost of which is the poverty line. This method is officially used in the USA (since 1964) and in West-Germany. In the USA only a food packet is composed, and the cost of this packet is multiplied by a coefficient of three to derive the poverty line (used by the American Social Security Administration). In West-Germany the budget method is used to set the level of the minimum income in social assistance (Bundessozialhilfe).

The advantage of this method is that it is in principle straightforward (first defining a certain minimum standard of living, then determining the level of resources needed) and that it

3

keeps close to the notion of absolute poverty. The disadvantage is that the contents of the baskets are in many senses arbitrary.

b) *The subjective method* works with estimations by the populations itself (obtained in surveys) about the minimum income level.

The most important advantage of this method is that the level of the poverty line is not fixed by experts (in a more or less arbitrary way), but defined by society itself. The subjective method is therefore a socially realistic method. In most cases, the subjective method produces poverty lines at a rather high level. Furthermore the poverty lines fluctuate over time depending on changes in the social reference group (e.g. due to an increase in the overall living standard of the elderly, they respond with a higher necessary minimum income) and on the period of reference (e.g. in a period of crisis aspirations might decline). Given the wide variations in economic and social circumstances between regions and countries, the subjective poverty lines are less suitable for comparative purposes across time and space. This method has been developed independently by Kapteyn, Van Praag and others at the Universities of Leyden and Tilburg (the SPL-method) and Deleeck at the Centre for Social Policy, University of Antwerp (CSP-line). The basic ideas are the same, but the operationalization is different.

c) *The statistical or relative method* defines the poverty line in relation to (as a % of) a macro-economic indicator, for instance national income per capita, average or median available household income or household equivalent income. This method is mostly used in international comparative studies, such as OECD, 1976; Beckerman, 1979; Commission of the EC, 1981; O'Higgins and Jenkins, 1990; Eurostat, 1990. Recognizing that poverty is relative, the statistical approach is used to obtain figures on poverty that are at least roughly comparable. (Similar considerations apply to a study of poverty in one country over longer periods of time.)

The disadvantage of this method is that the choice of the level and the equivalence scale of a statistical or relative poverty line is largely arbitrary. Some regard relative poverty lines as (crude) measures of income inequality, rather than poverty. The extent, but in particular the social distribution of poverty, is strongly influenced by the equivalence scale. If it is more flat the poverty risk for large households is relatively small. If the equivalence scale is steep, as the one currently recommended by OECD (1982), poverty appears to be more concentrated with large households.

The advantage is that with this type of poverty line, one is able to measure reliably changes and differences in the size and the composition of the poor (or rather low income groups). It yields more or less comparable poverty lines for countries with different levels of economic and social development. Therefore it seems to be more suitable for international comparative studies. Another advantage of the relative method is that it is easy to perform sensitivity analyses: to see to what extent the results depend on the particular level or equivalence scale of the poverty line used. If the results remain the same across a range of (relative) poverty lines, one can have more confidence in the conclusions reached. For an example of this approach, see Callan a.o. (1989, pp. 58-81).

d) *The legal or political method* takes a minimum income that is set by social security or tax regulations as the poverty line. Generally, the minimum guaranteed income in social assistance is used.

The legal poverty line has the advantage that it is exact, that it gives a more absolute poverty line and that it appears to be politically validated. However, the legal minimum is not only a reflection of what society defines as its guaranteed minimum, but also the result of other considerations, such as the government budget and the assumed effect on the labour market, which may play a (quite legitimate) role. The method presupposes what is often a subject of debate and research, namely that the level of the guaranteed minimum income is sufficient to stay out of poverty. Further more, many countries do not have a legal guaranteed minimum income, and in others its function within the whole of social security (and consequently its level) often varies significantly.

e) *Deprivation standards or indices* attempt to measure poverty through the non-possession of a number of goods, non-participation in certain activities and non-use of certain services (e.g. quality of food, clothing and dwelling, household appliances, use of health and educational facilities).
This method was pioneered by Townsend (1979) (objective deprivation: index composed of a number of goods and services) and developed and improved by Mack and Lansley (1985) (subjective deprivation: involuntarily not possessing goods and services which at least 50% of the population regards as necessary). The advantage of this method is that it reflects the multi-dimensional aspect of poverty. The disadvantage is that where exactly one draws the poverty line and how the choice of items is made, remains arbitrary. Furthermore, analysis of the results is complex and international comparability is not evident.

Poverty measures

Given a certain poverty line, there are several ways to express the total extent of poverty. Still the most popular overall measure of poverty is the "headcount", the number of poor persons or households. This measure has been criticized, notably by Sen (1976), because it takes no account of how far below the poverty line poor households actually are. Sen has devised a new poverty measure, which does not have the disadvantages of the "headcount". Following him, several authors have proposed alternative aggregate poverty measures (reviewed in Foster, 1984 and also in Hagenaars, 1987). Although we regard these criticisms as quite justified in theory, we will rely on the number of poor households as our most important indicator of the extent of poverty. This indicator has the important advantage that it is easily interpretable for the non-expert, even for the layman, which is not the case for the more sophisticated poverty measures. Moreover, the conclusions will probably very seldom be different. The results are more likely to be sensitive to the choice of the poverty line.

In addition to the "headcount", in this report the average poverty-gap or shortfall is used (the relative distance between the income of the poor and the poverty line), as well as the aggregate poverty gap (the total amount needed, theoretically, to raise the incomes of all poor households to the level of the poverty line).

Certainly as important as the overall extent of poverty is the social distribution of poverty. To describe this, we use three measures: 1) the poverty risk: the percentage of all households within a certain social category that are poor; 2) relative poverty risk: the poverty risk in a certain social category relative to the poverty risk in the whole sample; and

5

3) the composition of the poor: the share of a certain social category within the total number of poor.

1.3. The income concept

As explained above, poverty is measured by comparing total household income to an income poverty line. The most common income concept in poverty research, which is also used here, is *disposable money household income*. This is defined as income from work and property, plus social security cash transfers and minus income tax and social security contributions. Disposable income is the income concept most directly relevant to the spending power or command over resources, which determine a household's standard of living at a certain moment. However, income and benefits in kind (health, education, imputed rent from owner occupation of the house, use of company car etc.), are not included. An argument has been made, notably by Townsend (1979), for a broader-based income concept, which would include some of these items, as well as others. Inclusion of these items leads one into difficult problems of valuation, however.

In some cases, there are deviations from the concept of disposable household income. The most important of these is that in Lorraine income after taxes could not be measured. Neither could it be estimated from the income before taxes because of the complexity of the French tax system. Attempts to do this failed to agree with reality. Therefore all results on income for *Lorraine* refer to *income before taxes*. In Belgium income from movable assets was not asked for in the survey. This is anyway a notoriously underreported source of income in most socio-economic surveys.

To make incomes equivalent across countries in terms of spending power, *purchasing power parities* for household consumption, have been used, as official exchange rates do not always reflect differences in prices of consumer goods. All amounts are recalculated into ECU of January 1, 1988 by means of consumer price index figures for the various countries, the purchasing power parities with the Belgian Franc and the exchange rate Belgian Franc-ECU ([2]).

In this report all amounts are expressed *in monthly amounts*. In many countries, most incomes (wages as well as benefits) are paid out once a month, so that the month is the natural accounting period. In these cases, the amount asked for is the amount received in the current or last month. In some countries, notably Lorraine and Luxembourg, and for some sources of income (income from assets, for instance) the month is not the most appropriate accounting period, and then the receipts over a longer (year) or shorter period were asked. In some cases, the respondent could choose the period to which the amount referred. All amounts were then recalculated to monthly amounts. For more detailed information, we refer to the methodological appendices.

The recipient unit in this research project is the *household*. It is clear that the individual is not a suitable unit, because many people (notably children) share in the income / consumption of a wider unit. But there might be discussion whether the family (a couple or a single adult with or without dependend children) or the household is the most appropriate unit to use in analyzing poverty. A household is defined, somewhat loosely, as a group of related or unrelated individuals who live together under one roof, and generally eat together. The crucial question for poverty research is to which extent all members of the household share in the same level of economic welfare. This is a very difficult question, not only because income transfers within the household are difficult to observe, but also because transfers in kind of goods and services (food, transport) and the common use of rooms and amenities (television, washing-machine) are important determinants of the real living standard of individuals. The Luxembourg and Nancy research groups have tried to measure income transfers and differences in living standards within the household (see for instance: Jeandidier a.o., 1988; Dickes, 1988; Ray, 1989). Here we assume, however, that all members of a household share the same level of economic welfare.

Which persons in each concrete situation belong to which household is a decision that is made in the field, and that is generally left to the persons concerned themselves. There exist differences, between countries, though, in the treatment of *students*. In most countries, students that are financially dependent on their parents and return home to their parents regularly at week-ends and during the holidays are considered to be members of their parent's household. In The Netherlands and Lorraine, however, they are assumed to form seperate households on their own.

1.4. Standardized income and equivalence scales

In part I of the report, which treats the distribution of social benefits over income categories, *equivalent* or *standardized household income* is used in addition to disposable income. Although disposable income is a correct index of the command over resources of a household, it is obvious that a given amount of income represents quite different levels of need satisfaction or economic welfare for a family of four persons and for a single person. Therefore a distribution of social benefits over disposable income categories could be misleading if it is interpreted in terms of the equity of the distribution. If a large part of the benefits would not accrue to the lowest deciles, this would not necessarily mean that they would not go to those most in need. A large household in the third or fourth decile may well be worse off than a small household in the bottom decile of disposable income.

A crude way to take this into account would be to calculate income per capita for each household. But this seems to go too far. A four person household will not need four times as much as a single person to be as well off. There are probably substantial economies of scale due to the sharing of rooms, more efficient use of durable goods, etc. Moreover, children need less than adults. Therefore incomes of different kinds of household are usually made comparable or equivalent by the application of an *equivalence scale*. This is a series of index numbers, which vary by household type, by which household income is deflated into "real" income units. (A good introduction into the methodology is Deaton and Muellbauer, 1980; an overview of various methods and scales is given by Whiteford, 1985; Buhmann a.o., 1988 have applied a range of equivalence scales to the income distributions of several countries.)

The 'mapping' of income into economic welfare or satisfaction of needs may of course be affected by a large number of variables, among which are the age, sex and health of the household members, the region where the household is located and many others. The most important variable, however, and often the only one taken account of in empirical applications, is household size. There is in fact an enormous literature on equivalence scales, which we will not go into here. It suffices to say that so far no consensus has emerged on a particular equivalence scale.

Scales may be defined by experts, often for statistical purposes, sometimes on the basis of minimum budgets, or taken from the scales implicit in the structure of social benefits. Equivalence scales may also be derived empirically from survey data on consumer spending or respondent's subjective assessment of the adequacy of income. In the latter case the scales itself are an empirical finding, and not the result of expert judgment. But in either case, their use for the measurement of poverty or welfare always constitutes in a certain sense a normative choice.

For this report we have chosen the scale used by the OECD (1976), which is fairly close to the geometric mean derived from a number of equivalence scales in international research (see Whiteford, 1985, p. 109). The scale is as follows: single person: 0.666; two-person household: 1.00; three-person household: 1.25; four-person household: 1.45; five-person household: 1.60; larger households: +0.15 for every extra person. Dividing the disposable income of each household by the appropriate equivalence factor we get household standardized or equivalent income. This is used as an indicator of the real living standard or the level of economic welfare of a household. In the text equivalent income, standardized income and economic welfare are used as synonyms.

The choice of the 0.666-1.0-1.25 scale implies that the equivalence scale used in part I is different from the one incorporated in the EC-relative poverty line, used in the other parts. The EC-poverty line has been chosen in order to have some continuity with the work done in the first EC Programme to Combat Poverty, as well as some comparability with the results of O'Higgins and Jenkins (1990). But this does not imply that we consider the "EC" scale (1.0-0.7-0.5) to be the best one. Besides, an equivalence scale that is appropriate at the level of the poverty line, is not necessarily an appropriate one at other levels of income.

1.5. Duration of poverty and the panel approach

Most poverty research until now, at least in Europe, has measured poverty on the basis of cross-sectional surveys. In that way, it is possible to assess the extent and social distribution of poverty at one moment in time. However, the dynamic aspect of poverty is lost. For some households poverty may be a persistent condition, for others it may be only a temporary one. It does not become clear which events or circumstances cause people to fall into poverty. One might even argue that in cross-sectional surveys the extent of poverty is overestimated, because some households are counted as poor because of temporary income fluctuations, which they are easily able to bridge over, without an important fall in their standard of living.

To catch the dynamic aspect of poverty, longitudinal household data are necessary, which can only be provided by panel surveys. In panel surveys, persons are followed over time and information is gathered about them at regular intervals (most often each year). Either the person itself is interviewed, or a reference or contact person in the household. Persons are followed, and not households, because households are not stable across time, and it has been proven to be very difficult to define longitudinal households. However, because the household (or the family) is the basic unit of observation in research into poverty and economic welfare, in each wave the income and characteristics of the complete household in which a panel-person lives are measured.

Children born of panel members become panel members themselves, while persons who die or emigrate naturally are no longer part of the sample. As a consequence, the panel adequately reflects the changes that take place in the population at large, except for immigration. Therefore, with proper adjustment by weights, the panel sample remains representative with respect to all persons and households in the population at each survey-moment, with the exception of those persons who have immigrated after the initial sample was drawn.

The longest running example of this kind of panel is the Panel Study of Income Dynamics (PSID), organized by the ISR, University of Michigan, which started in 1968 with a sample of USA households. Its results have shown that there is indeed considerable mobility among the poor. However, as Bane and Ellwood (1986) have stressed, the poor are not homogeneous in this regard: many persons experience fairly short poverty spells, but many others are in poverty for a very long time. Moreover, the characteristics of these two groups do not appear to be the same.

In this project the scope for panel-analyses was rather limited by the availability of data. Only two waves were available for Belgium, Ireland, Lorraine, Luxembourg and The Netherlands, while Greece and Catalonia joined the project later, and it was not feasible for them to organize two waves in the short period left. Moreover, it takes much more time to construct a panel data-base than a corresponding cross-sectional data-base, as all teams who had a second wave discovered. Nevertheless, the results in this report are important, as they are the first comparative results on the duration of poverty and the mobility of the poor in Europe.

1.6. Data

The data are from *large-scale household surveys* in the several countries or regions. In most cases the surveys are in fact panel surveys of households. For Belgium, Ireland, Lorraine, Luxembourg and The Netherlands two waves have been used. Because Catalonia and Greece entered the project some years after its inception, they were able to realize only one wave.

The questionnaires were mainly concerned with the socio-demographic characteristics of the household and its members (including labour-market characteristics), and the various incomes received through earnings, social security and other sources. In addition, questions were asked about the subjective appreciation of income and the possession of some life-style indicators. Work has been done to coordinate the questionnaires. The formulations of key questions has been adapted. Much effort has been spent on making sure that in all countries the same concepts and the same methods have been used. More detailed information on this is given in Appendix 3.

The years and sizes of the surveys are given in Table 1.1. For more detailed information on the surveys (sampling, field work, reweighting etc.) the reader is referred to the full report.

For the *cross-country comparisons*, generally *the results of only one year* for each country were used. This was done in order to keep the analysis manageable, and because, as will become clear below, the differences between the results of two waves are generally small. The teams from The Netherlands and Lorraine made it clear that they preferred their second-wave data to be used for cross-country comparisons, mainly because of larger sample sizes in those waves. For the same reason, the Irish research team expressed more trust in the first-wave results. Luxembourg had no preference, but second-wave data have been used here, because there was more complete information for this wave. For Belgium, we rely on the first wave, because this is closer in time to the waves used for the other Benelux-countries.

Table 1.1
Overview of surveys

	First wave		Second wave	
	year	size of sample*	year	size of sample*
Belgium	1985	6471	1988	3779
The Netherlands	1985	3405	1986	4480
Luxembourg	1985	2013	1986	1793
Lorraine	1985	715	1986	2092
Ireland	1987	3294	1989	947
Catalonia	1988	2976		
Greece	1988	2958		

* Number of households in sample. Only households for which poverty-status could be established (which implies full income information) have been counted.

So the years used for cross-country comparisons are as follows: Belgium: 1985; Lorraine: 1986; Luxembourg: 1986; The Netherlands: 1986; Ireland: 1987; Catalonia: 1988; Greece: 1988. This implies that there is only one year difference between Belgium on the one hand and the other Benelux countries and Lorraine on the other. Between these countries and Ireland, Greece and Catalonia there is a gap of at most three years. But, as we will see, the differences between the "85-86" and the "87-88" group of countries are so large that the comparative conclusions are unlikely to be affected by the differences in the years of the surveys.

1.7. A system of social indicators

One of the preconditions to be able to produce comparable figures is to have a common framework for analysis. All reporting of results (national and comparative) within this research project has been done according to a standardized system of social indicators.

The system of social indicators is presented below:

PART A: **INDICATORS OF THE DISTRIBUTION OF EARNINGS AND SOCIAL SECURITY BENEFITS (DESCRIPITVE INDICATORS)**

I. Distribution by household disposable income deciles

1. Distribution of disposable income over income deciles (and income inequality)
2. Socio-demographic composition of income deciles
3. Position of households receiving benefits in the income distribution
4. Level of benefits over income deciles
5. Distribution of income from labour and of social security benefits over deciles

II. Distribution by household standardized income deciles

PART B: **INDICATORS OF POVERTY AND THE ADEQUACY OF SOCIAL SECURITY (RESULT INDICATORS)**

I. Indicators of poverty

1. Poverty lines (subjective standards, statistical standard, legal standard)
2. Number of poor households
   - based on income standards (objective insecurity)
   - based on the appreciation of income (self-report insecurity)
3. The social distribution of poverty
4. Possession of life-style indicators among insecure/secure households

II. Adequacy of social security

1. Number of poor households before and after social security payments
2. The poverty-gap

PART C: **DYNAMIC RESULTS ON POVERTY: POVERTY IN PANEL PERSPECTIVE**

11

Notes

(¹)   Some researchers, notably Townsend, have maintained that this is in fact the case, but their empirical evidence is not conclusive.

(²)   The "detour" via the Belgian Franc was necessary because there is no purchasing power parity associated with the ECU itself (as there is no country in which consumer goods are paid for in ECU). The choice of the Belgian Franc is of course purely arbitrary. (See appendix 2 for a more detailed description of the procedure followed.) Another choice would have produced nominally different amounts, which would stand in the same proportion to each other.

2 Indicators of the distribution of income and social transfers

2.1. Average level of income

As has been noted in the introduction, for the purposes of this report *disposable household income*, is the most relevant income concept. As official exchange rates do not always reflect differences in prices of household consumer goods, purchasing power parities ([1]) have been used to get comparable results across countries.

Table 2.1
Average disposable income of households and per head of population
monthly amounts in ECU, in prices of Jan. 1988

	Using purchasing power parities		Using official exchange rates	
	Households	Heads	Households	Heads
Greece	1013	329	676	220
Ireland	1058	308	1011	295
Catalonia	1619	469	1149	333
Belgium	1299	459	1299	459
Netherlands	1319	489	1291	478
Lorraine*	1331	477	1388	497
Luxembourg	1853	662	1678	599

* In Lorraine, income is measured *before* taxes.

Because the real living standard of a household is determined not only by its disposable income but also by the level of needs, in particular by the number of household members, *standardized (equivalent)* household income is used as an indicator of economic welfare. The equivalence scale applied is: 0.666, 1.00, 1.25, 1.45, 1.60 for households composed of one, two, three, four and five persons respectively; for each additional person 0.15 is added.

On the basis of average disposable household income, in purchasing power equivalent units, we can identify three groups of countries: the poorer ones: Greece and Ireland; the middle income countries: Belgium, The Netherlands and Lorraine, and the rich countries: Catalonia and Luxembourg. This is according to expectations, except for the position of Catalonia, which is rather surprising. Using official exchange rates, average household income in Catalonia is *below* that of the Benelux-countries. The purchasing power parity therefore plays a crucial role, and it is possible that the purchasing power parity for the whole of Spain, which has been used because of lack of more detailed information, is not the appropriate one for Catalonia. Part of the explanation is also that households in Catalonia tend to be larger and to include more earners than Benelux households. Average disposable income per head of the population in Catalonia is on the level of Belgium and Lorraine.

2.2. Income inequality

In this report deciles are used to indicate the inequality of the distribution of income and to show the relationship of income position with other characteristics of households, in particular the sources of income. Deciles are formed by ranking all households by the size of their disposable income. This distribution is devided into ten equal parts called deciles. The first decile includes the 10% group of households with the smallest amounts of income, the second decile the next 10% group, ... until the tenth decile which contains the households with the largest incomes.

There are several methods to express total income inequality in one number. Two of the more common indices are those of Gini and Theil. In table 2.2 these are given for the most representative years. Both coëfficients produce the same ranking of countries. Income inequality is greatest by far in Greece. In Ireland, the country which ranks second, income inequality is already considerably smaller. The least income inequality is found in the Benelux-countries, especially in Belgium [2].

Table 2.2
Income inequality of household disposable income,
as measured by the Gini and Theil-coëfficients

	Theil	Gini
Greece, 1988	0.335	0.409
Ireland, 1987	0.233	0.379
Catalonia, 1988	0.189	0.339
Belgium, 1985	0.120	0.277
Netherlands, 1986	0.138	0.292
Lorraine, 1986	0.144	0.319
Luxembourg, 1986	0.130	0.284

2.3. Demographic structure

There are some significant differences between countries as regards demographic structure. Household size is much higher in Catalonia and Ireland than in the other countries. In Ireland this is mainly due to the relatively large number of families with three children or more, which is reflected in the high number of children averaged over all households. In Catalonia it happens more often that several adults live together. This is because many persons marry late, and tend to live with their parents until they marry.

Table 2.3
Demographic characteristics

	average size of households	average number of children across all households	percent single non-elderly adults	percent of households with head 65 or over
Greece, 1988	3,08	0,83	5,6	19,9
Ireland, 1987	3,58	1,35	6,5	14,5
Catalonia, 1988	3,45	0,69 *	5,3	17,4
Belgium, 1985	2,83	0,84	7,2	20,7
Netherlands, 1986	2,70	0,80	14,7	15,9
Lorraine, 1986	2,88	0,89	8,8	19,5
Luxembourg, 1986	2,73	0,67	8,8	21,9

* Only persons of 16 years or younger.

Ireland and The Netherlands are characterized by a relatively low proportion of households headed by elderly persons; The Netherlands also by a large proportion of single non-elderly people.

2.4. Demographic structure and the income distribution

The demographic characteristics of a household are strongly related to its position in the income distribution. In all countries the *average size of households* increases as income level rises.

Generally, in the tenth decile the average size of households is 2.5 to 3.5 times as large as in the first decile. Looking at the individual countries, we find that in the Benelux-countries and Lorraine the patterns are rather similar. But in Greece and Catalonia, households in the bottom deciles are on average considerably larger than in the Benelux-countries. In Ireland, on the other hand, average household size in the lowest deciles does not exceed that of the Benelux-countries, and the largest differences are found in the middle and higher deciles.

The finding that there is a positive correlation between household size and decile number, does not imply that large households tend to be better off than small households. After taking into account the greater needs of larger households, by using standardized deciles, we find that there is virtually no relation between household size and the position in the

15

income distribution. Only in Belgium, Luxembourg and Catalonia are households in the bottom quintile somewhat smaller than average.

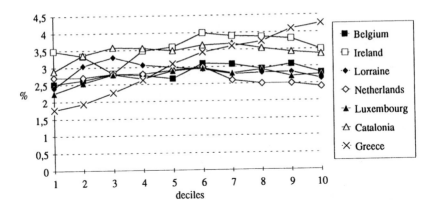

Figure 2.1 Average size of household by standardized income deciles

Table 2.4
Percentage of all children in the bottom part of standardized and unstandardized income distribution of household income

| | percent of children by standardized income: | | percent of children by unstandardized income: | |
	in bottom quintile	in bottom and 2nd quintiles	in bottom quintile	in bottom and 2nd quintiles
Greece, 1988	5,8	15,8	8,8	25,5
Ireland, 1987	24,4	42,5	5,1	24,1
Catalonia, 1988	22,2	49,0	10,0	34,3
Belgium, 1985	18,5	40,4	3,5	15,4
Netherlands, 1986	26,3	51,3	5,0	22,5
Lorraine, 1986	20,5	47,2	5,1	20,4
Luxembourg, 1986	20,3	44,8	4,8	19,3

Strongly linked to the household size is of course *the number of children* (figure 2.2). The results refer to *dependent* children. These are persons who are 15 years or younger, or are 16 years or over and in full-time education, and are living in their parent's (or guardian's) household. However, in the Catalonian survey only persons under 16 years are regarded as children. The averages by decile are calculated over all households, including those without children.

We generally find that, from the lowest decile upwards, the average number of children strongly increases till the fifth or sixth decile, and then levels off. Only in Belgium do we find more children in the highest deciles than in the middle deciles, while in Ireland and The Netherlands the number of children falls off towards the highest income groups. The lowest deciles contain more children in Catalonia and Greece, than in the other countries.

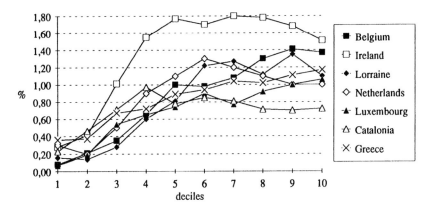

Figure 2.2   Average number of children per household over income deciles

Again, these results should not be taken to imply that children tend to live in households that are relatively well-off. After taking needs into account by standardizing, we find that children are fairly evenly distributed over the deciles, or are even somewhat concentrated in the lower deciles (figure 2.3). In particular in Ireland and The Netherlands a larger than proportionate number of children live in the bottom quintile of economic welfare (table 2.4).

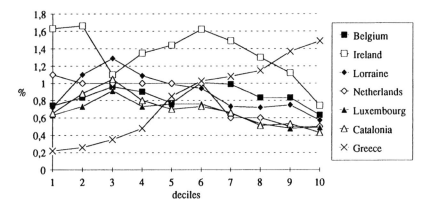

Figure 2.3   Average number of children per household by standardized income deciles

Contrary to the number of children, the percentage of *households with an elderly head* falls as we move up the disposable income distribution. In the Benelux-countries, Lorraine and Catalonia about half of all households with an elderly head are in the bottom income quintile. In fact, in most countries (except The Netherlands, due to its low overall number of elderly heads of households) these households form the majority in the lowest decile or quintile. In Greece and Ireland, on the other hand, only one-third of all elderly heads of households are in the bottom quintile and relatively many in the middle and higher deciles.

As can be seen in table 2.5 and figure 2.4, the effect of standardization on the distribution of elderly heads is the opposite of its effect on the distribution of children: the elderly tend to move to higher deciles through standardization. Still, they remain clearly concentrated in the lower income groups, except in Ireland, where elderly heads of households are much *less* than proportionally represented in the bottom quintile of economic welfare. Perhaps they are "pushed upwards" by large households with a non-elderly head.

Table 2.5
Percentage of households with an elderly head in lower parts of
standardized and unstandardized distributions of household income

| | percent of households with an elderly head: | | | |
| | by standardized income: | | by unstandardized income: | |
	in bottom quintile	in bottom and 2nd quintiles	in bottom quintile	in bottom and 2nd quintiles
Greece, 1988	35,4	60,4	33,0	55,7
Ireland, 1987	14,0	46,8	30,1	65,1
Catalonia, 1988	36,1	58,7	46,1	66,0
Belgium, 1985	32,2	58,0	51,0	76,1
Netherlands, 1986	N.A.	N.A.	43,4	70,4
Lorraine, 1986	27,8	49,5	45,2	67,0
Luxembourg, 1986	34,7	55,4	48,3	73,9

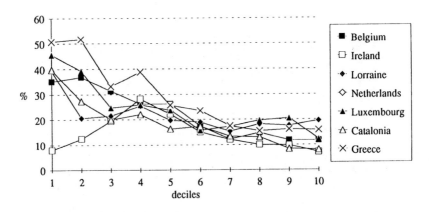

Figure 2.4   Percentage of households headed by an elderly person by standardized income deciles

2.5. Number of earners and income providers

In the Benelux-countries, Lorraine and Ireland there is on average about one person at work (^{3}) in each household. In Greece and Catalonia this figure is about 1,3 per household. This difference is partly due to the age structure of the population in the southern countries (less elderly), partly to household formation: more adults living together, in particular adult children living with their parents. Consequently, these countries also have a rather low proportion of households with no persons at work, or with only one income provider. In Ireland, on the other hand, average household size is also rather large, but the results on the number of persons at work and income providers per household are similar to those for the Benelux. In fact, only Belgium has fewer households with at least one person at work than Ireland. Among the causes of this situation are the low labor market participation rate of women, and the high unemployment rate in Ireland.

Table 2.6
Some data on household income providers

	Average number of persons at work	percent of households with 2 persons at work	percent of households with no persons at work	percent of households with only one income provider
Greece, 1988	1,28	31,5	23,3	44,9
Ireland, 1987	1,06	20,4	31,8	58,4
Catalonia, 1988	1,30	29,1	21,3	38,7
Belgium, 1985	1,02	27,9	33,3	50,5
Netherlands, 1986	1,0	24,0	29,6	59,5
Lorraine, 1986	1,02	26,9	30,9	51,1
Luxembourg, 1986	1,10	25,9	28,7	56,4

* including households with no income provider.

The number of income providers is an important determinant of the total income of which a household disposes. Not surprisingly, in all countries (except Greece) the proportion of households with only one income provider falls steadily as we move up the income distribution, both of standardized and unstandardized income (figure 2.5). In the lowest deciles, almost all households have only one income provider. Nevertheless, the individual distribution of income is sufficiently unequal, so that one-income households are still a significant minority in the higher deciles, especially in The Netherlands and Ireland. The curves are a little flatter in the standardized than in the unstandardized distribution, indicating that households with only one income provider are on average somewhat smaller than others. Greece is an exception to this pattern: even in the bottom four deciles the percentage of households with only one income provider is only around 50%, while it is not much lower in the higher deciles.

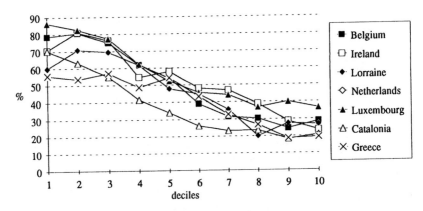

Figure 2.5   Percentage of households with only one income provider over standardized
income deciles

Conversely, the *number of persons at work* rises very strongly with decile number. The pattern is a little less pronounced for the standardized distribution than for the unstandardized one. In the lowest decile few persons are at work; in the highest deciles almost all households include at least one person with paid work, and most include several. In Greece, however, the lowest deciles comprise many persons at work, and the average number increases only very moderately with decile number. Among the other countries Catalonia stands out for having a higher average number of persons at work in most deciles; Ireland for having a lower average in deciles 3 through 8 (figure 2.6).

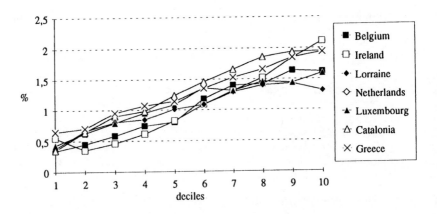

Figure 2.6   Average number of persons at work per household over standardized income
deciles

2.6. Overall proportions of households receiving certain sources of income

The differences in demographic and socio-economic structure obviously influence the proportion of households receiving incomes from certain sources. But especially as regards social security, these proportions are also to a great extent determined by institutional arrangements. For instance, in many countries one observes that many men aged 55 to 64 withdraw from the labor market. In some countries early retirement schemes are specifically aimed at this group, which implies a rise in the proportion of persons receiving pensions. In other cases, earnings are replaced by unemployment allowances or invalidity allowances. Another example are the presence or absence of limits to the length of time one can enjoy unemployment allowances.

Table 2.7
Percentage of households receiving certain kinds of income

| | Source of income | | | | | | |
	earnings	replacement income	pensions	unemployment allowances	sickness or invalidity allowances	social assistance	family allowances
Greece, 1988	84,1	44,8	42,0	2,2	1,7	0,3	3,0
Ireland, 1987	61,5	58,9	34,0	21,6	12,3	1,2	45,0
Catalonia, 1988	94,3	40,3	30,1	4,7	8,0	2,9	6,8
Belgium, 1985	67,3	46,4	32,1	12,1	7,3	0,7	46,5
Netherlands, 1986	71,2	39,7	21,5	6,8	9,5	7,6	41,7
Lorraine, 1986	73,0	42,8	29,4	9,0	10,6	1,0	35,2
Luxembourg, 1986	72,1	45,4	36,5	1,5	10,2	1,6	41,8

Looking at table 2.7, one is struck by the high proportion of households receiving *income from labour* in Greece and Catalonia. As has been noted above, this is probably partly explained by demographic circumstances: less elderly persons than in the other countries and more adult children living with their parents. As the same circumstances also apply in Ireland, it is significant that the proportion of households receiving earnings is on the same level as that of Belgium.

Surprisingly many households receive *pensions* in Greece, while the incidence of other replacement incomes is very low in Greece. It appears that some allowances which are awarded because of invalidity are in fact classified as pensions. In the Netherlands relatively few households have a pension. This is probably partly due to demographic reasons. In all countries pensions include early retirement benefits.

A very high proportion of households receive *unemployment allowances* in Ireland. Obviously, the economic situation is responsible for this. At the other end of the spectrum is Luxembourg. Rather many households have unemployment allowances in Belgium, too. This is related to the fact that there is no restriction in time on these benefits in Belgium.

The incidence of *sickness or invalidity allowances* is again rather high in Ireland. The Netherlands have the highest proportion of households partially or wholly dependent on *social assistance.*

There is a striking difference in the number of households drawing *family allowances* between the northern European countries and the southern ones. In the former countries all or virtually all families with children are covered by a family allowance scheme. In the southern countries only special or selective schemes exist. In Lorraine family allowances for the first child are selective; for larger families they are universal.

Table 2.8

Average amounts received of income from various sources, by households actually benefiting, as a percentage of median total household income in each country

				Source of income			
	earnings	replacement income	pensions	unemploy- ment allowances	sickness or inva- lidity allowances	social assistance	family allowances
Greece, 1988	113	49	51	11	8	7	3
Ireland, 1987	133	50	46	41	42	23	7
Catalonia, 1988	106	38	36	35	30	11	3
Belgium, 1985	108	53	57	33	36	22	13
Netherlands, 1986	112	60	68	42	53	19	8
Lorraine, 1986	104	57	68	23	22	5	15
Luxembourg, 1986	107	54	57	22	32	14	9

Table 2.8 shows the amounts of each source of income averaged over recipient households only, and expressed as proportions of median total household income. (The absolute amounts are shown in table A.1, in appendix.) Some caution is necessary in interpreting these figures, as total household income is of course to a greater or lesser extent determined by the source of income in question. Also, sometimes certain transfers are the sole source of income of a household, in other cases it is only a supplement. There may be differences between countries in this regard.

Average *income from labour* is generally only a little higher than median income, except in Ireland, where it exceeds median income considerably. The average level of replacement incomes is much lower than that of earnings in all countries (most so in Catalonia). Among replacement incomes, *pensions* are generally highest, while social assistance provides the lowest amounts on average. More often than is the case with other replacement incomes, pensions are the sole source of income in a household. Comparing across countries, pensions are relatively high in The Netherlands and Lorraine and relatively low in Catalonia. In The Netherlands pensions include fixed amount state pensions and earnings related pensions based on collective labour agreements. *Unemployment allowances* seem relatively generous in The Netherlands and in Ireland. In Lorraine they are rather low; in Greece they are very low.

Sickness or invalidity allowances are a rather heterogenous category, comprising short-term earnings-related sickness allowances, earnings-related compensation for labor accidents or diseases (often fairly generous), but also fixed-amount benefits for persons who have never been able to work. In The Netherlands these benefits are highest in relative terms. Sickness or invalidity allowances are on average low in Catalonia and Lorraine and very low in Greece. Amounts granted by *social assistance* are at their highest relative level in Ireland. In many countries, including certainly The Netherlands, the average amounts are depressed by many small grants given to households as supplements to incomes from other sources.

Average *family allowances* are at a high level in Lorraine (but the system there is somewhat selective), and fairly high in Belgium too. In Greece and Catalonia they are much lower.

2.7. Distribution of income from labour

Earnings are by far the largest component of aggregate household income, and determine to a large extent its distribution. Social security can be seen as a correction to the unequal distribution of earnings.

It comes therefore as no surprise that the proportion of households with earnings rises strongly as the level of - standardized as well as unstandardized - income increases (figure 2.7). The curve is generally a little less steep for the standardized distribution, as households with earnings tend to be larger than average. In the three top deciles 80-95% of all households have income from earnings. This is true for all countries. The differences across countries are greater in the lower and middle deciles. In the Benelux-countries, Lorraine and Ireland only a minority of households in the lowest quintile receive income from earnings. Ireland has the most pronounced concentration of households with earnings in the distribution of income and welfare: a comparatively small proportion of these households are found in the bottom and second quintile (table 2.9). In Lorraine, on the other hand, a larger proportion of all households with earnings are in the bottom quintile than in the Benelux or Ireland ([4]). The situation is very different in Catalonia and, to a lesser extent, Greece, where almost all households have earnings. Even in the lowest decile, a majority of all households enjoy income from earnings. Nevertheless, in these countries too, households without earnings are concentrated in the lower deciles ([5]).

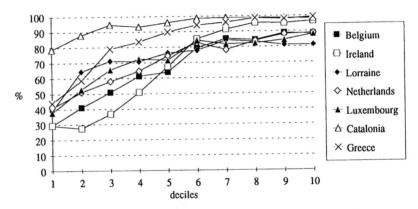

Figure 2.7   Percentage of households with income from labour by standardized income deciles

Table 2.9
Proportion of households with earnings in bottom quintile of
standardized and unstandardized distributions

	percent in bottom standardized quintile	percent in bottom unstandardized quintile
Greece, 1988	12,2	13,1
Ireland, 1987	8,4	6,4
Catalonia, 1988	17,6	17,0
Belgium, 1985	10,5	5,7
Netherlands, 1986	12,9	7,0
Lorraine, 1986	14,2	9,2
Luxembourg, 1986	12,6	8,1

There appear to be even greater inequalities in the *level of earnings* than in the number of earners. Especially average earnings in the tenth unstandardized decile stand out. In the Benelux-countries they are six to eight times higher as those of recipient households in the bottom decile; in Catalonia, Greece and Ireland this ratio exceeds 20. In the standardized distribution the inequalities are only a little more moderate. The unequal distribution of average earnings is of course partly explained by the higher number of earners in high income households, partly by the inequality of individual earnings.

The two tendencies mentioned (increasing proportion of households with earnings, and increasing average earnings as decile number rises) combine to make the *distribution of aggregate earnings* over disposable income deciles, as well as standardized income deciles, very unequal. The top unstandardized decile receives one quarter (the Benelux-countries, Lorraine, Catalonia) to one third (Greece, Ireland) of total earnings, which is much more than all five bottom deciles combined. The proportions are a little less unequal by standardized deciles, but still the top decile receives between 22% (Belgium, Lorraine,

Luxembourg) and 32% (Ireland), more than the four bottom deciles together. Despite some differences the similarity of the distributions across countries is notable. Only in Ireland is the share of the five bottom deciles much smaller than in the other countries.

2.8. Distribution of pensions

Contrary to households with earnings, the *proportion of households* with an income from pensions generally falls as we move up the scale of disposable household income (see figure 2.8). In many countries the majority, or almost so, of households in the bottom deciles receive pensions. But also in the highest deciles a large minority (esp. in Greece, Luxembourg and Lorraine) of all households have an income from pensions. As table 2.10 shows, the concentration of households with pensions in the bottom quintile is greatest in The Netherlands and Belgium, and least in Greece and Ireland. Pensions as defined here include retirement, survivors and early retirement pensions. In Greece, some benefits, which are granted because of invalidity, are included in pensions.

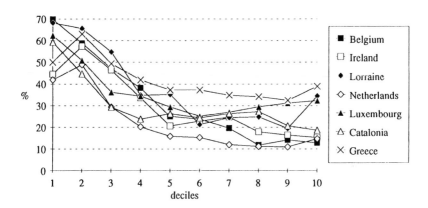

Figure 2.8   Percentage of households with a pension by income deciles

The results by household disposable income should not be interpreted in the sense that households with pensions are generally worse off than the average household. Most of these households are small (single or couple with no children), so the distribution by standardized (welfare) deciles is quite different (figure 2.9). In Catalonia, Belgium and Luxembourg, households with pensions are represented more than proportionally in the bottom quintile of economic welfare, but not very markedly. In Lorraine the distribution is virtually uniform, and in The Netherlands almost so. In Ireland, only 15% of all households with pensions are in the bottom standardized quintile; they are concentrated in the second quintile (table 2.10).

Table 2.10
Proportion of all households with pensions in bottom quintile of
standardized and unstandardized income

| | percent of households with pensions: | |
	by standardized income in bottom quintile	by unstandardized income in bottom quintile
Greece, 1988	27,4	27,0
Ireland, 1987	14,5	33,9
Catalonia, 1988	27,6	34,6
Belgium, 1985	26,8	39,9
Netherlands, 1986	19,4	38,6
Lorraine, 1986	20,5	31,4
Luxembourg, 1986	25,7	33,5

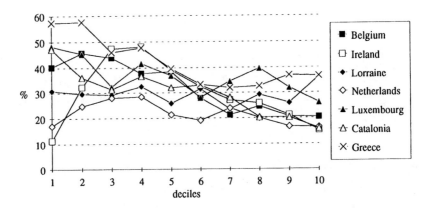

Figure 2.9   Percentage of households with a pension by standardized income deciles

Though the *average pension* received rises with household disposable or standardized income decile number in all countries, it does not do so very strongly, compared with earnings. Even in the top deciles, the average pension received is generally below median household income or not much above it (except in Lorraine). The Netherlands has, in relative terms, the highest pensions in most deciles, while the opposite is true for Catalonia.

The finding that the average amount received in the top deciles is not very large, suggests that in most of these cases the household is only in a favourable income position because of other incomes of the person receiving the pension himself or because of other persons in the household. In the bottom deciles, on the other hand, the pension generally will be the only source of income.

It is remarkable that the distribution of *aggregate pensions* is in no country skewed towards households in the bottom half of the distribution of economic welfare. In Belgium and Catalonia aggregate pensions are distributed fairly evenly, while in Luxembourg there is a small, and in Lorraine and Greece a rather pronounced concentration in the top decile. By *un*standardized income, a larger than proportional amount of aggregate pensions flows to the bottom deciles in Belgium, the Netherlands, Ireland and Catalonia. The concentration in the top quintile in Lorraine and Greece remains.

2.9. Distribution of unemployment allowances

In several countries, notably Ireland and the Netherlands, households receiving unemployment allowances are found disproportionally in the bottom quintile of economic welfare (standardized income) (table 2.11). (This is also true for Luxembourg, but unemployment allowances are rare in Luxembourg.) To a somewhat lesser extent, the same is true for Belgium and Catalonia. In Lorraine, however, households with unemployment allowances are distributed rather evenly, and in Greece they are concentrated in the middle standardized income deciles. But in the other countries too, many unemployment allowances go to households in the upper half of the distribution of economic welfare. Looking at the deciles of unstandardized income, we find similar concentrations of unemployment allowances beneficiaries in the bottom quintile in the Netherlands and Catalonia, but in Belgium and Lorraine they are found more or less proportionally in all deciles, and in Ireland predominantly in the second quintile. This is an indication that, especially in Ireland, and also in Belgium, households receiving unemployment allowances tend to be larger than average (see figure 2.10).

Table 2.11
Proportion of all households with unemployment allowances
in bottom quintiles - standardized and unstandardized

| | percent of all households with unemployment allowances: | | | |
| | by standardized income | | by unstandardized income | |
	in bottom quintile	in bottom and 2nd quintiles	in bottom quintile	in bottom and 2nd quintiles
Greece, 1988	9,3	27,8	10,8	40,0
Ireland, 1987	37,6	58,4	18,0	50,1
Catalonia, 1988	29,1	45,5	29,1	49,0
Belgium, 1985	29,7	55,0	19,6	41,2
Netherlands, 1986	34,8	56,2	35,3	58,4
Lorraine, 1986	20,8	38,8	16,0	31,2
Luxembourg, 1986	37,3	60,7	26,0	49,3

While comparing these results across countries, one must keep in mind that not all persons in unemployment receive unemployment allowances.

The Lorraine results are affected by the fact that all incomes have been measured over a yearly period. All households that have in the course of a year received unemployment allowances during one or several months are counted as receiving unemployment allowances, and the amount per month is calculated as the total amount received over a year divided by twelve. Compared with a situation where income is measured for one month only, this procedure will tend to depress average amounts, and at the same time will probably make the income position of households receiving unemployment allowances appear more favourable.

Average unemployment allowances received show little variation by income deciles, standardized or unstandardized (except Luxembourg).

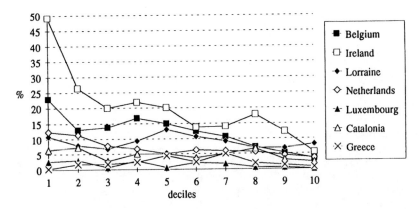

Figure 2.10 Percentage of households with unemployment allowances by standardized income deciles

This implies that the position of these households is determined not by the level of the benefit but by the absence or presence of other incomes in the household. To explain these distributions, one would have to take into account the position of unemployed persons in the household (main breadwinner, wife to main breadwinner, child living with parents) and the way unemployment allowances are regulated (the length of time during which one can remain entitled, how and when one can become entitled, to what extent payments are earnings related, whether there are minimum or maximum benefits).

The *distribution of aggregate unemployment allowances* over standardized or unstandardized deciles generally follows that of households receiving these allowances.

2.10. Distribution of sickness or invalidity allowances

The label "sickness or invalidity allowances" covers in most countries a rather heterogeneous collection of schemes, some of which are short-term, others long-term, some are earnings-related, others provide fixed amount benefits, some are only for employees, others cover the whole population. In many cases, partial invalidity leads to relatively small allowances. Given this heterogeneity it is not surprising that the distributions of households receiving sickness or invalidity allowances over income deciles show little pattern. Only in Catalonia are these households clearly overrepresented in the two bottom deciles; in the other countries there is a certain preponderance in the middle and lower middle deciles. This is true for the standardized as well as the unstandardized distributions. On the whole, aggregate sickness or invalidity allowances are rather evenly distributed over the income distribution.

2.11. Distribution of social assistance

As could be expected, given that social assistance is generally only provided to persons or households with no other means of subsistence, and after a means test, households receiving social assistance are strongly concentrated in the bottom quintile of economic welfare (table 2.12). But nevertheless, one might be surprised that in all countries, except Lorraine, 40-50% of all social assistance beneficiaries are *not* in the bottom quintile, and some are even found at the top of the distribution. It has to be kept in mind though, that in many cases (excluding The Netherlands) these figures refer to only a small number of households in the sample. Apart from measurement error (misunderstandings and mistakes in the interviewing or data-processing stages) the incidence of social assistance in higher income groups could be explained by allowances for special needs, or by the means-test sometimes disregarding the incomes of certain household members (such as children or parents).

Table 2.12
Proportion of all households with social assistance in
bottom quintile - standardized and unstandardized

	percent of all households with social assistance in:	
	bottom standardized quintile	bottom unstandardized quintile
Greece, 1988	49,6	62,2
Ireland, 1987	50,0	24,0
Catalonia, 1988	54,8	50,8
Belgium, 1985	51,4	57,1
Netherlands, 1986	49,9	48,7
Lorraine, 1986	81,0	62,0
Luxembourg, 1986	49,4	52,5

By *un*standardized deciles, the results are very similar, except in Ireland, where most social assistance receiving households are in the third, fourth and fifth decile. This is an indication that in Ireland social assistance goes mainly to rather large households. This is confirmed by the fact that the average amount is the largest in the bottom standardized decile in Ireland. In other countries there is no clear pattern regarding the amounts received.

2.12. Distribution of family allowances

In the northern countries, the *proportion of households* benefiting from family allowances increases from below 10% in the lowest unstandardized decile to between 50% and 60% around median income, and it is fairly constant above this level. In Lorraine, the proportion of households receiving family allowances is lower than in the other northern countries, perhaps because the system is selective for households with only one child. In Greece and Catalonia family allowances are unimportant and are more or less evenly distributed over income groups (figure 2.11).

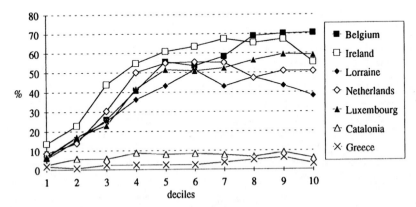

Figure 2.11 Percentage of households with family allowances by income deciles

These results using unstandardized deciles should not mislead one into thinking that households with family allowances are relatively well off. The distribution of beneficiaries of family allowances over deciles of economic welfare (standardized income) is fairly even in Belgium and Luxembourg, and shows a concentration in the bottom quintile in Ireland and the Netherlands (table 2.13).

Table 2.13
Proportion of all households with family allowances in
bottom quintiles - standardized and unstandardized

| | percent of all households with family allowances: | | | |
| | by standardized income | | by unstandardized income | |
	in bottom quintile	in bottom and 2nd quintiles	in bottom quintile	in bottom and 2nd quintiles
Greece, 1988	5,6	11,2	7,9	23,6
Ireland, 1987	22,1	39,2	7,0	26,2
Catalonia, 1988	20,1	45,3	11,8	32,9
Belgium, 1985	18,0	37,9	4,5	18,9
Netherlands, 1986	24,5	47,4	5,4	24,8
Lorraine, 1986	21,1	47,8	6,7	24,1
Luxembourg, 1986	18,9	42,0	5,8	21,3

In Lorraine there is a concentration in the second quintile. In general, in the Benelux-countries and Ireland, the shape of the curve describing the distribution of households receiving family allowances, rather unsurprisingly, follows closely that of the average number of children (figure 2.12).

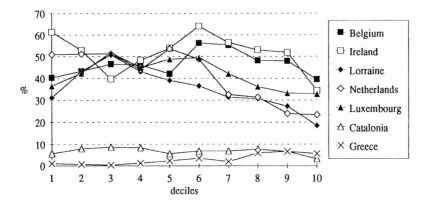

Figure 2.12 Percentage of households with family allowances by standardized income deciles

The *average amount of family allowances*, outside Greece and Catalonia where these benefits are insignificant, is more or less constant across deciles of economic welfare. The same is true in the *un*standardized distribution, except in Belgium, where the average amount increases moderately with decile number.

As there is not much variation in the amount received across deciles, the *distribution of the aggregate sum of family allowances* mainly follows that of benefiting households. In all but a few rare cases, family allowances are only a small part of a household's income. As family allowances are a universal benefit or only partially selective, their distribution follows that of households with children. Many of these have one or more income from earnings, which is the most important reason why the incidence of family allowances is highest in the upper half of the unstandardized distribution of income.

2.13. Overall distribution of replacement income and social security income

Finally we have a look at the distribution of all replacement incomes together and of all social security income combined, i.e. replacement incomes plus family allowances. Social assistance is treated as a replacement income and therefore as part of social security. Although this may be incorrect from a formal or legal standpoint, social assistance, as a social safety-net, in fact provides income when all other sources have failed, and thus functions socially as a kind of replacement income.

By deciles of economic welfare or standardized income, households with replacement incomes are represented more than proportionally in the bottom quintile in all countries, except Lorraine where this overrepresentation is rather limited (table 2.14, figure 2.13).

Table 2.14
Proportion of all households with replacement incomes in
bottom quintiles - standardized and unstandardized

| | percent of all households with replacement income: | | | |
| | by standardized income | | by unstandardized income | |
	in bottom quintile	in bottom and 2nd quintiles	in bottom quintile	in bottom and 2nd quintiles
Greece, 1988	26,8	48,9	26,6	48,5
Ireland, 1987	26,8	52,8	29,1	57,0
Catalonia, 1988	30,2	51,5	34,8	52,9
Belgium, 1985	27,8	52,4	34,0	58,4
Netherlands, 1986	27,2	51,5	36,7	61,9
Lorraine, 1986	21,9	42,6	28,7	48,8
Luxembourg, 1986	27,0	48,0	32,7	56,3

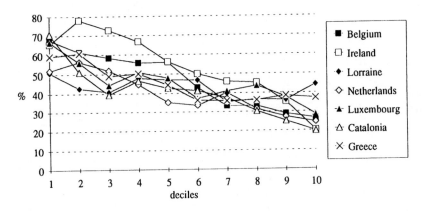

Figure 2.13 Percentage of households with a replacement income by standardized income deciles

In the bottom decile of *un*standardized income 70% or more of all *households* have a *replacement income* (except in Greece). In the higher deciles this proportion falls, but in the highest deciles there is still a large minority that receives a replacement income (from 20-25% in The Netherlands and Belgium, to 35-40% in Luxembourg, Lorraine, Ireland and Greece). In Ireland, the large number of unemployment allowances makes the proportion of households with replacement incomes very high in all deciles, and especially in the lower middle deciles (see figure 2.14).

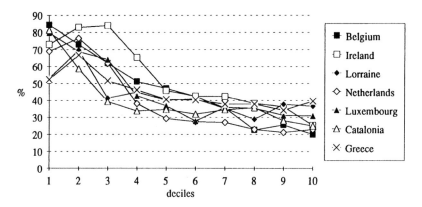

Figure 2.14 Percentage of households with a replacement income by income deciles

In Catalonia and Greece, the distribution of *social security* virtually equals that of replacement incomes, simply because there are very few family allowances. In the other countries a large majority of all households in all standardized deciles have some income from social security (except the top two deciles in the Netherlands). Nevertheless, in most countries, the proportions of households with replacement incomes is somewhat higher in the bottom half of the distribution of economic welfare. In Ireland and Lorraine, however, the proportions remain virtually equal across deciles.

By *un*standardized deciles, the picture is somewhat different. In Belgium and Luxembourg there is no systematic difference across deciles in the proportion of households with social security system at all; in Ireland and the Netherlands this proportion is somewhat lower than average in the highest deciles. This even distribution of the incidence of social security income is the result of the fact that replacement incomes, especially pensions, and family allowances tend to be distributed in opposite and complementary patterns: replacement incomes go mainly to the lower income groups, in particular the elderly, family allowances more to families with earnings in the higher income groups.

The *amounts* households with *replacement incomes* receive are rather lower than average in the bottom decile, and tend to rise with decile number. This is true for the standardized as well as for the unstandardized distribution. The variations in amounts received across deciles are most pronounced in Lorraine and Greece.

By *un*standardized deciles the *average amounts of social security transfers* generally do not display a marked pattern. In Belgium, the Netherlands, Luxembourg and Ireland, the amounts are highest in deciles 2 through 4 or 5, and somewhat lower than average in the bottom decile and the top five deciles. In Lorraine and to a lesser extent in Catalonia, the amounts are highest in the top quintile. Only in Greece do the amounts show a strongly rising curve. These patterns may be a little surprising, as both average replacement income and average family allowances tend to rise with decile number. The reason is that as we move up the income distribution the composition of households receiving social security income changes: less households with replacement incomes and more households with (lower) family allowances.

By deciles of economic welfare the patterns are somewhat different. In Lorraine, Luxembourg and Catalonia the amounts of social transfers are clearly highest in the top deciles. In Belgium and Ireland there are no important differences across countries. These patterns come about because, compared with the unstandardized distributions, households with replacement incomes and those with family allowances are both spread more evenly across deciles.

The distribution of the *total sum of replacement income* across deciles of economic welfare is characterized by its evenness. A strong concentration is only found in Lorraine, but it occurs in the *top* decile. In Belgium, Ireland and Catalonia, the bottom five deciles do receive slightly more than a proportional share, but the difference is rather small. The share of the bottom quintile nowhere exceeds 23%. In fact, in all countries the distribution of aggregate replacement income displays a remarkable resemblance to that of aggregate pensions. This is not surprising, as pensions constitute the bulk of all replacement incomes.

The resemblance to pensions can also be seen in the distribution of aggregate replacement income across *un*standardized deciles. In Belgium, the Netherlands and Catalonia, the bottom quintile has a relatively large share (27-28%). In Lorraine and Greece, the bottom quintile receives less than proportional. In Ireland there is a concentration in deciles 4 and 5, and in Greece and Catalonia in the top deciles.

The distribution of *aggregate social security transfers*, across standardized as well as unstandardized deciles, is very similar to that of replacement incomes. This is because replacement incomes form between 80% (Belgium) and 99% (Greece) of all social security cash transfers. In addition, family allowances are rather evenly spread across standardized deciles (figures 2.15 and 2.16).

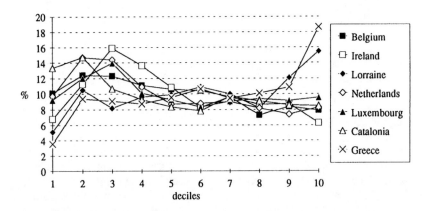

Figure 2.15 Distribution of aggregate social security income by income deciles

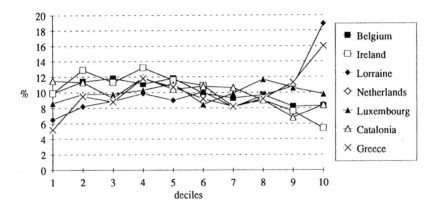

Figure 2.16 Distribution of aggregate social security income by standardized income deciles

It is remarkable that, despite large differences between countries in economic, social and demographic conditions and institutional arrangements, we find everywhere that social security transfers as a whole are widely distributed across equivalent as well as disposable income groups. This does not imply that social security is hardly or not redistributive. To measure the redistribution brought about by social security, one would have to study the incidence of social security on the distribution of incomes *before* transfers, and compare pre- and post-transfer distributions of income.

What we can say, on the basis of the present results, is that social security does not serve solely, or even mainly, to relieve poverty, if we understand by that the lifting of pre-transfer poor households to the level of the poverty line, without giving anything in excess and without giving anything to pre-transfer non-poor. This result is not very surprising, as relieving poverty is the explicit aim of only a small part of social security, namely social assistance. Most of social security consists of social insurance schemes, providing replacement incomes when certain social risks occur, which cause the loss of earnings. Usually these are granted on an individual, not a household, basis. Furthermore there are allowances in case of certain conditions, such as child allowances.

Nevertheless, these findings have a policy implication that is not unimportant. A general, across the board increase of all social security transfers would not only be of very limited effectiveness as regards poverty, its redistributive or equalizing effect would also at best be rather moderate. This may be obvious to some, but it still is a fact that is not universally recognized.

Notes

(1) The exact method used to make national data comparable is described in appendix II.

(2) These conclusions are not affected if one takes into account the results for the other years (Belgium, 1988; Ireland, 1989; Lorraine, 1985; The Netherlands, 1985; Luxembourg, 1985).

(3) i.e. private and state employees and self-employed persons.

(4) Part of the explanation for this difference might be methodological: in Lorraine data are gathered for each of the 12 months of the year instead of a single month. This might increase the proportion of households with earnings, especially in the lower income groups, where we would tend to find persons with intermittent earnings. However, Luxembourg provided results showing the average number of employed by decile during a single month and during 12 months, and these indicate that the difference between the two series of figures is rather small.

(5) The number of households with earnings in Catalonia may appear excessively high. It seems that some households in Catalonia have a little income from earnings even though there are no persons at work. Presumably some persons who define themselves as retired, incapacitated, student or otherwise inactive, still perform some paid work (part-time jobs, small-scale farming or trading).

3 The poverty lines

3.1. Poverty lines adopted in this study

As has been noted in the introduction, the concept of poverty is ambiguous. A single scientifically validated poverty line does not exist at the moment. In applied poverty research five approaches to the measurement of poverty can be distinguished: budget, subjective, relative or statistical, and legal income poverty lines, and deprivation indices. In the introduction, some of the advantages and disadvantages of the various approaches have been indicated.

The discussion of the advantages and disadvantages of the various poverty line methods would be largely academic, if empirically all methods would produce the same, or very similar, results. Unfortunately, this appears to be far from true (cf. Hagenaars and De Vos, 1988; De Vries, 1985). The estimates of numbers in poverty vary widely, and the groups of people in poverty according to different poverty lines do not overlap completely. In the context of social policy, this would not be so bad, if all methods would agree on which social groups and categories are at high risk of poverty. But this is also not the case. In this respect, the equivalence scale is of great importance. Using a poverty line with a very "steep" equivalence scale, large families will appear to be more at risk of poverty than if a poverty line with a "flatter" equivalence scale would have been used, and the reverse, of course, holds for small households, especially single people. Many important characteristics correlate with household size, such as age, labour market status of husband and wife, type of income, sex of head of household; and their correlation with poverty will consequently also be affected (cf. Buhmann a.o., 1988).

Subjective methods produce, in general, poverty lines that are much higher than, for instance, relative poverty lines. In many cases, the poverty line is at such a level that it would be very difficult to maintain that all households below it are poor, in the sense of being socially excluded. The term "insecurity of subsistence", meaning a situation in which households encounter some (financial) difficulty in participating in the average or most widely shared life-style, would be more appropriate. However, because "insecurity of subsistence" is a rather cumbersome phrase, and to avoid confusion, we will continue to use generally the words "poor" and "poverty".

In the research project which is reported here, four poverty lines have been adopted. These are:

1) the "EC" poverty line, as defined by O'Higgins and Jenkins (1990) which is an elaboration of the poverty line used in the first EC-programme against poverty. It is defined as 50% of average equivalent household income for single-person households. The equivalence factors used are 1,0 for the first adult, 0,7 for other adults and 0,5 for children.
The EC-standard is a relative or statistical poverty line.

2) the legal poverty line, defined as the guaranteed minimum income.

Two subjective standards:
3) the CSP-poverty line, introduced by the Centre for Social Policy, Antwerp.

4) the Subjective Poverty Line (SPL), developed by Kapteyn, among others.

Both subjective methods have as their aim the estimation of a minimum level of income, with which it is still possible to live "decently". Therefore this minimum income level is derived from declarations made by the population itself (i.c. the sample). In fact, the households in the sample have been asked the following question: "What is the minimum amount of income that your family, in your circumstances, needs to be able to make ends meet?". Empirically, one finds that the answers to this question rise systematically with the actual income of the household. To derive one income standard, it is assumed that only households, that are just able to balance their budget, i.e., that are on the brink of insecurity of the means of subsistence, are able to give a correct estimate of what level of income is necessary to participate in the normal standard of living. The views of households, whose incomes are either above or below the minimum level, are biased, because of the differences in style of living. Now, it is not self-evident which households are in a state of budgetary balance. The difference between the two subjective methods lies precisely in the way they identify those households.

In the *CSP-method* a second question is asked for this purpose, namely: "With your current monthly income, everything included, can you get by: with great difficulty, with difficulty, with some difficulty, fairly easily, easily, very easily, for your household?". Households that answer "with some difficulty" are supposed to be just able to balance their budgets. On the basis of their declarations on the minimum level of income, the CSP-standard is calculated.

The CSP-standards are computed separately for each type of household. The type of a household depends on its size and composition, i.e. on the number of persons at active age, the number of elderly, and the number of children. Because of data limitations, reliable estimates of the CSP-standards can only be computed directly for the 8 or 10 most common household types. CSP-standards for the other household types are derived from these estimates. The technical details of the procedure are described in appendix 5.

The SPL takes as its point of departure the notion that households that put their estimate of the minimum income (Ymin) at a level equal to their actual income (Y), are just able to balance their budgets. The argument is illustrated in figure 3.1.

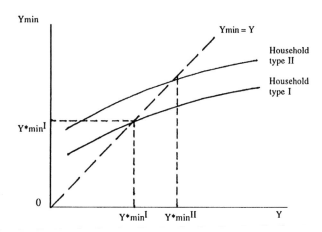

Figure 3.1   The relation between Y and Ymin, for two types of household.

Figure 3.1 shows that the answer to the minimum income question (Ymin) rises with actual income. Of interest now is the point where Ymin is equal to Y: at that income level, Y*min, households of a particular type are, on average, just able to make ends meet. Above this income level the budgets are more than sufficient, while below it, households feel that they cannot make ends meet: their minimum income is higher than their actual income.

The level at which the income the household deems necessary is (on average) equal to actual income will vary with the size of the household. Larger households (type II in figure 3.1) will need larger amounts of money to make ends meet.
These levels are calculated with the help of regression equations, with which the curves are estimated. In appendix 4 this is explained in more technical detail. It has to be emphasized that the SPL as applied here, is a rather simple version of this method. In Muffels, a.o. (1990), a more fully developed model is presented, in which age of children and reference-group effects are taken into account.

3.2. Levels of the poverty lines

Table 3.1 shows the levels of the poverty lines in seven countries expressed in ECU in prices of Jan. 1988, for ten important types of household. France, Luxembourg and Spain

Table 3.1
Level of poverty lines, in monthly amounts (ECU, in prices of Jan. 1988) by type of household*

CSP-standard

	Belg. '85	Neth. '86	Lux. '86	Lor. '86	Irl. '87	Cat. '88	Greece '88
single elderly	509	528	637	478	305	361	368
single active	560	570	771	587	325	556	549
two elderly	662	706	845	723	532	624	416
one active, one elderly	769	747	978	832	482	794	534
two actives	806	789	1112	940	551	798	666
two actives, one child	933	836	1249	1100	796	973	796
two actives, 2 children	1023	863	1330	1195	831	1094	890
two actives, 3 children	1051	882	1395	1262	855	1296	829
one active, one child	736	617	908	746	570	731	594
one active, 2 children	817	644	1016	841	606	852	653

SPL-standard

	Belg. '85	Neth. '86	Lux. '86	Lor. '86	Irl. '87	Cat. '88	Greece '88
single elderly	639	616	747	685	385	706	378
single active	639	616	747	685	385	706	607
two elderly	797	743	902	816	531	925	495
one active, one elderly	797	743	902	816	531	925	584
two actives	797	743	902	816	531	925	707
two actives, one child	875	830	1007	928	642	1084	863
two actives, 2 children	935	897	1089	1033	734	1213	871
two actives, 3 children	991	953	1168	1134	815	1223	942
one active, one child	762	743	902	816	531	925	762
one active, 2 children	850	830	1047	928	642	1084	715

EC-standard

	Belg. '85	Neth. '86	Lux. '86	Lor. '86	Irl. '87	Cat. '88	Greece '88
single elderly	313	367	474	341	223	314	194
single active	313	367	474	341	223	314	194
two elderly	530	624	805	579	380	534	330
one active, one elderly	530	624	805	579	380	534	330
two actives	530	624	805	579	380	534	330
two actives, one child	683	808	1049	750	491	690	465
two actives, 2 children	838	991	1281	920	603	847	602
two actives, 3 children	996	1174	1586	1091	715	1004	738
one active, one child	465	551	745	511	335	478	330
one active, 2 children	624	734	1088	682	447	628	466

Legal standard

	Belg. '85	Neth. '86	Lux. '86	Lor. '86	Irl. '87
single elderly	336	482	519	275	204
single active	336	478	519	280	211
two elderly	465	688	710	401	349
one active, one elderly	465	722	710	406	369
two actives	465	694	710	409	425
two actives, one child	491	745	789	497	490
two actives, 2 children	588	805	869	577	560
two actives, 3 children	722	874	948	673	609
one active, one child	364	684	599	416	288
one active, 2 children	465	755	678	519	375

* elderly: man 65 or over; woman 60 or over.
active: non-elderly adult.
child: person of 16 years or younger, or in full-time education.
The list of household types is not exhaustive.

40

and Greece had no nationally guaranteed minimum income (and thus no legal standard) at the time of the first waves ([1]).

It can be remarked that most poverty-standards incorporate some differentiation by age: the CSP, EC and legal standards differentiate between children and adults, while the CSP-standard, as well as the legal standard in The Netherlands and Ireland, also distinguish elderly and adults. Only the SPL, in the rather unsophisticated variant used here, takes no account of the age of household members.

To make sense of the large number of figures in table 3.1, it is useful first to look at the level of the poverty line, and then at its equivalence scale. To represent the level of a poverty line, one might use two different kinds of indicators: one is the amount for a standard type of household (for instance the active couple), the other is some sort of average amount over a range of types of household. Here we have used the latter, namely the *geometric mean*, as shown in table 3.2 and in figure 3.2, but the first indicator would lead to the same conclusions, as the reader can check.

Table 3.2
Geometric means ([2]) of social subsistence minima, in monthly amounts (ECU, in prices of Jan. 1988)

	CSP-standard	SPL-standard	EC-standard	LEGAL-standard
Greece, 1988	607	669	366	-
Ireland, 1987	552	570	418	376
Catalonia, 1988	760	956	552	-
Belgium, 1985	767	801	547	457
Netherlands, 1986	708	764	645	681
Lorraine, 1986	826	844	599	430
Luxembourg, 1986	996	932	852	693

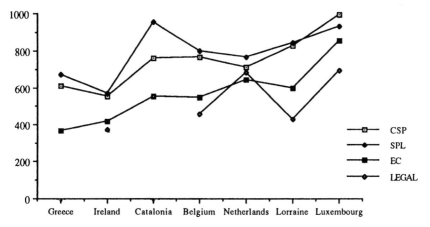

Figure 3.2   Geometric means of social subsistence minima, in monthly amounts (ECU, in prices of Jan. 1988).

41

Using the EC-standard, one can distinguish three groups of countries: Greece and Ireland, where the EC-standard is rather low, the Benelux countries, Catalonia and Lorraine, where the EC-standard is at an intermediate level, and Luxembourg where it is highest. This ranking is of course to a great extent determined by the levels of average household income, but also by average household size. Mainly because of this latter factor, Catalonia ranks lower by the EC-standard, than by average household income. Finally, the lower the correlation between household income and household size (and as long as this correlation remains positive), the higher average equivalent income, and thus the higher the EC-standard. Though this effect is in general rather unimportant, it may account for the relatively high level of the EC-standard in The Netherlands.

The subjective poverty lines are in most countries much higher than the EC-line. They also show a tendency to increase with average income, but with some important deviations. First, the SPL makes a peculiar "jump" in Catalonia. Secondly, the subjective standards are much higher in Lorraine than in The Netherlands, with Belgium in between, although these three countries have about the same level of average income. In comparison to the EC-standard, the subjective norms appear to be at a relatively low level in The Netherlands, and at a high level in Lorraine. Thirdly, the CSP-standard is at the same level in Lorraine and Luxembourg, in contrast to the SPL.

The observation that, in general, when average disposable or equivalent income is higher the subjective standards are higher too, can be explained as a kind of reference-group effect. As economic conditions improve, the average style of life moves to a higher level, and more things are considered necessary. It is sometimes argued that welfare and poverty are completely relative, so that if average welfare increases with everything else remaining the same, poverty rates will not drop (at least not in the longer run). From these data it is hard to ascertain whether poverty is completely or only partly relative. If we use the EC-standard (which is proportional to average equivalent household income), as an indicator of economic welfare, we find that both subjective standards are at their highest relative level in Greece, the poorest country. This would support the hypothesis that poverty is partly relative. But among the other countries the levels of the subjective standards relative to the EC-standard show no clear pattern.

The fluctuations of the subjective standards around the general trend across countries are harder to explain. Two variables that possibly play a role are the level of collective services and the level of social security. It is obvious that the welfare level of a household depends not only on its cash income, but also on non-cash allowances from government services, such as health care, education, et cetera. If government expenditures on these services are higher in one country than in another, households may feel they need less money to be secure of subsistence. It is hard to substantiate this hypothesis with statistics, especially because what matters, of course, is not the financial input, but the output in terms of services to households. Social security may also influence the level of the minimum incomes, by reducing uncertainty about future income. According to Hagenaars (1986) (expectations of) fluctuations in income may induce people to state a higher minimum income, because they have to save for bad times. A high level of social security may reduce this need. However, it does not seem very likely that these variables account for all unexplained fluctuations. Especially the large differences in the level of the subjective standards between Belgium and The Netherlands, two countries that are rather similar, are very peculiar.

Another reason for the fluctuations could be that the models used here are rather simple, and do not take into account many variables that might have a (differential) effect on the estimates.

Finally, and rather trivially, the possibility that small differences in the wording of the minimum income question have an appreciable influence on the answers cannot be excluded.

More surprising, perhaps, than the fluctuations across countries, are the divergent levels of the SPL and CSP-standards *within* countries. In most countries they are fairly close together, the SPL being generally somewhat higher (except in Luxembourg) but in Catalonia the SPL is much higher than the CSP-standard. Because the CSP and SPL-standards share the same theroretical background, the differences must be due to the more technical details. Among these, the fact that the CSP-method averages over minimum income *or* actual income, whichever is the lowest amount, may well explain the lower average level of the CSP-standard.

The legal standard is below the EC-standard in all countries, except The Netherlands. It also appears that guaranteed minimum income is at least partly relative to the average level of economic welfare.

3.3. The equivalence scales

The equivalence scales of the various standards are shown graphically in figure 3.3. Figure 3.3 shows clearly that the *EC-standard* has by far the steepest equivalence scale in all countries. The equivalence scales of the *subjective standards* are much flatter in all countries, but to different degrees: in Ireland and Catalonia they are fairly steep, while being rather flat in other countries, especially the CSP-standard in The Netherlands. Despite these differences, the results of the subjective standards, especially those of the SPL, seem to converge within a fairly narrow range, where the cost of a couple with three children is 130 % to 140 % of that of a childless couple.

Within the scope of this report it is impossible to explain these differences in the equivalence scales: among the variables involved may be differences in the costs that different types of household face (e.q. education for households with children, health care for the elderly) and reference group effects (high-status families may have more or less children than others). Some variables, like the degree of urbanisation of the place where one lives may play a double role: encompassing both differences in costs and reference group effects. Some interesting differences between the CSP and SPL equivalence scale can be noted. In the first place, the CSP-standard produces equivalence factors for types of household consisting of elderly persons, that are always lower than the equivalence factors for corresponding types of household with the same number of adults of active age. In some countries like Lorraine and Greece the difference is very large in others, like Ireland, it is very small. As the SPL does not take the age of household members into account, it cannot show similar differences.

Equivalence scales implied by the CSP-standard (2 adults = 100)

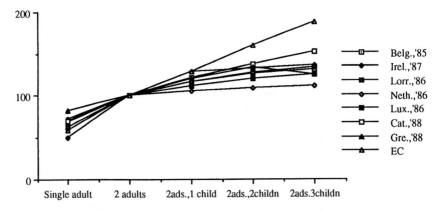

Equivalence scales implied by the SPL-standard (2 adults = 100)

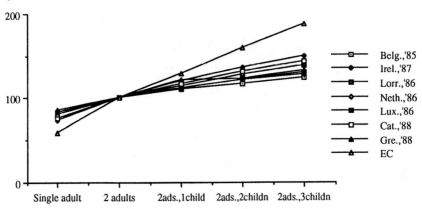

Equivalence scales implied by the Legal-standard (2 adults = 100)

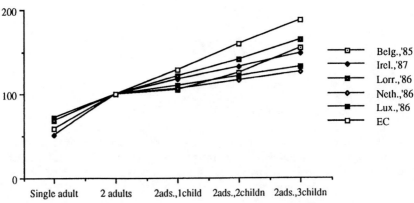

Figure 3.3   Equivalence scales of four poverty lines in seven countries

Secondly, the SPL for single persons is rather high, in all countries, both in comparison with the CSP-standard and compared to the SPL for two-person households.

Thirdly, in several countries one observes that the equivalence scale of the CSP is relatively steep for households with one or two children, but is much flatter for households with more children, as if the cost of children is not so much dependent on their number, but on whether there are any children or not. It is possible that people who get many children have less monetary needs than others have. This characteristic could be prior to, or induced by, the presence of many children. Again, the SPL cannot show such an effect, as the logarithmic form of the regression imposes a smooth curve on the equivalence scale.

Looking finally at the equivalence scale of the *legal standard*, one again observes rather large differences between countries, with The Netherlands at the low end of the spectrum and Lorraine at the high end. Furthermore, we find that elderly persons enjoy in most countries (almost) the same legal minimum as persons of active age, except in Ireland, where the minimum for an elderly couple appears to be about 20% lower than the minimum for an active couple ([3]). The legal minimum for single people is about 70% of that of couples. As figure 3.3 makes clear, families with many children are relatively favoured in Belgium and The Netherlands, while Luxembourg shows a more flat rate. The pattern for Belgium and The Netherlands is explained by the fact that the amount of child allowance per child rises with the rank number of the child and also with age (children in households with many children are on average older).

3.4. Changes across time

Another important aspect of the poverty lines is their *behaviour across time*. Table A.2 in appendix shows the changes in the levels of the poverty lines (in real terms) from the first to the second wave for the five countries for which we have two wave data. The EC-standard rises in all countries, and, by definition, a constant percentage applies to all types of household. The subjective standards often show more substantial changes. The SPL rises strongly in The Netherlands, while it falls considerably in Luxembourg. The CSP-standard has more overall stability, but it produces sometimes large fluctuations in the poverty line for certain types of household.

These drastic changes in the subjective standards across years appear implausible. They may be due to the rather simple models applied here, which do not take sufficiently all relevant factors into account. Muffels, Kapteyn a.o. (1990, pp. 137-175) report that more refined models produce more stable results in The Netherlands.

Notes

([1])   In the meantime, France has instituted one. The Luxembourg guaranteed income went into effect in 1986, one year after the first wave was conducted. The Legal-standard for those countries has been calculated by deflating to the relevant year.

([2])   Geometric rather than average (arithmetic) means have been used to give an estimate of the "average" level of the standards over the various types of household, because the geometric mean provides a better estimate of the central tendency, if one wants to compare two series of figures, and to give equal weight to all amounts (a 5% increase in a low amount has the same effect as a 5% increase in a high amount). These means have no direct relationship to an average standard, computed over the individual households in the sample, which would be influenced by the distribution of the sample over different types of household. The figures presented here make possible a comparison "in the abstract", independent of the demographic composition of the samples.

(3)   In fact, the rates of support paid by the main social security schemes in Ireland are higher for the elderly, but the treatment of housing costs is such that the effective support to the elderly may turn out to be less because they have, on average, lower housing costs.

4 The incidence of poverty

4.1. The extent of poverty

Table 4.1 and figure 4.1 present the poverty rate according to the different poverty standards for the seven European countries.

Table 4.1
Percentage of all households, whose means of subsistence are insecure

	CSP-standard	SPL-standard	EC-standard	Legal-standard
Greece, 1988	42,6	42,0	19,9	-
Ireland, 1987	29,6	31,6	17,2	8,1
Catalonia, 1988	31,3	37,3	15,1	-
Belgium, 1985	21,4	24,9	6,1	2,9
Netherlands, 1986	10,9	15,9	7,2	7,2
Lorraine, 1986	30,8	26,5	10,8	4,0
Luxembourg, 1986	14,5	12,5	7,6	5,0

Using the *EC-standard*, the countries can be divided into two groups: the Benelux-countries, which have a low number of poor households, on the one hand, and on the other, Greece, Ireland and Catalonia, where the poverty rate is between two and three times as high. Lorraine seems to be situated between these two groups. The "poorer" countries, as measured by average household income, thus have more poor ([1]). This is *not* self-evident, as the EC-standard is defined as a proportion of average equivalent household income. It means, of course, that there is more income inequality in the "poorer" countries, *after* standardisation for family size, at least in the lower part of the distribution. In fact, we have seen that Ireland, Greece and Catalonia were the countries in which disposable household income was most unequally distributed.

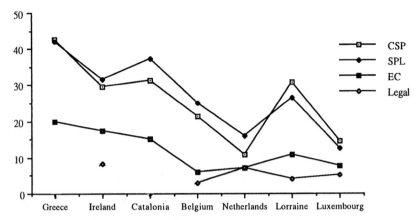

Figure 4.1   Percentage of all households whose means of subsistence are insecure, Belgium, 1985; The Netherlands, Luxembourg, Lorraine, 1986; Ireland, 1987; Catalonia and Greece, 1988

Looking at the *subjective standards*, the same pattern emerges, but far less clearly. Again Greece, Catalonia and Ireland have the largest number of households in poverty, but the difference between these countries and Belgium and Lorraine in particular is much reduced. In The Netherlands and Luxembourg the number of poor is much smaller than in Belgium (and Lorraine). It can further be remarked that the poverty rate using the SPL-standard is in most countries somewhat higher than the one obtained with the CSP-standard. These differences within and between countries are of course to a large extent the result of the divergent levels of the standards. In particular the relatively low amounts in The Netherlands are important.

The poverty rates produced by the *Legal-standard* follow a completely different pattern (not unexpectedly, as this poverty line is of a different nature). Ireland has the highest poverty rate, followed by The Netherlands, Luxembourg, Lorraine and Belgium (in this order). Greece and Catalonia have no guaranteed minimum income. Except perhaps for Belgium, these percentages appear rather high. In the case of Luxembourg and Lorraine they can be explained by the fact that in both countries the guaranteed minimum income was not yet in effect at the time of interviewing. (The Legal-standard has been calculated by deflating to that period.) In Ireland, some groups are not covered by the guaranteed income scheme, such as students, some self-employed persons and some full-time employees. But "the majority of families which fall below the (Legal-standard) do so not because they are ineligible for income support, but because, for whatever reason, they do not receive the support to which they are entitled" (Callan, Nolan a.o., 1989, p. 51). It is not clear what the causes of this non-take-up are, but lack of information seems to be one of them.

In The Netherlands the guaranteed minimum income does cover the whole population (except students), and it has been established for a long time, which makes it all the more surprising that the incomes of no less than 7% of all households fall short of it. The calculation of the guaranteed minimum income for The Netherlands is rather complicated, involving some special means-tested allowances, which people may not have taken up. The effect of non take-up on the number of people below the Legal-standard may be especially strong in The Netherlands, because a large number of households in The Netherlands receive flat-rate allowances under the general old-age social insurance scheme, or other general insurance schemes, and for many of these households this benefit is their only source of income. As the level of the allowances is generally on or near the guaranteed minimum income, even small short-falls will push these households below the Legal-standard. In Belgium, Luxembourg and Ireland on the other hand, social insurance schemes are to a greater extent earnings-related, or have minimum benefits, that are higher than the legal minimum income.

The changes across years in the poverty rates are shown in table 4.2. The poverty rates based on the EC-standard change very little. There is more change in the subjective poverty rates, in particular those based on the SPL. This is of course mainly an effect of the fluctuations in the poverty lines.

Table 4.2
Percentage of households in poverty by four standards in two waves

		CSP-standards	SPL-standard	EC-standard	Legal-standard
Ireland	1987	29,6	39,6	17,2	8,0
	1989	32,0	39,6	17,3	5,0
Belgium	1985	21,4	24,9	6,1	2,9
	1988	22,4	20,7	5,7	2,7
Netherlands	1985	12,4	8,6	7,1	8,5
	1986	10,9	15,9	7,2	7,2
Lorraine	1985	26,6	29,1	9,7	5,7
	1986	30,8	26,5	10,8	4,0
Luxembourg	1985	14,7	23,2	7,6	6,4
	1986	14,5	12,5	7,6	5,0

4.2. Poverty and subjective insecurity of subsistence

Table 4.3 shows how many households are, in their own evaluation, insecure of the means of subsistence. This means that they have at least some difficulty in making ends meet. In Ireland, Catalonia and The Netherlands a small majority of all households feel themselves financially insecure. In Belgium and Greece a majority considers itself financially secure, while in Lorraine, and especially in Luxembourg relatively few households have difficulties in making ends meet. Although feelings of not being able to make ends meet occur the least in the richest country, among the other countries there is no correlation between average household income, or the poverty rate, and the rate of subjective feelings of insecurity. Alternatively, one might suppose that people refer to the average standard of living in a country. Under this hypothesis, a higher degree of income inequality would produce more feelings of not having enough. But the country with the highest income inequality (Greece) has only a moderate rate of subjective insecurity.

Table 4.3
Percentage of all households that say they experience (at least some) difficulties in making-ends meet, by poverty status according to four standards

	Overall	CSP		SPL		EC		Legal	
		poor	non-poor	poor	non-poor	poor	non-poor	poor	non-poor
Greece, 1988	43,7	63,5	29,0	63,5	29,4	70,0	37,2	-	-
Ireland, 1987	50,7	75,7	40,2	70,9	40,2	80,0	44,6	70,7	51,1
Catalonia, 1988	53,8	83,2	40,5	78,1	39,5	89,3	47,5	-	-
Belgium, 1985	42,0	73,6	33,5	68,5	33,3	83,0	39,5	82,9	40,8
Netherlands, 1986	60,9	69,6	35,5	70,0	33,6	69,6	36,8	35,0	37,1
Lorraine, 1986	32,2	52,8	23,2	51,9	25,2	62,5	28,7	64,9	31,0
Luxembourg, 1986	18,8	43,6	14,6	57,0	15,4	54,8	15,9	49,4	17,2

Comparing self-report financial insecurity with the poverty status on the basis of each of the four standards, we find that self-evaluation correlates quite strongly, though far from perfectly, with the evaluation of the financial situation using the income standards. This is the case in all countries, for all standards: among poor households, self-report financial insecurity is much more important than among non-poor households.

Nevertheless, there are also large discrepancies. Between 20 and 40% of all households experience their financial situation otherwise than the standards indicate. The extent and direction of these discrepancies appear to be mainly a function of the overall subjective insecurity rate and to a lesser extent of the level of the income standards. If the subjective insecurity rate is high, and/or the level of the standard is low, there will be more non-poor people who feel themselves insecure, and less poor people who report no difficulty in making ends meet; and, of course, the reverse also holds.

In themselves these differences are not surprising or disturbing. It is clear that a statistical standard does not need to correspond to the feelings of the population, and the same is true for the Legal-standard. And the subjective standards too are designed to represent an average view of (certain groups of) households, not to capture individual perceptions. They are 'intersubjective', not subjective, in fact. Except in the case of total social agreement, there is not necessarily a close correspondence between such a standard and self-rating. Many variables influence the evaluation of its income by a household. Among these are the number, age and health status of the members of the household, the urban or rural environment, the standard of living of the social reference group and of the household itself in the past etc. The poverty standards used here take only the number and, to some extent, the age of household members into account. Many other characteristics could be incorporated into a more detailed set of poverty lines. Other variables, such as reference group, would probably be considered irrelevant from the point of view of social policy, even though they have a real effect on the subjective welfare of households.

4.3. The social distribution of the risk of being poor

The risk of poverty is distributed unequally over subgroups of the population. In this section we will therefore focus on the number of households that are in poverty in various subgroups of the population. As the overall number of households in poverty, has been discussed in the previous section, we will in this section concentrate more on the distribution of the risk of poverty over different groups in the population. To facilitate comparisons across countries of these distributions, we will use the *relative risk of insecurity* (poverty), i.e. the percentage of poor households in each social category in proportion to the overall percentage of households in poverty in the sample ([2]).

Risk of poverty by the labour market status of the head of household

In table A.3 in appendix figures are given for the risk of poverty according to the labour market status of the head of household. They show remarkable consistency, across standards, as well as across countries.

The figures clearly bring in evidence the all-important role the *employment* of the head of household plays in poverty. In all countries the percentage in poverty of households, whose heads are employed, is far below the average, while that of households whose head is not employed is far above. In The Netherlands, using the subjective standards, the risk of being in poverty for heads that are not employed, is no less than ten times as great as the risk for the employed heads. In Belgium (except on the basis of the Legal-standard) the percentage of households in insecurity is between three to five times as great if the head of household is not employed, than if he/she is employed. In Luxembourg, Lorraine and Ireland the difference in risk of poverty between the employed and the not employed seems to be somewhat smaller, but it is still considerable. In Greece, the poverty risk of employed heads of households is close to the average risk.

If we look at the category of not employed heads of households in more detail, it appears that the group that is most at risk of poverty (excluding "other" not employed, which is a rather heterogeneous rest-category) are the households whose head is *unemployed* (table 4.4). In Belgium (except according to the Legal-standard) more than 60% of all households headed by an unemployed person live in poverty. In The Netherlands the CSP-standard yields similarly high percentages at risk for the unemployed, but the SPL- and Legal-standards give lower estimates (which are still three to four times higher than average). In Luxembourg and Greece the risk of being in poverty rises above 70% for unemployed heads of households, and in Lorraine and Catalonia it is also extremely large. In Ireland too, households whose head is unemployed are far more at risk of financial insecurity than any other group (75% according to the CSP-standard, 59% even using the strict EC-standard). This is especially significant, because in Ireland this group of households is rather large (11%). In the other countries the number of households with a head that is unemployed is relatively small, comprising between 1% (Luxembourg) and 5,5% (Belgium) of all households.

Table 4.4
Relative risk* of being in insecurity of subsistence
for households with an unemployed head

	CSP-standard	SPL-standard	EC-standard	Legal-standard
Greece, 1988	171	180	183	-
Ireland, 1987	252	213	342	272
Catalonia, 1988	203	174	288	-
Belgium, 1985	287	238	430	283
Netherlands, 1986	394	321	271	325
Lorraine, 1986	208	222	380	503
Luxembourg, 1986	427	419	538	624

* average risk = 100

The *retired* are a group that is traditionally considered to be a group at great risk of poverty. However, from these figures their situation does not seem as bad as might be expected. The proportion in poverty is lower for retired heads of households than for the not employed in general, and the average insecurity score of poor retired heads of households is higher, indicating that they fall less deeply below the minimum income. Also, in comparison with the overall percentage, the situation of the retired in general does not appear very dramatic, which is brought out in table 4.5. This shows the risk of poverty for retired heads of households, relative to the risk for all households. The figures are not fully comparable, because in Luxembourg, Lorraine and Ireland, only persons, who have in the past participated in the labour force, can be retired. This excludes many widows. In the other countries all persons above retirement age are considered retired (as well as persons that have been retired early).

Table 4.5
Relative risk* of insecurity of subsistence for retired heads
of household, according to various standards

	CSP-standard	SPL-standard	EC-standard	Legal-standard
Greece, 1988	109	129	109	-
Ireland, 1987	61	111	46	51
Catalonia, 1988	129	156	146	-
Belgium, 1985	139	190	108	179
Netherlands, 1986	150	182	33	122
Lorraine, 1986	94	135	86	83
Luxembourg, 1986	103	132	97	80

* average risk = 100

The picture varies somewhat according to which standard one uses. The EC-standard generally produces a lower relative risk for the retired and the elderly than the other standards, because of its steep equivalence scale. On the basis of this standard, the risk to be in poverty for these households is only in Catalonia significantly higher than average. In Ireland and The Netherlands it is very much below the average risk. Using the subjective standards, retired households unequivocally face a higher than average risk in Belgium, The Netherlands and Catalonia. In Ireland it is below average by the CSP-standard, around average by the SPL-standard. In Greece, Lorraine and Luxembourg the results are mixed: the CSP-standard indicates a risk of poverty for households with retired heads that is about average, the SPL-standard a significantly higher one.

The *sick and disabled* heads of households form a rather diverse group, which comprises people who have been disabled after a long working career, as well as people who have been invalids all their life. Depending on the cause of the disablement and on other factors they are subject to different income replacement schemes, some of which may be earnings-related, while others are not. Using the CSP- and EC-standards, their risk of poverty is higher than that of retired heads of households in all countries. Using the SPL this is only the case in Luxembourg, Ireland and Catalonia.

Risk of poverty by profession of the head of household

Table A.4 in appendix shows to what extent social status as indicated by the profession of the head of household, influences the risk of poverty. Only results for employed heads of households are given, because these were available for all countries. The figures show that this risk falls strongly with rising socio-professional status, going from, generally, somewhat above the average for unskilled or semi-skilled manual workers, to half the average risk for higher clerical workers, managers, etc. This pattern can be observed in all countries, for all standards.

The position of small self-employed and farmers rather varies across the seven countries. Some caution is advisable in interpreting the statistics for these groups. The incomes of self-employed and farmers who still run their businesses can fluctuate a great deal from year to year, and is often not precisely known to the recipients themselves. Because of these fluctuations, income measured over a longer time-span, or even life-time income, would perhaps be more appropriate for these groups. Farmers are a group at high or very high risk of poverty in all countries, except Luxembourg. In most countries they form only a very small part of the population, but in Ireland and Greece they are an important group. It is noteworthy that the Irish research team has put special efforts into obtaining reliable measures of farm income (see Callan, Nolan a.o., 1989, p. 48-49). They also indicate that the year 1986, for which data were collected, was a distinct low point for farm income in Ireland. The results for the small self-employed are mixed.

Risk of poverty by education of the head of household

Education is another indicator of social status. The education an individual has got, is an important factor determining his opportunities in the labour market, and his chances of obtaining a sufficient income. The risk of poverty falls systematically with increasing level of education (see table A.5 in appendix). Heads of households with only primary education always suffer a relatively high risk of poverty.

Despite the similarity in the relation between level of education and poverty between countries, there are also some interesting differences. In Luxembourg and Lorraine as well as in Greece and Catalonia, about half of all heads of households seem to have had only primary education. In Belgium, one-third of all heads have only got primary education, and in The Netherlands 10%. The relative risks of poverty of other groups are affected by these differences in proportions, in the sense that lower cycle secondary education suffices to have a lower than average risk of insecurity in Luxembourg and Lorraine, but not in The Netherlands, and barely so in Belgium.

In the interpretation of these figures it has to be kept in mind that the average level of education is generally lower among older people. Because within each category of education, retired persons have a lower income than active persons, the differences regarding the rate of poverty between groups with different levels of education are partially due to the effects of age and retirement.

Risk of poverty by marital status of the head of household

If we break down insecurity of the means of existence by marital status of the head of household, we can observe some similarities as well as some differences between the seven countries (table A.6 in appendix). Using the EC-standard, *married heads of households* have a risk of being in poverty that is about average; using the SPL their risk is below average, although this is less the case in Catalonia and Greece; using the CSP-standard the difference is generally smaller, and becomes nonexistent in Ireland, Catalonia and Greece. In the Benelux and Lorraine, *unmarried* heads of households find themselves at a relatively high risk of poverty. In Greece and Catalonia, however, their risk is markedly lower than average. For Ireland, the results are mixed.

Widowed persons are by all standards at a high risk of poverty in Catalonia, Lorraine and to a lesser degree in Greece. For the Benelux-countries and Ireland, the results are equivocal, however. Using the subjective standards, widowers and widowers in the Benelux are much more likely to find themselves in poverty than the average household (twice as likely by the SPL). Using the EC-standard, on the other hand, their risk is below poverty. For Ireland, only the SPL indicates a higher than average risk for widowed persons (table 4.6).

Table 4.6
Relative risk* of being in insecurity of subsistence for households with widowed head

	CSP-standard	SPL-standard	EC-standard	Legal-standard
Greece, 1988	134	142	111	-
Ireland, 1987	79	165	38	65
Catalonia, 1988	150	172	181	-
Belgium, 1985	154	222	75	162
Netherlands, 1986	215	268	32	188
Lorraine, 1986	136	205	143	240
Luxembourg, 1986	132	254	70	164

* average risk = 100

Households headed by *divorced or separated persons* are in all countries at a relatively high risk of poverty. In Lorraine and Luxembourg only, the CSP-standard produces a somewhat lower than average risk for these households. Their poverty rate seems particularly high in Ireland (table 4.7).

Table 4.7
Relative risk* of being in insecurity of subsistence for households, of which the head is divorced or separated.

	CSP-standard	SPL-standard	EC-standard	Legal-standard
Greece, 1988	121	117	136	-
Ireland, 1987	180	185	192	265
Catalonia, 1988	107	119	140	-
Belgium, 1985	142	138	149	193
Netherlands, 1986	155	206	118	160
Lorraine, 1986	82	130	108	118
Luxembourg, 1986	96	99	153	204

* average risk = 100

Risk of poverty by age of the head of household

The percentages of households in poverty by age of the head of household are shown graphically in figure 4.2. This shows that by age the risk of insecurity often (except in Ireland and Catalonia) follows a U-like curve: insecurity of subsistence is high among households headed by persons 16-24 years old, lowest among the 25-50 years olds, and then rises steadily with age. The results from the CSP- en EC-standard do not always conform to this pattern, which probably has to do with the fact that the CSP-standard specifies lower minimum incomes for the elderly than it does for persons at active age. The EC-standard does not distinguish between elderly and non-elderly, but it is relatively low for small households, which may have a similar effect.

This pattern may be, at least partially, explained by reference to the typical employment career. The youngest age group probably contains many persons in unemployment or on low wages. In the age group between 25 and 50 years almost all men are employed, as well as many women. Many people reach the peak of their income. Labour market participation becomes much lower for women between 50 and 65 years old. For men as well it drops significantly, because of early retirement and invalidity. Over 65 years, labour market participation, of course, is virtually nihil, and almost all households fall back on pensions, which are generally at a lower level than their former wages. The oldest age-group, 75+ years, contains a disproportionally high percentage of widows, whose financial position is often vulnarable.

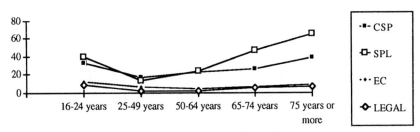

Belgium, 1985

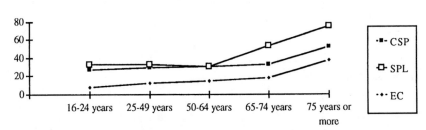

Catalonia, 1988

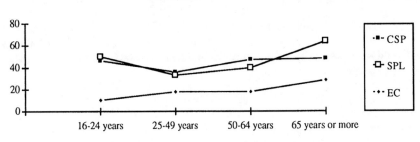

Greece, 1988

Ireland, 1987

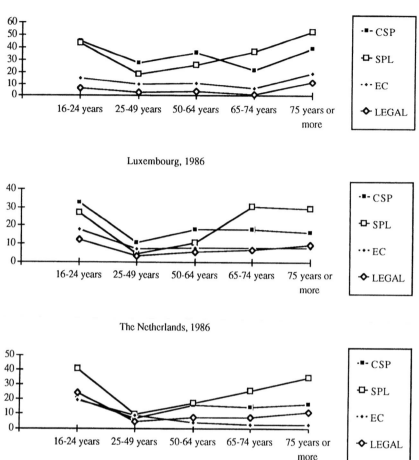

Figure 4.2   Percentage of households insecure of subsistence according to four poverty
standards by age of the head of household in seven countries

Despite these similarities across countries, there are also important differences. In Belgium
both very young and elderly heads of households are at high risk of being in poverty.
Using the subjective standards the risk of the elderly exceeds that of the young, but the
reverse holds if one uses the EC-standard. In The Netherlands and Luxembourg heads of
households aged 16-24, are the age group at highest risk. Only on the basis of the SPL
can the elderly be said to be at relatively high risk in these two countries. In Lorraine both
the young and the very old (75+) are at a high risk of poverty. Ireland presents a rather
different pattern: it is the only country where the risk of insecurity of subsistence is higher

for heads of households at active age than for elderly heads of households (except by the SPL-standard). In Catalonia the risk of insecurity rises steadily with the age of the head of household, and is particularly high for the very old. In Greece there are only modest differences between age groups as regards the risk of insecurity, though for the elderly this risk is somewhat higher than average.

It would not be easy to explain the differences across countries, and at this stage only some of the variables involved can be identified. In the fist place, *household formation* is obviously important. In some countries, young people may tend to live with their parents until they have sufficient income to form their own household. In other countries, they may leave their parental houses earlier. It is perhaps significant that the rate of insecurity of subsistence among very young households is relatively highest in countries where the number of these households is also relatively high (such as The Netherlands). Similarly, in some countries (perhaps Ireland, Greece and Catalonia) many elderly people may live with their adult children, especially if they have low incomes. Among persons aged 25-64 years the number of people who divorce or never marry is probably important. Secondly, *economic factors* will have an effect. Especially among adults at active age the number of households without earnings will be an important determinant of the poverty rate. In this context, the high unemployment rate in Ireland may be mentioned. Thirdly, the way *social security*, in particular the pension system, is organised must be taken into account. Pensions may be earnings-related in various degrees, they may have minimum amounts at various levels, there may exist one or several regimes for different socio-professional groups, these may cover the whole population or not.

Risk of poverty by sex of the head of household

Table A.8 in appendix makes clear that, except in Ireland, female headed households are at much greater risk of being poor than households headed by males are. This is not surprising, because (to make figures comparable) for all couples the man is taken to be the head of household, except in some special cases. Therefore, a woman can only be the head of a broken or "incomplete" family: single people, widows, one-parent households. These types of household are, for various reasons (see above and below) economically more vulnerable.
The relatively secure situation of female headed households in Ireland is probably due to the fact that widows (as the elderly in general) are relatively well of in Ireland (see above).

It may be observed that, while the CSP- and Legal-standards give estimates of the percentage of poor households that are about 1,5 to 2 times higher for female-headed than for male-headed households, the SPL-standard yields estimates with a ratio of 1 to 3 or 4. This is probably due to the fact that the SPL-standard specifies higher minimum incomes for single elderly persons than the other standards do. The majority of females who are head of their household are elderly widows.

On the other hand, by the EC-standard the situation of the female headed households appears to be much more favourable. This can be explained by the fact that the EC-standard gives relatively low minima for small households, in particular for single people.

Risk of poverty by nationality of the head of household

Households, whose head does not have the nationality of the country he lives in, have a higher risk of insecurity than the average household (table A.9 in appendix). This applies particularly to people from outside the EC. The risk of insecurity for heads of households with the nationality of another EC-country is generally not much greater than the risk for people with the nationality of the country itself.

Risk of poverty by type of household

The distribution of the risk of poverty over different types of household involves a large number of figures (see table A.10 in appendix). To simplify matters, we will first look at the elderly, secondly at adults at working age without children, thirdly at couples with children, and lastly at one-parent families.

The households in which the *elderly* live are mainly of three types: single elderly persons, elderly couples and households composed of one adult and one elderly person. The majority of households of the last type are couples but it also includes elderly single persons with one adult child.

Single elderly persons are at higher than average risk by all standards in Lorraine, Greece and Catalonia (table 4.8). For the other countries the results are mixed. Using the EC-standard, which is rather low for single persons, the poverty rate for single elderly is slightly below average in Belgium and Luxembourg, and much below average in The Netherlands and Ireland. On the basis of the SPL, their risk is two to three times as high as that of the average household in all countries. The CSP-standard produces somewhat lower estimates, which are still above average in all countries, except Ireland.

Table 4.8
Relative risk* of being in insecurity of subsistence for single elderly persons

	CSP-standard	SPL-standard	EC-standard
Greece, 1988	131	168	121
Ireland, 1987	91	222	17
Catalonia, 1988	147	230	194
Belgium, 1985	172	273	82
Netherlands, 1986	209	301	22
Lorraine, 1986	136	274	179
Luxembourg, 1986	177	368	93

* average risk = 100

Most households composed of *two elderly persons* are elderly couples, though sometimes other kinds of relationships may be involved. The poverty rate among these households is by all standards above average in Greece and Catalonia, and also in Belgium (table 4.9). Using the EC-standard it is also higher than average in Luxembourg and Ireland, and below average in Lorraine and especially The Netherlands. By the subjective standards, elderly couples are at relatively low risk of poverty in The Netherlands and in Ireland, while the results for Lorraine and Luxembourg are mixed.

Table 4.9
Relative risk* of being in insecurity of subsistence
for households consisting of two elderly persons

	CSP-standard	SPL-standard	EC-standard
Greece, 1988	120	168	169
Ireland, 1987	50	90	49
Catalonia, 1988	123	211	200
Belgium, 1985	127	202	185
Netherlands, 1986	74	89	44
Lorraine, 1986	76	123	85
Luxembourg, 1986	92	142	151

* average risk = 100

On the basis of the subjective standards, the poverty rate among elderly couples seems to be lower than among single elderly, but the reverse is true if the EC-standard is used. Most single elderly are of advanced age and/or widows, and often have relatively low pensions. Elderly couples are generally younger, and may have a higher occupational pension, or even enjoy two pensions.

Comparing across countries, the general picture that emerges is that households consisting of one or two elderly persons are at relatively high risk in Catalonia and Greece, and also in Belgium. In Ireland, on the other hand, the poverty rate for these households is at its lowest relative level. The results for The Netherlands seem very divergent.

Except in Catalonia, the risk of being in poverty for households, consisting of one elderly person and one non-elderly person, is around or below average.

When we turn to households, consisting of persons of active age, we find that in the northern countries and using the subjective standards, *single adults of active (working) age* are more at risk of insecurity than the average household (table 4.10). By the EC-standard (with its relatively low poverty line for one-person households), this is much less the case. In Catalonia and Greece the poverty rate of single persons is around average (subjective standards) or clearly below it (EC-standard). The group of single adults generally includes several groups whose financial position is often rather precarious. Some of them may be young persons, who have started recently to live on their own, with low income from employment, or with none at all, because of unemployment or because they are students. Others may be divorced persons, who also have a high risk of unemployment.

Households consisting of two persons of active age - most of them are married couples with no children - are at relatively low risk of poverty in all countries by all standards.

Table 4.10
Relative risk* of being in insecurity of subsistence for single adults

	CSP-standard	SPL-standard	EC-standard
Greece, 1988	106	85	37
Ireland, 1987	150	166	118
Catalonia, 1988	89	107	67
Belgium, 1985	140	163	95
Netherlands, 1986	211	242	118
Lorraine, 1986	96	165	116
Luxembourg, 1986	143	154	92

* average risk = 100

The results for *households consisting of two adults* and *one or more dependent children* (table 4.11) vary according to which standard one uses. Using the EC-standard one observes that the risk of being in insecurity of subsistence increases as the number of children rises. For couples with one child the poverty rate is almost always below average, for couples with three or more children it is always above average; in The Netherlands and Ireland it is even far above average. This result for Ireland is rather disturbing, as families with three children are very numerous in Ireland. For couples with two children the insecurity of subsistence rate is generally around or below average, except in The Netherlands where it is higher.

Table 4.11
Relative risk* of being in insecurity of subsistence for households consisting of two adults and one, two or three children

Country	Number of children	CSP-standard	SPL-standard	EC-standard
Greece, 1988	1	88	78	52
	2	88	66	72
	3	100	113	189
Ireland, 1987	1	120	75	99
	2	124	83	112
	3	132	114	199
Catalonia, 1988	1	71	75	36
	2	119	124	96
	3	129	136	117
Belgium, 1985	1	86	59	82
	2	71	43	88
	3	53	25	139
Netherlands, 1986	1	50	34	63
	2	37	35	150
	3	39	37	265
Lorraine, 1986	1	96	69	67
	2	87	52	65
	3	105	69	121
Luxembourg, 1986	1	87	37	68
	2	78	17	99
	3	38	7	229

* average risk = 100

The subjective standards produce rather different results, mainly because of their much flatter equivalence scales. There are also some differences between the CSP- and SPL-standards, possibly for the same reason. In the Benelux countries, both the CSP and SPL poverty rate among couples with one, two or three dependent children is lower than average, and moreover falls as the number of children increases. For Lorraine, the poverty rate for couples with one, two or three children is around average by the CSP-standard, but below it by the SPL-standard. The results of the subjective standards for Ireland, Catalonia and Greece are somewhat different. Both standards indicate that the risk of financial insecurity rises quite strongly as the number of children increases. In other respects too, the patterns are fairly similar to those of the EC-standard. The risk of couples with three children substantially exceeds the average risk; couples with one child have a relatively low risk; couples with two children are in between (in Catalonia somewhat above average risk, in Greece below it).

As a general conclusion on the situation of couples with dependent children we can say that small families - couple with one or two children - face a risk of insecurity of subsistence that is in no country very great. Although much depends on the equivalence scale used, it appears that in several countries, notably Ireland, families with three or more children are at high risk of insecurity of subsistence or of poverty.

An explanation of these findings would have to take account of many variables. Who are the people that get few, and who are the ones that get many children? At what stage in their lives do they get children? What are the consequences of having children, for instance for the labor market participation of the mother? Does financial support for families with children exist and how is it organized, in the tax system, through family allowances, study grants, in-kind benefits, etc.? As regards family allowances, it can be remarked that family allowances are virtually non-existent in Catalonia and Greece, that in Belgium they are very high for third and subsequent children, and that in Ireland they are relatively low, and do not depend on the rank of the child.

It is fair to say that *one-parent families* are a category of households that are generally recognised to be at high risk of poverty (table 4.12). We indeed do find very high relative rates of insecurity of subsistence among these households, in particular in Belgium, Catalonia, Ireland and Luxembourg. In The Netherlands, on the other hand, the results of the various standards are completely at odds with one another. Furthermore, it can be observed that one-parent families form a rather small part of the population (between 1,1% in Catalonia, and 3% in The Netherlands). This implies small sample sizes for this group, with consequences concerning the reliability of results.

It is noteworthy that the *household typology* used here is *not exhaustive*. In particular, complex households in which several adults live together, such as adult but unmarried children living with their parents, are not included. In the Benelux-countries and Lorraine the typology covers between 78% and 88% of all households, but in Ireland 74%, in Greece 66% and in Catalonia only 52% of all households (in Catalonia all persons of 18 years or older are regarded as adults). In the Benelux and Ireland, most of the poor are also found in households that fall within the typology (at least 78%). This is somewhat less the case in Lorraine for the EC-standard (72%). In Greece, however only between 62% and 70% of all poor households are covered by the household typology, and in

Catalonia only between 49% and 64%. This implies that some of the excluded types of household may be at relatively high risk of poverty.

Table 4.12
Relative risk* of being in insecurity of subsistence for households
consisting of one adult and child

	CSP-standard	SPL-standard	EC-standard
Greece, 1988	107	105	152
Ireland, 1987	154	214	112
Catalonia, 1988	137	140	158
Belgium, 1985	242	217	123
Netherlands, 1986	30	213	46
Lorraine, 1986	124	198	88
Luxembourg, 1986	324	376	337

* average risk = 100

Risk of poverty by number of income providers and by number of persons at work

Table 4.13 (also table A.11 in appendix) shows that a single income provider is in many cases not able to make a household secure of subsistence. This is true in all countries, except to some extent in Greece. With two income-providers however, the risk of insecurity is always below average; in the northern countries it is only half the average, or even less. Any additional income-providers do not seem to make much difference, probably because these are generally children with their own income.

Table 4.13
Relative risk* of being in insecurity of subsistence of households with one and
two income providers (persons with an income from earnings or a replacement income)

Country	Number of income providers	CSP-standard	SPL-standard	EC-standard
Greece, 1988	0 or 1	115	119	98
	2	85	85	94
Ireland, 1987	0 or 1	141	148	149
	2	55	45	40
Catalonia, 1988	0 or 1	154	163	165
	2	74	76	67
Belgium, 1985	0 or 1	156	163	146
	2	40	33	39
Netherlands, 1986	0 or 1	143	152	138
	2	27	23	35
Lorraine, 1986	0 or 1	141	163	153
	2	52	36	41
Luxembourg, 1986	0 or 1	147	161	132
	2	47	24	59

* average risk = 100

63

We have seen that households where the head is not at work are at a relatively high risk of poverty. This is even more true if there is no person at work at all in the household. In Greece, though, the risk of poverty of these households by the CSP- and EC-standards does not very much exceed the average risk.

It is perhaps more surprising that one income from work is in several countries, namely Luxembourg, Lorraine, Catalonia and Greece, not sufficient, or only just so, to provide more than average security of subsistence. Only in The Netherlands does one earned income appear to be enough to reduce the risk of poverty to a level very much below the average. Two or more incomes from work do reduce the risk of being in poverty in most countries, but in Greece, additional persons with earnings over and above the first one do not make very much difference. There can be two reasons behind this observation: either average earnings per worker fall as the number of persons at work in a household increases, or the number of earners correlates strongly with household size.

Risk of poverty by whether household owns or rents house

Table A.12 in appendix shows that if the household owns the house it lives in, the risk of insecurity of subsistence is smaller than if the house is rented, except in Greece. It has to be remembered that imputed rent from owning one's own house is not included in total income.

The difference between *owners and tenants* appears to be greater in The Netherlands than in the other countries. This probably has some connection with the fact that ownership of one's own house is less widespread in The Netherlands, than in the other countries. In Belgium, many elderly people, who presently may be living on low incomes, own their own house.

4.4. Composition of the poor

A somewhat different perspective on poverty is provided when we look at the composition of the poor. Some social categories are important among the poor, even though their risk of poverty is relatively low, simply because they form a large part of the population. Other groups with a high rate of poverty, but which are few in numbers, may form only a small minority among the poor. These characteristics provide clues to the proximate causes of poverty in EC-countries (tables A.13 - 17 in appendix).

The divergences between the standards used again make it difficult to obtain a clear picture of the characteristics of the poor. Nevertheless, the following observations can be made. In many poor households the *head is working*. By the strict EC-standard this is the case for around 40% of all poor households, except in Belgium where the proportion of working poor heads of households seems to be somewhat lower, and in Greece where it is considerably higher. By the subjective standards fewer among the poor households in the Benelux have working heads. In the majority of these households the head is the only bread-winner.

Table 4.14
Relative risk* of being in insecurity of subsistence of
households with no, one or two persons at work

Country	Number of persons at work	CSP-standard	SPL-standard	EC-standard
Greece, 1988	0	125	150	120
	1	99	96	92
	2	84	75	9
Ireland, 1987	0	175	216	176
	1	81	58	75
	2	47	33	56
Catalonia, 1988	0	185	206	233
	1	120	117	103
	2	37	28	25
Belgium, 1985	0	190	224	193
	1	89	63	77
	2	17	11	26
Netherlands, 1986	0	249	262	161
	1	45	40	90
	2	20	16	43
Lorraine, 1986	0	137	191	182
	1	113	89	84
	2	40	20	31
Luxembourg, 1986	0	182	269	167
	1	99	50	97
	2	30	9	43

* average risk = 100

In countries where a large part of the population is employed in agriculture (here Greece and Ireland), many of the poor are in *farmer's* households.

In several countries, *unemployed* heads of households are an important group among the poor. This is true in particular for Ireland, to a lesser extent for Belgium, and also for The Netherlands, Lorraine and Catalonia. In all countries unemployment allowances seem to be inadequate for many, if not most unemployed heads of households. The variations across countries are mainly related to the proportion of these households in the entire population.

Households where the head is *retired* and/or elderly are in most countries an important group among the poor, though by no means a majority. Inadequate retirement and survival pensions for *some* elderly are still an important cause of poverty. In Ireland, however, the retired and elderly seem to form only a small minority among the poor. Using the EC-standard, this is also true for the Netherlands. In Belgium these households form a larger proportion of all poor than in other countries.

Even though the poverty rate among *one-parent families* is generally very high, they are few in number. Therefore, only a small proportion of all poor households are one-parent households. This is rather in contrast to the situation in the USA.

In Ireland, more than one-third of all poor households by the EC-standard, and about one-quarter by the subjective standards, are two-parent *families with three or more children*. By the same standard, but not by the subjective standards, almost half of all poor Dutch households are two-parent families with two or more children. In the other countries, these households are much less represented among the poor by all standards.

In the northern countries, around three-quarters or more of all poor households have only *one, or no, income provider* (i.e. a person with an income from earnings or social security). In Greece, and to a lesser extent in Catalonia, many poor households have two or even more income providers.

4.5. Deprivation and poverty

In the previous sections we have been concentrating on poverty or insecurity of the means of subsistence, as measured by income standards. Here we will look at the *living standards of households* as measured by eight *life-style indicators*. These indicate whether a household possesses a certain household appliance or amenity or not. Households, whose means of subsistence are insecure will be compared to households that are secure. Unfortunately, these data were not available for Greece, and only partly for Lorraine.

The choice of the items has been dictated by what was common to the surveys. Unfortunately, this has limited the list to only eight items, which all refer to durables or to aspects of the housing quality.

Possession and non-possession of eight life-style indicators

In the first place, it is interesting to see how widespread these possessions are. From table 4.15 it appears that the items which we might call necessaries - refrigerator, indoor toilet, bath or shower, washing machine and dry dwelling - are possessed by the great majority of households in all countries. However, for each necessary item, the proportion of households not possessing it, is greater in Ireland than in the other countries (esp. as regards a washing machine). The exception is a damp dwelling, which seems to be more prevalent in Lorraine and Luxembourg. This item is possibly less reliable than the others, because the dampness or dryness of a dwelling is a matter of degree, and some people may have higher standards than others. Somewhat surprisingly, regarding only these "basic" amenities, Catalonia scores better than all other countries!

The "luxury"-items: colour television, car and central heating, are less widespread. For these also Ireland lags behind the other countries. Some of the findings, such as the prevalence of refrigerators and the relative absence of central heating installations in Catalonia clearly reflect climatic conditions.

Table 4.15
Percentage of all households who do *not* possess certain life-style indicators

	Belgium 1985	Netherlands 1986	Luxembourg 1985 [a]	Lorraine 1986	Ireland 1987	Catalonia 1988
Refrigerator	2,3	1,0	2,4	N.A.	4,5	0,4
Indoor toilet	3,1	1,5	5,8	4,1	6,3	1,7
Bath/shower	9,1	N.A.	7,6	N.A.	8,3	2,4
Washing machine	11,9	8,1	7,3	5,6	19,9	5,8
Dry dwelling	5,6	10,7	19,4	21,8	10,0	18,7
Colour TV	17,0	10,9 [b]	18,7 [b]	6,2	19,4	10,6
Car	27,1	30,0	27,7	24,5	37,4	31,1
Central heating	37,8	23,4	21,9	N.A.	44,8	71,4

[a] For Luxembourg, 1985 instead of 1986 results have been used, because the item "central heating" was lacking in the 1986 survey.

[b] Black and white *or* colour television

Deprivation and insecurity of subsistence

The lack of any item by itself does not indicate a lower living standard. It is *the cumulation* of not possessing several items that constitutes deprivation or poverty. Rather arbitrarily, we have considered all households, which do not possess three or more life-style indicators, to be living in deprivation (table 4.16). We find that, by this definition, Irish households are most at risk of being in deprivation, Dutch households the least [3]. The proportion of households in deprivation in Catalonia is barely higher than in Belgium and Luxembourg, and if we would omit the item "central heating", which is presumably less relevant in Catalonia, the proportion would very probably be lower. This is rather in contrast to the results of the income standards.

Table 4.16
Percentage of households, whose means of subsistence are secure/insecure, which do not possess three or more life-style indicators, out of eight.*

	All households	CSP		SPL		EC		Legal	
		sec.	insec.	sec.	insec.	sec.	insec.	sec.	insec.
Belgium, 1985	15,2	10,4	33,1	7,8	37,3	14,0	32,3	13,9	42,3
Netherlands, 1986*	7,5	6,1	19,0	4,5	23,3	6,7	17,2	5,9	26,2
Luxembourg, 1985	14,8	10,9	37,2	9,0	34,6	13,0	37,5	12,4	49,3
Lorraine	N.A.								
Ireland, 1987	22,3	18,3	32,4	15,5	37,7	21,3	28,1	21,9	30.0
Catalonia, 1988	15,4	10,9	24,9	9,1	26,4	12,7	30,4	-	-

* in The Netherlands only seven indicators were used.

Table 4.16 also shows that the probability of being in deprivation is much greater if one is financially insecure or poor, but that, nevertheless, *more than two-thirds of all poor or insecure households are not deprived, while a substantial minority of non-poor or secure households is.* Many possible reasons can be quoted for this finding that the correlation is far from perfect. In the first place, differences in living standards are possibly underestimated, because the quality of the items, which may vary a great deal for things like cars and baths or showers, is not taken into account. Secondly, insecurity of the means of subsistence depends only on the income in the current period, while whether one can afford items as these is also determined by the level of income in the past, and, if one takes loans or mortgages, by expectations about income in the future. Thirdly, the conditions in which households find themselves may vary in such a way, that certain items are more necessary for one household than for another. For instance, in rural areas with little or no public transport, it may be very difficult to live without a car. On the other hand, some people who can afford it, may simply prefer not to have a car or a colour television. Fourthly, the quality of a dwelling (indoor toilet, dryness etc.) may be only indirectly linked to household income, if the house is rented, especially if housing is heavily subsidised. Lastly, the cost of most of these items is not much smaller for a single person than for a family of five. In other words, the economies of scale for a colour television or a refrigerator are probably quite large. This means that a large family which is financially insecure, may still be better able to afford an item than a small family with an income (just) above the standard, because for the first family the cost is relatively lower.

It is noteworthy in this respect, that all items are either durable goods or aspects of the quality of the house, to which the arguments given above may apply more strongly, such that they depend less on current disposable or equivalent income than the material style of living as a whole. The results of Callan, Nolan a.o. (1988, pp. 111-123) for Ireland show that a more balanced deprivation index may well have a higher correlation with current income.

From a methodological point of view, these results can be interpreted in two ways. On the one hand, one might draw conclusions as regards to validity of the various income standards and the deprivation index. One might observe that generally poverty-status by the SPL has the strongest correlation, and poverty-status by the EC-line the weakest correlation with deprivation as measured here. However, because of the unsatisfactory nature of the deprivation index, as has been indicated above, no conclusions regarding the validity or reliability of either the income standards, or deprivation standards in general seem to be warranted on the basis of these results.

From a different perspective, the results might also be taken to indicate that the number of households that are really poor, in the sense that their style of life is very much below what is common in their society, is very small, smaller even than the poverty rates produced by the more stringent income poverty lines. Possibly many poverty spells are not long enough to have an important effect on the style of life. Detailed panel studies of households would be required to clear up this important issue. This interpretation may apply better to the richer countries than to those with a lower general living standard. Unfortunately, lacking data for Greece, only results for one of the 'poorer' countries, namely Ireland, are available.

Notes

(1)   Whether Catalonia can be considered a relatively "poor" region in the EC, is somewhat unclear as has been noted above.

(2)   The overall percentage of households in poverty can be computed as the average of the risks of insecurity in different groups, weighted by the proportions the groups form in the total sample. Therefore, the relative risk of a group, as defined here, will not only depend on its risk of insecurity, compared with the risk of other groups, but also on its weight in the overall sample. This means that the figures must be used with some caution. This effect will only be significant, however, if the size of a group is both large and varies strongly across countries.

(3)   Some calculations indicate that this is not only due to the fact that in The Netherlands only seven indicators could be used.

5 The adequacy of social security transfers

5.1. Introduction

In this chapter the social security system is assessed in terms of the objective of reducing poverty and insecurity of subsistence; other, possibly equally important, aims of social security are ignored. The method used is that of comparing pre-transfer and post-transfer incomes to the poverty lines. Pre-transfer income is defined simply as actual disposable income less actual social security transfers received. Post-transfer income is equal to disposable income. Pre-transfer income cannot be equalled with a hypothetical income in the absence of social security: social security contributions and taxes are not added to it, and behavioural changes are not taken into account. However, this relatively simple numerical exercise can serve as a first indication of the adequacy of social security.

This chapter is divided into two parts. Sections 2 to 4 treat the adequacy of social security as a whole, for the population as a whole. The second part focuses on the adequacy of social security by sector. Four sectors are discussed: pensions, unemployment allowances, sickness or invalidity allowances and family allowances. These four sectors cover most of social security in any country.

5.2. Reduction of the head-count

In the first place the question can be asked, how many households would be non-poor on the basis of their pre-transfer-income alone, and how many would be poor without transfers, but are lifted above the poverty line by social security transfers. Obviously the answers depend on the level of the poverty line, but there is less variation by standard in the poverty rate before social transfers are granted than after. This is the case because after subtracting social security transfers, many households have either no income at all, or an income from earnings that is above any standard.

This is especially true as regards the first part of the above question: how many households do not need social security transfers to be non-poor or secure of the means of subsistence (table 5.1)?

Table 5.1
Proportion of households whose means of subsistence are secure before social transfers

	CSP-standard	SPL-standard	EC-standard	Legal-standard
Greece, 1988	42,9	45,8	61,9	-
Ireland, 1987	47,1	49,9	53,8	57,5
Catalonia, 1988	55,3	52,2	69,2	-
Belgium, 1985	48,5	50,4	59,0	65,2
Netherlands, 1986	62,9	61,3	60,2	63,6
Lorraine, 1986	43,3	50,3	60,6	71,3
Luxembourg, 1986	56,7	64,0	61,1	68,3

Using the EC-standard, almost 70% of all households in Catalonia are not in insecurity of subsistence, even without social security. In Ireland, about half of all households are not in poverty before social security transfers. In the other countries, this percentage is around 60%. Using the CSP- and SPL-standards, the proportions of households whose means of subsistence are secure before social security transfers are generally lower, except in The Netherlands. The relative positions of countries are also somewhat different. In The Netherlands more than 60% of all households have an income before social security above the level of the subjective standards. High percentages are also given for Luxembourg and Catalonia. But, again, in Ireland and Lorraine, as well as in Greece, the number of households that do not need social security for their security of subsistence is relatively low.

To account for these differences the primary factor is probably the proportion of household with at least one person at work. Almost all households without a person at work will have only income from social security. (Few households have significant income from wealth). Households without a person at work form a smaller group in Greece and Catalonia, and to a lesser extent in Luxembourg, than in the other countries. In Ireland, by contrast, this group is very large. The correlation is far from perfect, however, because if the level of the standard is rather high, many incomes out of earnings will be insufficient to stay out of poverty, especially if the household is large. This may occur particularly frequently in Greece.

The second part of the question is: how many households are secure of the means of subsistence only after social transfers are granted? Using the EC-standard we find that in Belgium, The Netherlands, Lorraine and Ireland about one-third of all households are secure due to social security. In Luxembourg this proportion is a little lower, and in Greece and Catalonia it is only about one in six of all households. On the basis of the subjective standards, the proportions are somewhat lower, but the relative results for different countries are roughly the same.

But of course this comparison does not take into account that in some countries there are more households that can be lifted out of poverty by social transfers than in others. In table 5.2 are given the proportions of households that are non-poor or secure due to social transfers, of those that were poor or not secure before them.

Table 5.2

Proportion of households, insecure before social security, that are
secure of subsistence due to social security transfers

	CSP-standard	SPL-standard	EC-standard	Legal-standard
Greece, 1988	25,4	22,5	47,8	-
Ireland, 1987	44,2	36,9	62,8	80,9
Catalonia, 1988	29,9	22,0	51,0	-
Belgium, 1985	58,4	49,7	85,1	91,6
Netherlands, 1986	70,6	58,9	82,0	80,2
Lorraine, 1986	45,7	46,7	72,6	86,4
Luxembourg, 1986	66,4	65,6	80,5	84,2

By all standards (except the Legal-standard) the effectiveness of social security, defined in this way, is highest in the Benelux-countries. Using the EC-standard more than 80% of the poor before social security are not poor after it; using the subjective standards the pecentages vary between 50% and 70%. In Lorraine the proportions are somewhat lower. In Greece and Catalonia the effectiveness is much lower, and it is in fact very low indeed. By the EC-standard only half of all households that would be poor without social security are non-poor thanks to it; only one-quarter of these households are lifted to the level of the subjective standards. Ireland occupies a position between the Benelux and the southern countries.

The most proximate reasons for the differences could be three: either there is less social security in Ireland, Catalonia and Greece, i.e. the aggregate amount of social transfers is smaller, or the size of the problem is larger (more pre-transfer poor) or the available means are inefficiently used, i.e. less targeted at situations of poverty or insecurity of subsistence. In the next sections we will investigate what in fact is the case.

The findings presented above are very important for the evaluation of social security. Despite the very substantial (financial as well as administrative) resources of social security, the results in terms of lifting households out of poverty or insecurity of subsistence are not exactly brilliant. Only in the Benelux countries, and even there only when using the most strict standards, is the number of households left in poverty rather small.

The results, based on the Legal-standard, are particularly interesting. Because the Legal-standard is part of the social security system, we might say that using the Legal-minimum income is to evaluate the social security system by its own standard. In Belgium, 90% of all households whose income would be below the Legal-standard without social security, are brought above this level of income by the social transfers, but in Ireland and in The Netherlands social security succeeds in making secure of subsistence only 80% of the households that are insecure without it. The other countries are in between. It is not clear why a small group of households in all countries are below the legally guaranteed minimum. Lack of entitlement plays a role in some countries, non take-up of certain allowances is probably an important reason in most countries.

5.3. Reduction of the average poverty gap

In this section the financial accounts of social security are made up in terms of the security of the means of subsistence of households, based on the four standards. Despite the divergence in the levels of these standards, the results show a great deal of consistency.

It appears that households, that would be secure without social transfers, have a much greater pre-transfer income than the other categories of households. This is hardly surprising. More interesting is the finding that the average pre-transfer income of households that are secure after social transfers (but insecure before) is about equal to or only a little higher than the pre-transfer income of households that are insecure, even after social security. This suggests that the reason why the latter group of households are in poverty lies in the inadequacy of social security.

Table 5.3 makes clear that households which become secure of subsistence due to social security receive, on average, the largest amount of social transfers. The last remark applies especially to Greece. In most countries households that are already secure before social transfers, receive less than half of the average amount.

The category of households that remains financially insecure, even after social transfers, benefits much less from social security than households that become secure of their means of subsistence due to social security. In Belgium, The Netherlands, Ireland and Catalonia the former kind of households receive about the average amount, in Greece, Luxembourg and Lorraine they actually get even less than this.

Finally post-transfer income (i.e. total disposable income) can be computed as the sum of the two previous ones, and therefore presents no surprises. Households, that are secure before social transfers have the highest average amount of income, households whose security is due to social security are next, and households, insecure of subsistence, receive the lowest amounts of income.

Deficits and surpluses can be calculated by comparing the minimum income (according to each standard) with household income, before and after social security transfers. Households that are secure anyway have, on average, a large surplus of income excluding social transfers, and, of course, an even larger surplus including them. The income surplus of households that are made secure by social transfers (who, evidently, have a deficit before transfers), is much smaller.

Table 5.3
Social transfers per household, as a percentage of average transfers by security of subsistence status

	CSP	SPL	EC	Legal
GREECE, 1988				
Households:	CSP	SPL	EC	Legal
- secure before social transfers	47	43	49	-
- secure due to social transfers	368	408	327	-
- insecure after social transfers	60	73	51	-
IRELAND, 1987				
Households:	CSP	SPL	EC	Legal
- secure before social transfers	48	47	49	50
- secure due to social transfers	188	215	182	184
- insecure after social transfers	114	117	122	93
CATALONIA, 1988				
Households:	CSP	SPL	EC	Legal
- secure before social transfers	43	43	52	-
- secure due to social transfers	328	340	305	-
- insecure after social transfers	103	110	108	-
BELGIUM, 1985				
Households:	CSP	SPL	EC	Legal
- secure before social transfers	37	40	44	49
- secure due to social transfers	198	207	195	207
- insecure after social transfers	102	114	101	78
NETHERLANDS, 1986				
Households:	CSP	SPL	EC	Legal
- secure before social transfers	40	42	41	41
- secure due to social transfers	293	301	263	292
- insecure after social transfers	120	124	91	67
LORRAINE, 1986				
Households:	CSP	SPL	EC	Legal
- secure before social transfers	39	44	45	52
- secure due to social transfers	233	247	227	246
- insecure after social transfers	73	78	74	43
LUXEMBOURG, 1986				
Households:	CSP	SPL	EC	Legal
- secure before social transfers	41	49	44	51
- secure due to social transfers	225	239	214	229
- insecure after social transfers	83	99	80	75

The average pre-transfer poverty gap of households that live in insecurity of subsistence, is generally larger than the poverty gap of households that are secure due to social transfers, but not much so. Taking into consideration that average pre-transfer income is not much different between these two categories of households, this implies that the average level of needs, as indicated by the poverty-standards, is also about equal (the pre-transfer poverty gap is defined as poverty-standard minus pre-transfer income). What differentiates these categories households most from each other, is the level of social security transfers. We might therefore say, that some households are made secure of subsistence, while others are not, not because some households have more pre-transfer income than others, but because social security is directed more towards certain categories of households. Perhaps the fact that some social risks, notably retirement, are better protected by social security than other risks, such as unemployment, is one among several reasons for this.

The average shortfall of poor households (how far do they have to live below the poverty line?) is presented by the (post-transfer) *average poverty gap* for insecure households. This indicator reflects the intensity of poverty for households living in poverty. Although, of course, social transfers everywhere fall short of completely closing the poverty gap for households insecure of the means of their subsistence, they do so to a varying extent as is shown in table 5.4. In Belgium, The Netherlands and Luxembourg the disposable income of these households is on average around 20% below the poverty line. In Ireland and Lorraine the average shortfall is equal to about one-quarter of the poverty line and in Greece it exceeds 35% of the poverty line. It is remarkable that, within each country, the average shortfall does not vary much by standard.

Table 5.4
Average poverty gap after social security transfers, of households
insecure of subsistence, as a percentage of the standard

	CSP-standard	SPL-standard	EC-standard	Legal-standard
Greece, 1988	- 35	- 38	- 35	-
Ireland, 1987	- 27	- 27	- 27	- 33
Catalonia*	N.A.	N.A.	N.A.	N.A.
Belgium, 1985	- 19	- 21	- 17	- 20
Netherlands, 1986	- 20	- 22	- 23	- 28
Lorraine, 1986	- 24	- 26	- 25	- 32
Luxembourg, 1986	- 20	- 22	- 19	- 15

* For Catalonia the average poverty gap in a percentage of the standard is not given.

5.4. Reduction of the aggregate poverty gap

Looking at the distribution of the aggregate amounts of social security transfers, we observe that more than half of all social transfers is directed to households that only become secure of subsistence through them.

Table 5.5 shows which percentage of all social transfers is received by households, whose pre-transfer income is below the minimum income. By the EC-standard, this share is somewhat lower in Greece and especially in Catalonia, than in the other countries, where it varies remarkably little, between 73% and 79%. Using the subjective standards, no clear pattern emerges.

Table 5.5
Share in total aggregate social transfers, received by households,
insecure of subsistence before social transfers, based on four standards

	CSP-standard	SPL-standard	EC-standard	Legal-standard
Greece, 1988*	79,2	80,3	69,5	-
Ireland, 1987	77,5	76,6	73,6	70,8
Catalonia, 1988	76,2	77,3	64,3	-
Belgium, 1985	81,7	79,7	74,1	68,2
Netherlands, 1986	78,1	77,4	79,1	77,6
Lorraine, 1986	83,1	77,8	73,0	62,7
Luxembourg, 1986	76,7	68,6	73,2	64,9

The most important statistic in this context is the *poverty gap after social transfers are granted* (this is equal to the total income deficit of all households, insecure of subsistence). The poverty gap is the sum of money that would be theoretically sufficient to solve the problem of insecurity of subsistence, by handing out to each household, insecure of subsistence, the amount of income that it needs to reach the level of social subsistence, supposing this could be done with perfect targeting. In order to facilitate interpretation, in table 5.6 the poverty gap is given as a percentage of aggregate income of all households.

Table 5.6
The post-transfer poverty gap as a percentage of aggregate income of all households

	CSP-standard	SPL-standard	EC-standard	Legal-standard
Greece, 1988	N.A.	N.A.	N.A.	-
Ireland, 1987	5,0	4,5	2,7	1,7
Catalonia, 1988	5,3	7,0	1,8	-
Belgium, 1985	2,6	3,0	0,5	0,2
Netherlands, 1986	1,0	1,6	0,9	0,9
Lorraine, 1986	5,4	4,0	1,4	0,4
Luxembourg, 1986	1,6	1,3	0,8	0,3

The poverty gap appears to be relatively large in Ireland, Catalonia and Lorraine (1,4% to 2,7% by the EC-standard, 4% to 7% by the subjective standards). In the Benelux-countries the poverty gap is a relatively insignificant amount: less than 1% of aggregate household income by the EC-standard, between 1% and 3% by the subjective standards. Unfortunately, there are no results on this point for Greece, but because both the number of poor and the average poverty gap exceeds those in any of the other countries, it seems likely that the poverty gap in Greece is much larger - relatively - than anywhere else.

The data also enable us to compute some of the *Beckerman ratios*, through which we can evaluate the effectiveness and the efficiency of the social security system. By effectiveness we understand the extent to which social security succeeds in "relieving the poor", i.e. how far the poverty gap before social transfers is eliminated by social security. The measure of efficiency, on the other hand, indicates what part of social security actually helps in making households secure of subsistence, and what part is received by households who are financially secure already. The latter part includes transfers received by households, that are financially insecure before social transfers, over and above what they strictly need to reach the minimum income level. This is illustrated in figure 5.1.

Here we assess "efficiency" and "effectiveness" purely in terms of minimum income standards. It has to be kept in mind that relieving insecurity of the means of subsistence is certainly not the only aim of social security. Historically, the primary aim of social insurance (as distinguished from social assistance) has been the protection of the standard of living of persons who experienced certain social risks, such as unemployment, invalidity or retirement.

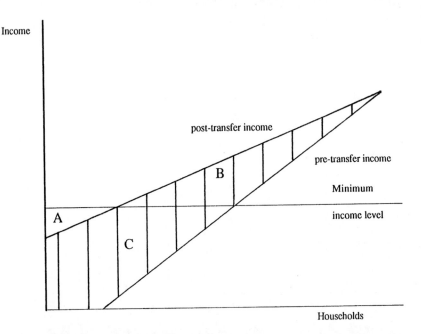

The shaded area (B+C) represents social transfers. Area A is the poverty gap, Areas A and C together form the poverty gap before social security. Area B stands for the part of social transfers that is received by households which do not strictly need it for their security of subsistence. Thus we can measure effectiveness by C/(A+C) and efficiency by C/(B+C).

Figure 5.1   Illustration of Beckerman ratios

From table 5.7 it appears that social security is most *effective* in the Benelux-countries: using the EC-standard or Legal-standards, more than 90% of the pre-transfer poverty gap is eliminated; using the subjective standards 85% or more is closed. In Lorraine and Ireland the effectiveness of social security is slightly less. In Catalonia social security seems relatively ineffective: using the EC-standard less than three-quarters of the poverty gap is eliminated, by the subjective standards barely half of the poverty gap is closed.

Table 5.7
Effectiveness of social security: percentage of
pre-transfer aggregate poverty gap eliminated by social transfers

	CSP-standard	SPL-standard	EC-standard	Legal-standard
Greece, 1988	N.A.	N.A.	N.A.	-
Ireland, 1987	75,0	76,9	83,0	86,6
Catalonia, 1988	57,9	52,7	74,8	-
Belgium, 1985	86,5	84,7	95,7	98,2
Netherlands, 1986	90,9	86,9	90,9	91,3
Lorraine, 1986	73,3	77,3	88,3	94,0
Luxembourg, 1986	88,1	89,9	92,6	96,7

Generally speaking, there can be three reasons for a low effectiveness: either the size of the problem (the pre-transfer poverty gap) is relatively large, or the resources of social security are insufficient, or these resources are not sufficiently targeted towards the poor (low efficiency). The pre-transfer poverty gaps as a percentage of aggregate household income using the EC-standard are as follows: Ireland: 15,6%; Catalonia: 7,0%; Belgium: 12,6%; The Netherlands: 10,0%; Lorraine: 11,5% and Luxembourg: 10,8%. The size of the problem, therefore seems to be one of the reasons why the Irish social security system is less effective than the Benelux ones, but this is not true for Lorraine and certainly not for Catalonia.

From the point of view of eliminating poverty and insecurity of subsistence, all social security systems are rather *inefficient* (table 5.8): between 35% and 60% of aggregate social transfers goes to households that are non-poor before social transfers or to households in excess of what they strictly need to stay above the poverty line. By all standards, the Irish system is one of the least inefficient: using the CSP-standard, only 38% of total transfers is "wasted". Table 5.8 also shows that the relatively low effectiveness of social security in Catalonia is not primarily due to lower efficiency: the efficiency of social security in Catalonia is not lower than in the Benelux-countries.

Table 5.8
Efficiency of social security: percentage of
aggregate social transfers that helps to close the poverty gap

	CSP-standard	SPL-standard	EC-standard	Legal-standard
Greece, 1988	N.A.	N.A.	N.A.	-
Ireland, 1987	62,3	61,5	53,7	45,0
Catalonia, 1988	57,0	61,1	41,4	-
Belgium, 1985	59,1	59,7	42,7	43,8
Netherlands, 1986	49.8	51.8	42.3	46.7
Lorraine, 1986	55,6	51,8	38,5	23,2
Luxembourg, 1986	47,9	44,0	39,3	33,7

5.5. Adequacy of social security by sector

This chapter focuses on the adequacy of social security by sector. Four sectors are discussed: pensions (retirement, survival, early retirement), unemployment allowances, sickness or invalidity allowances and family allowances. Together these four sectors cover almost all of social security. The sectors are not legal concepts, any sector may encompass several different schemes. Because results on the adequacy of social assistance were available for only three countries (Belgium, The Netherlands and Catalonia), and in two of these countries were based on a very small number of households, it did not make much sense to do a comparative analysis of the adequacy of social assistance.

Unfortunately, data on the adequacy of social security by sector were not available for Ireland and Greece.

The approach in this chapter is basically the same as in the preceding chapter on the impact of social security as a whole. Pre- and post-transfer incomes are compared to the poverty line. However, there are some important differences. In the first place, the analysis is carried out only for households receiving the particular type of transfer income (thus, households with pensions, households with unemployment transfers, ...), not for all households (as in the preceding chapter). Secondly, pre-transfer income is defined as available household income minus the particular type of transfer, not minus all transfers. Thus, while analyzing the adequacy of unemployment allowances, pre-transfer income excludes these payments, but it may include other transfer payments, such as family allowances, or invalidity allowances (of course it includes all non-social security income).

The method chosen has important implications for the interpretation of the results. In the first place, because only households actually receiving a certain kind of transfer are considered, inadequacies due to lack of entitlement or non-take-up are not measured. Ignoring non-coverage may have different impacts in the various countries, especially as regards unemployment allowances. However, apart from the group of households actually receiving a transfer, it would have been very difficult to define an appropriate target group in a comparable way across countries.

Secondly, the definition of pre-transfer income (disposable income minus the particular kind of transfer under consideration) implies that the effect of each kind of transfer is assessed, in the situation that all other kinds of transfer have already been received. What is in fact measured is the *'marginal'* effect of a particular kind of transfer. The results by sector cannot be interpreted as a kind of decomposition of the overall effect of social security.

For each sector, the following results are presented and discussed. Firstly *the number* of poor and non-poor households before and after a certain social security benefit. Secondly the *average amounts* of incomes and allowances, and the average income surpluses and income shortages relative to the poverty line (the latter is called the "average poverty gap", which reflects the intensity of poverty for poor beneficiary households). Thirdly the *total amounts*, transferred to households non-poor or secure before, non-poor or secure due to, and poor or insecure after receiving the benefit under consideration.

5.6. Adequacy of pensions

The number of poor/non-poor before and after pensions

As table 5.9 shows, in most countries a large majority of households receiving pensions would be poor without the existence of pension schemes. According the EC-standard the proportion of households whose means of subsistence are insecure without pensions is the largest in The Netherlands and in Belgium (around 80%). In Lorraine and Luxemburg this percentage is somewhat lower (respectively 77 and 73%). In Catalonia a relatively high number of households receiving pensions do not need this transfer for their security of subsistence.

Table 5.9
The number of households with a pension *secure before pensions,*
as a percentage of all households with pensions

	CSP	SPL	EC	Legal
Belgium, 1985	11	11	19	22
The Netherlands, 1986	15	15	19	16
Luxembourg, 1986	22	28	27	33
Lorraine, 1986	15	17	23	31
Catalonia, 1988	28	27	41	N.A.

Using the CSP and the SPL-standards the differences between the countries are smaller. The number of beneficiary households poor without pensions in Lorraine is now comparable to that in Belgium and the Netherlands. Again in Catalonia, but now also in Luxembourg, fewer households with pensions are poor before receiving a pension than in the other countries.

Households with pensions can be non-poor before pension transfers either because of other income of the pensioners themselves (earnings, income from capital), or because of other persons in the household with a non-pension income. This latter factor may be particularly important in Catalonia.

A second question is, how many households are lifted above the poverty line because of pension income? Using the EC-standard, the impact of pensions is very large in the Netherlands: 81% of all households with a pension are becoming secure of subsistence due to pensions. The impact is not much smaller in Belgium. In Luxembourg and Lorraine about two thirds of all households receiving pensions are lifted above the poverty line by pensions. In Catalonia, however, this proportion is only one third. The results according the Legal-standard are very similar. On the basis of the subjective standards the proportions are lower, in particular for Belgium, but the pattern across countries is roughly the same.

But it makes more sense to express the number of households becoming non poor due to pensions, as a % of all households in poverty before pensions (table 5.10).

Table 5.10
The number of households receiving pensions, *becoming secure due to pensions,*
as a percentage of all households insecure before pensions

	CSP	SPL	EC	Legal
Belgium, 1985	69	51	93	94
The Netherlands, 1986	90	75	99	96
Luxembourg, 1986	80	69	91	92
Lorraine, 1986	67	60	88	96
Catalonia, 1988	48	34	67	-

In most countries, a large majority of all pension receiving households that would be poor without them, are non-poor due to these transfers. Using the EC standard we find that the impact of pensions is extremely large in the Netherlands: almost all beneficiary pre-transfer poor households made secure by pensions. In Belgium, Luxembourg and Lorraine too, the impact of pensions for beneficiary households is very large. Catalonia registers a much smaller impact compared to the other countries.

On the basis of the subjective standards the impact of pensions is smaller in all countries, but the main differences between the countries remain. Pensions are the least effective in Catalonia and the most effective in the Netherlands. According the Legal-standard pensions have a strong poverty reducing impact for households receiving a pension in all countries.

A final question to be answered is, how many households receiving pensions remain poor despite their pension income (table 5.11)?

Table 5.11
The number of households with pensions *insecure after pensions*,
as a percentage of all households with pensions

	CSP	SPL	EC	Legal
Belgium, 1985	28	44	6	5
The Netherlands, 1986	8	21	1	4
Luxembourg, 1986	16	22	7	6
Lorraine, 1986	28	34	9	3
Catalonia, 1988	38	48	19	N.A.

On the basis of the EC-standard the risk of poverty for households with a pension income after receiving this benefit is almost non-existent in The Netherlands, but rather high in Catalonia. Using the subjective standards the proportions of households being in poverty after pensions are granted are much higher. The relatively low number for the Netherlands is partly explained by the low subjective CSP standard for this country.

Reduction of the average poverty gap

In terms of poverty reduction it is not only important to know how many households are falling below the poverty standard before and after a social benefit is granted but also to see how far they do fall on average below a certain minimum income level (this is the average poverty gap). This result is determined by the level of the pre-transfer income, and by the level of the transfer itself.

As could be expected, the average *pre-transfer* income of households, who are secure before transfer is substantially higher than that of the average beneficiary household . In Catalonia this is less the case (twice as high), in Belgium most (four times as high).

82

A second observation is that households becoming non-poor due to pensions receive on average the largest amount of *benefit* (see table 5.12), next are households that are already secure before pensions, while households who remain in poverty due to pensions receive the lowest average amounts.

Table 5.12

Average pensions for beneficiary households secure before, secure due to and insecure after pensions, as a percentage of overall average pensions

	CSP	SPL	EC	Legal
Belgium, 1985				
- secure before	82	82	84	85
- secure due to	116	126	108	108
- insecure after	73	78	57	52
The Netherlands, 1986				
- secure before	89	89	88	90
- secure due to	106	115	103	103
- insecure after	59	62	21	55
Luxembourg, 1986				
- secure before	81	86	82	85
- secure due to	117	125	112	113
- insecure after	58	60	57	47
Lorraine, 1986				
- secure before	94	96	90	89
- secure due to	122	136	110	108
- insecure after	58	58	46	22
Catalonia, 1988				
- secure before	94	92	94	N.A.
- secure due to	129	137	120	N.A.
- insecure after	78	85	72	N.A.

As a result of pre-transfer and pension transfer income the *average post-transfer* income for households receiving pensions is at the highest level for households already secure without pension income, followed by households becoming secure due to pensions and finally lowest for households remaining poor despite pensions.

Table 5.13 presents the average surpluses and deficits (poverty gaps) for household receiving pensions before and after pensions are granted, as a percentage of the average poverty line per category of household.

Households secure before pensions have a substantial surplus income before pensions and an even larger one after transfers. In most countries, the pre-transfer poverty gap of post-transfer poor households is only a little bit larger than that for households becoming non-poor due to pensions. For Catalonia, however, the differences between these two categories are much larger.

The average post-transfer poverty gap for poor households with pensions is in most countries below 20%. In Catalonia and Lorraine it is somewhat higher; in The Netherlands it is much lower (except by the EC-standard, but this figure is based on very few cases).

Table 5.13
Average poverty gaps and income surpluses of households with
pensions before and after pensions, as a percentage of the average poverty line,
by security status before/after pensions*

	CSP		SPL		EC		Legal	
	before	after	before	after	before	after	before	after
Belgium, '85								
- secure before	+ 46	+ 106	+ 55	+ 117	+ 62	+ 148	+ 72	+ 168
- secure due to	- 71	+ 41	- 68	+ 40	- 78	+ 71	- 82	+ 84
- insecure after	- 92	- 17	- 95	- 21	- 91	- 18	- 93	- 16
The Netherlands, '86								
- secure before	+ 148	+ 240	+ 158	+ 251	+ 152	+ 259	+ 139	+ 230
- secure due to	- 73	+ 58	- 70	+ 58	- 73	+ 88	- 73	+ 63
- insecure after	- 93	- 10	- 91	- 13	- 64	- 32	- 84	- 17
Luxembourg, '86								
- secure before	+ 56	+ 115	+ 87	+ 167	+ 63	+ 132	+ 100	+ 194
- secure due to	- 70	+ 58	- 78	+ 63	- 73	+ 78	- 84	+ 90
- insecure after	- 85	- 19	- 92	- 19	- 89	- 18	- 92	- 16
Lorraine, '86								
- secure before	+ 52	+ 131	+ 66	+ 154	+ 80	+ 185	+ 146	+ 310
- secure due to	- 69	+ 59	- 71	+ 61	- 73	+ 91	- 76	+ 157
- insecure after	- 79	- 23	- 86	- 24	- 79	- 20	- 87	- 28
Catalonia, '88								
- secure before	+ 71	+ 109	+ 77	+ 113	+ 89	+ 139		
- secure due to	- 39	+ 31	- 33	+ 27	- 47	+ 43	N.A.	N.A.
- insecure after	- 64	- 25	- 74	- 31	- 68	- 20	N.A.	N.A.

* The average poverty line for each category of households has been estimated because figures on the poverty gaps and income surpluses expressed as a percentage of the standard of each individual household, and then averaged (as in table 5.4), were not available.

estimated poverty line = average post-transfer income - average surplus or deficit

Reduction of the aggregate poverty gap

The aggregate amounts allow us, by means of the Beckerman ratio's, to answer two important questions. Firstly, to what extent is the poverty gap before pensions reduced by pensions for beneficiary households? The answer to this question is an indicator of the effectiveness of pension transfers. Secondly, how is the total amount spent on pensions divided over various households and what part of pensions is actually directed toward closing the poverty gap? This answer indicates the efficiency and non-efficiency of pensions in terms of a minimum income guarantee.

Table 5.14 presents the *effectiveness* of pensions. According to the EC- and Legal-standards, the effectiveness of pensions for beneficiary households is almost complete in the Benelux countries and in Lorraine, and only a little less effective in Catalonia. On the basis of the subjective standards the effectiveness is somewhat lower, especially in Catalonia, but still very high.

Table 5.14

Effectiveness of pensions: percentage of pre-pension aggregate poverty gap for households with a pension eliminated by pension transfers

	CSP	SPL	EC	Legal
Belgium, 1985	93	87	98	99
The Netherlands, 1986	99	96	100	99
Luxembourg, 1986	95	93	98	99
Lorraine, 1986	89	88	96	99
Catalonia, 1988	75	66	87	N.A.

Defining the efficiency ratio as the share of aggregate pensions that is flowing to poor households in so far as they strictly need this pension transfer to be lifted out of poverty, we observe (table 5.15) that pensions are nowhere terribly efficient, though they are less inefficient in Belgium than in the other countries. Using the EC-standard, in Belgium 46% of all pensions serve to close the poverty gap, in the other countries this proportion is 40% or less. By the subjective standards, the efficiency is higher in all countries, and again highest in Belgium.

Table 5.15

Efficiency and inefficiency of pensions

	CSP			SPL			EC			Legal		
	(1)	(2)	(3)	(1)	(2)	(3)	(1)	(2)	(3)	(1)	(2)	(3)
Belgium, '85	65	26	9	70	21	9	46	38	16	41	40	18
The Netherlands, '86	51	36	14	54	33	13	38	45	17	47	39	14
Luxembourg, '86	49	33	18	48	28	24	40	38	22	36	36	28
Lorraine, '86	54	32	14	54	30	16	38	42	21	24	48	28
Catalonia, '88	54	20	26	60	15	25	39	23	39	N.A.	N.A.	N.A.

(1) part of aggregate pensions flowing to poor households before pensions, up to the level of the poverty line, but not in excess of the poverty line (= efficiency-ratio)

(2) 'spill over effect': part of aggregate pensions flowing to households that are poor before pensions, but in excess of the poverty line.

(3) part of aggregate pensions flowing to households already non-poor before pensions.

(1) + (2) + (3) = 100.

The inefficiency in most countries is mainly due to the spill-over effect, i.e. a relatively large share of all pensions goes to households in excess of what they strictly need in terms of a minimum income guarantee. This is explained by the fact that pensions in most countries also aim at protecting the living standard of retired persons. In Belgium the spill-over is somewhat lower than in the other countries. In Catalonia, however, the inefficiency is mainly caused by the relatively large share flowing to households, who are already secure before pensions.

5.7. Adequacy of unemployment allowances

Reduction of the head-count

Table 5.16 shows that in all countries a large proportion (at least one-third) of all households receiving unemployment allowances are already secure before these transfers are granted. This is much more than is the case for pensioners. Except some that are part-time employed, few unemployed persons will have much other sources of income, but many of them live in households where other persons have other sources of income. This applies in particular to married women, and to young persons living with their parents.

Table 5.16
Number of households with unemployment allowances *secure before unemployment allowances,* as a percentage of all households with unemployment allowances

	CSP	SPL	EC	Legal
Belgium, 1985	32	39	55	63
The Netherlands, 1986	40	40	41	41
Luxembourg, 1986	42	64	62	71
Lorraine, 1986	41	59	68	82
Catalonia, 1988	35	33	46	N.A.

Nevertheless large differences across countries can be noticed. By the EC-standard, the number of beneficiary households secure before unemployment transfers is at a significantly lower level in the Netherlands than in the other countries. In Catalonia too, relatively few beneficiary households are secure before unemployment allowances. On the other hand, in Lorraine (and also in Luxembourg) a substantial group of beneficiary households are secure before unemployment allowances.

The number of households made secure by unemployment allowances, as a proportion of all households who were poor before transfers, can be found in table 5.17. By all standards the strongest reduction in poverty is found in The Netherlands. Belgium is ranked in the second position. In Luxembourg and Lorraine less than half of pre-transfer poor beneficiary households are made secure by unemployment allowances.

Table 5.17
Number of households with unemployment allowances becoming
secure due to unemployment allowances, as a percentage of all beneficiary
households poor before unemployment allowances

	CSP	SPL	EC	Legal
Belgium, 1985	50	53	74	90
The Netherlands, 1986	64	56	80	88
Luxembourg, 1986	34	40	48	80
Lorraine, 1986	40	40	48	82
Catalonia, 1988	38	36	59	N.A.

The final result, i.e. the number of households remaining poor despite unemployment allowances is shown in table 5.18. According to the EC-standard, poverty among households with unemployment allowances is the largest in Catalonia, even after these transfers are granted. Also in Luxembourg and Lorraine the poverty risk is relatively high. In Belgium and The Netherlands households benefiting from unemployment allowances are facing a lower poverty risk. In Belgium this is the result of fewer households in poverty before allowances and of a moderate impact of unemployment allowances. In the Netherlands we observe a reverse situation: more households in poverty before unemployment allowances, but also a higher impact. The final result in Belgium and the Netherlands is quite similar. Using the CSP-standard the differences between the countries are much larger. The low poverty risk for the Netherlands, is partly due to the low level of the CSP poverty line in the latter country.

Table 5.18
Number of households with unemployment allowances *poor despite unemployment allowances,* as a percentage of all households with unemployment allowances

	CSP	SPL	EC	Legal
Belgium, 1985	34	29	12	4
The Netherlands, 1986	22	26	12	7
Luxembourg, 1986	38	22	20	6
Lorraine, 1986	36	25	17	3
Catalonia, 1988	40	43	22	N.A.

Reduction of the average poverty gap

The average pre-transfer household income of households with an unemployment benefit, that are secure before benefit, is higher than that of the other categories of beneficiary households. This observation is true for all countries and for all standards. We find furthermore that the *pre-transfer poverty gap* of households that are made secure by unemployment allowances, is smaller than that of beneficiary households that are left in poverty (table 5.19). The reason for this, however, is a different one according to the standard used. On the basis of the EC-standard, there is for most countries little difference (except for Luxembourg, but sample numbers are very small) in the level of pre-transfer income between these two kinds of households, but the poverty-lines do differ and therefore the level of needs. Households remaining in poverty have higher needs than households becoming secure due to unemployment allowances. According to the more generous subjective poverty lines we find the reverse picture: pre-transfer income is significantly higher for households becoming secure due to unemployment allowances than for households remaining in poverty after benefit, while with regard to the level of poverty line there does not seem to be any consistent difference.

Not only do needs differ between the various household categories, but also the level of *average unemployment transfers* received by these categories. A general pattern is that households already secure of subsistence always receive less than average. Households becoming secure due to unemployment transfers receive on average the highest benefits, except in Belgium, where the benefits received by households remaining in poverty are, surprisingly, equally high. In the other countries the latter kind of households get slighty less than average (except Luxembourg, where the number of households with unemployment allowances is very small).

Table 5.19

Average poverty gaps and income surpluses for households with unemployment allowances before and after unemployment allowances, as a percentage of their average poverty line, by security status before/after unemployment allowances *

	CSP		SPL		EC		Legal	
	before	after	before	after	before	after	before	after
Belgium, 1985								
- secure before	+ 31	+ 60	+ 42	+ 76	+ 47	+ 89	+ 76	+ 129
- secure due to	- 24	+ 21	- 27	+ 24	- 46	+ 31	- 56	+ 44
- insecure after	- 72	- 20	- 80	- 22	- 71	- 13	- 82	- 21
Netherlands, 1986								
- secure before	+ 64	+ 104	+ 77	+ 126	+ 59	+ 90	+ 65	+ 112
- secure due to	- 53	+ 29	- 65	+ 62	- 53	+ 39	- 59	+ 29
- insecure after	- 79	- 14	- 79	- 14	- 70	- 20	- 69	- 14
Luxembourg, 1986								
- secure before	+ 32	+ 51	+ 72	+ 103	+ 39	+ 63	+ 85	+ 118
- secure due to	- 10	+ 20	- 21	+ 10	- 60	+ 26	- 49	+ 21
- insecure after	- 56	- 18	- 74	- 12	- 44	- 16	- 73	- 1
Lorraine, 1986								
- secure before	+ 44	+ 66	+ 60	+ 86	+ 75	+ 108	+ 147	+ 196
- secure due to	- 16	+ 19	- 17	+ 31	- 26	+ 26	- 29	+ 44
- insecure after	- 46	- 26	- 49	- 24	- 43	- 21	- 49	- 9
Catalonia, 1988								
- secure before	+ 55	+ 93	+ 62	+ 99	+ 85	+ 137	N.A.	
- secure due to	- 33	+ 23	- 30	+ 22	- 36	+ 37	N.A.	
- insecure after	- 69	- 31	- 76	- 35	- 74	- 28	N.A.	

* The average poverty line for each category of households has been estimated because figures on the poverty gaps and income surpluses expressed as a percentage of the standard of each individual household, and then averaged (as in table 5.4), were not available.

estimated poverty line = average post-transfer income - average surplus or deficit

In the Benelux countries the total disposable income of poor households receiving unemployment allowances falls short of the poverty line by on average less than 20%. In Catalonia the post-transfer average poverty gap is much larger.

Reduction of the aggregate poverty gap

On the basis of the data of the distribution of the aggregate amounts, it is possible to calculate that unemployment allowances are most effective in the Netherlands and Belgium: by the EC-standard the poverty gap before unemployment transfers are granted, is reduced by more than 90%. Unemployment transfers have relatively low effectiveness in Lorraine. According the Legal-standard we notice a very effective working of unemployment schemes for all countries (table 5.20).

Table 5.20

Effectiveness of unemployment allowances: percentage of
pre-transfer aggregate poverty gap (for households with
unemployment allowances) eliminated by unemployment transfers

	CSP	SPL	EC	Legal
Belgium, 1985	79	80	92	97
The Netherlands, 1986	92	91	90	97
Luxembourg, 1986	72	87	77	100
Lorraine, 1986	51	61	66	94
Catalonia, 1988	65	62	76	N.A.

In all countries unemployment allowances are rather inefficient from the perspective of a
minimum income guarantee. Around 40% according to the EC-standard (more on the basis
of the subjective standards; less based on the Legal-standard) of the means of
unemployment protection are directed towards closing the poverty gap, in all countries,
except in Lorraine, where efficiency is much less (table 5.21).

Table 5.21

Efficiency and inefficiency of unemployment allowances

	CSP			SPL			EC			Legal		
	(1)	(2)	(3)	(1)	(2)	(3)	(1)	(2)	(3)	(1)	(2)	(3)
Belgium, '85	59	17	25	52	17	31	39	17	44	28	20	52
The Netherlands, '86	50	17	33	51	26	34	44	24	32	46	20	34
Luxembourg, '86	51	12	37	41	4	55	40	9	54	32	9	59
Lorraine, '86	46	17	37	31	18	52	25	11	64	11	12	77
Catalonia, '88	54	12	34	55	13	32	37	18	45	N.A.		

(1) part of aggregate unemployment allowances flowing to poor households before unemployment
allowances, up to the level of the poverty line, but not in excess of the poverty line (= efficiency
ratio).

(2) 'spill over' effect: part of aggregate unemployment allowances flowing to households that are poor
before unemployment allowances, but in excess of the poverty line.

(3) part of aggregate unemployment allowances flowing to households already non-poor before unemployment allowances.

(1) + (2) + (3) = 100.

In the Netherlands the "spill over" effect is rather important. That is to say, households
becoming secure due to unemployment transfers receive more than they strictly need
according to their poverty standard. The inefficiency of the systems in the other countries
is mainly due to households receiving unemployment allowances that do not really need
them in terms of a minimum income guarantee. This pattern is the most striking for
Lorraine.

5.8. Adequacy of sickness or invalidity allowances

Reduction of the head-count

Table 5.22 shows that in all countries a substantial number of households benefiting from a sickness or invalidity allowance are already secure of subsistence before receiving this benefit. But, certainly on the basis of the EC-standard, large differences between the countries are found. In Lorraine and Belgium more than 60% of all households benefiting from a sickness or invalidity allowance are secure of subsistence without these benefits; in Luxembourg and Catalonia this percentage is around 50%; and in the Netherlands it is only 37%. By the Legal-standard fewer households are poor before sickness or invalidity allowances, but the countries are ranked in the same way. According to the subjective standards the differences between countries appear to be smaller, except that in Catalonia the proportion of households secure before sickness or invalidity allowances appears to be relatively low.

Table 5.22
The number of households with sickness or invalidity allowances,
who are *non-poor before sickness or invalidity allowances*,
as a percentage of all households with sickness or invalidity allowances

	CSP	SPL	EC	Legal
Belgium, 1985	42	41	61	67
The Netherlands, 1986	37	41	37	40
Luxembourg, 1986	42	53	50	59
Lorraine, 1986	43	51	69	80
Catalonia, 1988	30	29	47	N.A.

How many benefiting households who are poor before sickness or invalidity allowance are becoming non-poor due to this transfer? This is shown in table 5.23. Measured by this indicator the impact of sickness or invalidity allowances is the largest in the Netherlands, where by all standards more than three-quarters of all benefeciary households that would be poor without these transfers are lifted above the poverty line. In Belgium and Luxembourg the impact is less, but still considerable. The adequacy of sickness or invalidity allowances is much weaker in Lorraine and in Catalonia.

Table 5.23
The number of households with sickness or invalidity allowances,
that are *secure due to sickness or invalidity allowances*, as a percentage
of all households insecure before sickness or invalidity allowances

	CSP	SPL	EC	Legal
Belgium, 1985	58	62	83	92
The Netherlands, 1986	76	78	86	93
Luxembourg, 1986	55	70	72	83
Lorraine, 1986	42	47	58	62
Catalonia, 1988	34	34	51	N.A.

Table 5.24 shows that many households remain in poverty despite receiving a sickness or invalidity allowance, especially in Catalonia. This result for Catalonia is the consequence of a relatively high number of poor households before receiving these allowances on the one hand and of the relatively low impact of these allowances on the other. Both in the Netherlands and in Belgium the number of households remaining in poverty after receiving a sickness or invalidity benefit is relatively low. However this similar final result must be explained differently for both countries. Belgium appears to have a much higher number of beneficiary households that are already secure before sickness or invalidity transfers are granted, while the impact is lower than in the Netherlands.

Table 5.24
The number of households with sickness or invalidity allowances,
insecure after sickness or invalidity allowances, as a percentage
of all households with sickness or invalidity allowances

	CSP	SPL	EC	Legal
Belgium, 1985	24	23	7	3
The Netherlands, 1986	15	13	9	4
Luxembourg, 1986	26	15	14	7
Lorraine, 1986	33	26	13	8
Catalonia, 1988	46	48	26	N.A.

The Legal-standard produces the same ranking of the countries as the EC-standard. In general the subjective standards result in higher poverty risks after sickness or invalidity allowances for all countries, but the differences between the countries are much smaller. There is however no consistency between both subjective standards, except for the Netherlands where the lowest number of poor after sickness or invalidity allowance are registered according to both standards.

Reduction of the average poverty gap

The *pre-transfer income* of households with sickness or invalidity allowances is substantially higher for households already secure before this transfer is granted than for other categories of households. This is in particular the case for Catalonia. In Lorraine, differences in pre-transfer income between households secure before and the other household categories are smaller. The pre-transfer income for households secure due to sickness or invalidity benefit and those remaining insecure is much lower. According to the EC-standard the pre-transfer income is somewhat higher for the former type of households than for the latter. However, beneficiary households secure due to sickness or invalidity allowances have lower needs, as their poverty standard is situated at a lower level. This indicates that it concerns mainly smaller households. According to the subjective poverty lines differences in pre-transfer income of both categories of beneficiary households are significantly larger, but at the other hand, the level of needs, as indicated by the poverty lines, does not differ that much.

As a result of these differences, the *average pre-transfer poverty gap* for households secure due to sickness or invalidity allowances is considerably smaller than for households that remain in poverty (table 5.25).

Table 5.25

Average poverty gaps and average income surpluses before and after sickness or invalidity transfers for households receiving these transfers, as a percentage of the average poverty line, by security status before/after sickness or invalidity transfers*

	CSP		SPL		EC		Legal	
	before	after	before	after	before	after	before	after
Belgium, 1985								
- secure before	+ 48	+ 83	+ 59	+ 95	+ 71	+ 118	+ 95	+ 154
- secure due to	- 33	+ 28	- 32	+ 33	- 48	+ 43	- 50	+ 60
- insecure after	- 65	- 18	- 69	- 19	- 59	- 15	- 68	- 18
Netherlands, 1986								
- secure before	+ 60	+ 114	+ 67	+ 127	+ 67	+ 119	+ 60	+ 115
- secure due to	- 51	+ 41	- 53	+ 43	- 50	+ 50	- 56	+ 41
- insecure after	- 82	- 10	- 86	- 9	- 64	- 11	- 73	- 13
Luxembourg, 1986								
- secure before	+ 53	+ 79	+ 92	+ 131	+ 70	+ 102	+ 109	+ 155
- secure due to	- 44	+ 28	- 57	+ 36	- 49	+ 47	- 59	+ 54
- insecure after	- 67	- 20	- 73	- 30	- 60	- 16	- 76	- 27
Lorraine, 1986								
- secure before	+ 49	+ 64	+ 61	+ 80	+ 81	+ 108	+ 140	+ 181
- secure due to	- 24	+ 25	- 29	+ 30	- 33	+ 45	- 33	+ 67
- insecure after	- 51	- 28	- 50	- 25	- 50	- 24	- 70	- 24
Catalonia, 1988								
- secure before	+ 132	+ 159	+ 146	+ 175	+ 140	+ 178	N.A.	N.A.
- secure due to	- 28	+ 21	- 24	+ 19	- 41	+ 34	N.A.	N.A.
- insecure after	- 66	- 32	- 72	- 35	- 66	- 25	N.A.	N.A.

* The average poverty line for each category of households has been estimated because figures on the poverty gaps and income surpluses expressed as a percentage of the standard of each individual household, and then averaged (as in table 5.4), were not available.

estimated poverty line = average post-transfer income - average surplus or deficit

The *average sickness or invalidity transfer* is relatively at the highest level for households becoming secure of subsistence and at the lowest for households already secure before receiving these benefits. So, although financial needs before transfers are on average the largest for households remaining poor, nevertheless they do not receive the highest benefits. Of course sickness or invalidity schemes are not primarily directed at alleviating poverty. In the Netherlands, however, the differences between the household categories seem to be much smaller than in the other countries.

Comparing households not-poor due to sickness or invalidity allowances and households poor despite these transfers we can conclude that differences in financial need as well as differences in average transfers play a rol in making households secure of subsistence.

The average poverty gap for households left in poverty despite benefits is the smallest in the Netherlands, based on all standards, and appears to be relatively large in Lorraine and Catalonia.

Reduction of the aggregate poverty gap

Table 5.26 presents the degree to which the poverty gap among beneficiary households of a sickness or invalidity allowance is reduced by these transfers (effectiveness).

Table 5.26
Effectiveness of sickness or invalidity allowances: percentage of
pre-transfer poverty gap for households with sickness or invalidity
allowances eliminated by sickness or invalidity transfers

	CSP	SPL	EC	Legal
Belgium, 1985	84	84	94	96
The Netherlands, 1986	94	97	96	98
Luxembourg, 1986	84	88	91	93
Lorraine, 1986	58	67	73	78
Catalonia, 1988	61	59	75	N.A.

The sickness or invalidity schemes seem to be very effective in the Benelux, especially in the Netherlands. By the EC- and Legal-standards more than 90% of the pre transfer poverty gap of households receiving a sickness or invalidity benefit, is closed. Sickness or invalidity allowances appear to be less effective in Lorraine and Catalonia.

From the point of view of alleviating poverty, sickness or invalidity schemes are rather inefficient (table 5.27) around 40%, according to the EC-standard (more on the basis of the subjective poverty standards and less on the basis of the Legal-standards), of sickness or invalidity transfers help to close the poverty gap. The highest efficiency ratio is measured in Catalonia. According to the EC- standard sickness or invalidity schemes seem to be less efficient in Lorraine and in Belgium than in the Netherlands and Luxembourg, but on the basis of the subjective standards the differences between these countries are small. On the basis of the Legal-standard The Netherlands have the most efficient system. The inefficiency of sickness or invalidity schemes is for all countries mostly due to transfers flowing to households who are already secure of subsistence before receiving a sickness or invalidity allowance.

Table 5.27
Efficiency and inefficiency of sickness or invalidity allowances

	CSP			SPL			EC			Legal		
	(1)	(2)	(3)	(1)	(2)	(3)	(1)	(2)	(3)	(1)	(2)	(3)
Belgium, '85	48	21	31	44	24	31	31	22	47	22	24	54
The Netherlands, '86	46	25	29	43	25	32	40	32	29	41	28	30
Luxembourg, '86	54	19	27	41	20	39	39	27	34	32	25	43
Lorraine, '86	54	21	25	43	23	34	29	24	48	18	20	62
Catalonia, '88	60	14	26	62	13	25	43	17	41	N.A.	N.A.	N.A.

(1) part of aggregate sickness or invalidity allowances flowing to poor households before sickness or invalidity allowances, up to the level of the poverty line, but not in excess of the poverty line (= efficiency ratio).
(2) 'spill over' effect: part of aggregate sickness or invalidity allowances flowing to households that are poor before sickness or invalidity allowances but in excess of the poverty line.
(3) part of aggregate sickness or invalidity allowances flowing to households already non-poor before sickness or invalidity allowances.
(1) + (2) + (3) = 100.

5.9. Adequacy of family allowances

Reduction of the head-count

The number of households secure before receiving family allowances is presented in table 5.28. In all countries the majority of households is secure without family allowances. By the EC-standard more than 80% of benefiting households are not poor before receiving family allowances, except in Lorraine, where this proportion is significantly smaller. This may reflect the partially selective character of the French family allowance scheme. By the more generous subjective standards, the proportion of households that are secure before family allowances remains rather high in the Benelux, but is relatively low in Lorraine, and also in Catalonia.

Table 5.28
The number of households with family allowances *secure before family allowances,* as a percentage of all households with family allowances

	CSP	SPL	EC	Legal
Belgium, 1985	71	76	83	95
The Netherlands, 1986	91	87	81	92
Luxembourg, 1986	81	91	85	96
Lorraine, 1986	50	63	71	92
Catalonia, 1988	61	57	81	N.A.

Relatively few households with family allowances are lifted above the povertyline by these transfers. This can be explained by the fact that family allowances, compared with other social security benefits, involve lower amounts of benefit, and generally are not a main income source within total disposable income of beneficiary households.

Table 5.29 shows that, nevertheless in the Benelux and Lorraine a sizable proportion of all pre-family allowance poor households are secure after these benefits are granted. By the EC- and Legal-standards the impact is strongest in Belgium and Lorraine. Using the subjective lines, the Netherlands show clearly the strongest reduction of the number of poor households. In Catalonia the effect of family allowances is very small by any standard.

Table 5.29
The number of households with family allowances becoming *secure due to family allowances,* as a percentage of all households insecure before family allowances

	CSP	SPL	EC	Legal
Belgium, 1985	42	47	60	76
The Netherlands, 1986	52	52	48	57
Luxembourg, 1986	33	45	39	50
Lorraine, 1986	31	42	55	76
Catalonia, 1988	6	6	11	N.A.

By the EC-standard a relatively low number of households with family allowances are left in poverty in the Benelux (table 5.30). In spite of the relatively large number of households becoming secure due to these benefits in Lorraine, a larger number of beneficiary households are left in poverty. This is explained by a higher number of pre-allowance poor households. In Catalonia a substantial number of beneficiary households remain in poverty after family allowances are granted. This is due to the very small proportion of the population which becomes secure due to these allowances. The subjective poverty lines produce parallel results, except that in the Netherlands the proportion of poor among households with family allowances is very low.

Table 5.30
The number of households with family allowances *poor despite family allowances*, as a percentage of all households with family allowances

	CSP	SPL	EC	Legal
Belgium, 1985	17	13	7	1
The Netherlands, 1986	4	6	10	3
Luxembourg, 1986	13	5	9	2
Lorraine, 1986	35	21	13	2
Catalonia, 1988	37	40	17	N.A.

Reduction of the average poverty gap

The *pre-transfer income* of households secure before family allowances is significantly higher than that of the other household categories. Also households secure due to this benefit have a higher pre-transfer income than households remaining in poverty after family allowances are granted, but differences between the latter categories are somewhat smaller. This is reflected in the pre-family allowance poverty gap, which is rather small for households that become secure after family allowances (table 5.31).

One could suppose that there are differences in household size between the various household categories. The respective average poverty lines shows that there are no substantial differences in household size between the three categories. Households secure before family allowances are a bit smaller than households which are made secure due to family allowances. In general households remaining in poverty after family allowances are the smallest in size, except for Lorraine where households secure due to and households insecure after are more or less of the same average size.

Compared to other replacement benefits, the average level of family allowances is for all categories of households much lower, which implies that for most families they only form a relatively small part of total income. Except in the Netherlands, households secure due to family allowances receive, on average, the highest benefits. In the Netherlands the level of average family allowances is very similar for the three kinds of households. In Lorraine households insecure after family allowances receive relatively higher allowances than these households do in Belgium, Luxembourg and Catalonia. This might reflect the selective instead of universal character (as in the Benelux) of family allowances in France.

Table 5.31
Poverty gaps and income surpluses for households with family
allowances before and after family allowances, as a percentage of the
average poverty line, by security status before/after family allowances*

	CSP		SPL		EC		Legal	
	before	after	before	after	before	after	before	after
Belgium, 1985								
- secure before	+ 64	+ 78	+ 75	+ 89	+ 88	+ 104	+ 141	+ 164
- secure due to	- 12	+ 14	- 14	+ 15	- 15	+ 16	- 18	+ 33
- insecure after	- 30	- 17	- 30	- 16	- 36	- 15	- 41	- 21
Netherlands, 1986								
- secure before	+ 84	+ 96	+ 83	+ 95	+ 72	+ 82	+ 87	+ 99
- secure due to	- 6	+ 9	- 7	+ 7	- 7	+ 7	- 9	+ 9
- insecure after	- 36	- 25	- 31	- 20	- 31	- 18	- 42	- 29
Luxembourg, 1986								
- secure before	+ 68	+77	+ 107	+ 120	+ 79	+ 89	+ 143	+ 159
- secure due to	- 9	+ 12	- 9	+ 17	- 11	+ 8	- 11	+ 24
- insecure after	- 30	- 20	- 38	- 25	- 33	- 19	- 42	- 29
Lorraine, 1986								
- secure before	+ 58	+ 70	+ 68	+ 82	+ 79	+ 95	+ 148	+ 177
- secure due to	- 13	+ 12	- 15	+ 12	- 17	+ 13	- 29	+ 34
- insecure after	- 37	- 20	- 39	- 18	- 43	- 18	- 43	- 16
Catalonia, 1988								
- secure before	+ 69	+ 72	+ 73	+ 76	+ 92	+ 97	N.A.	N.A.
- secure due to	- 5	+ 23	- 9	+ 25	- 4	+ 7	N.A.	N.A.
- insecure after	- 26	- 23	- 26	- 23	- 25	- 21	N.A.	N.A.

* The average poverty line for each category of households has been estimated because figures on the
poverty gaps and income surpluses expressed as a percentage of the standard of each individual
household, and then averaged (as in table 5.4), were not available.

estimated poverty line = average post-transfer income - average surplus or deficit

Reduction of the aggregate poverty gap

Table 5.32 shows that, using the EC-standard, the pre-family allowance poverty gap for
beneficiary households is the most reduced by family allowances in Belgium and in
Lorraine; effectiveness is smaller for the Netherlands and Luxembourg and it is very small
in Catalonia. On the basis of the subjective standards, the effectiveness is lower, but the
ranking of countries remains roughly the same.

Table 5.32
Effectiveness of family allowances: percentage of pre-transfer poverty
gap for households with family allowances eliminated by family transfers

	CSP	SPL	EC	Legal
Belgium, 1985	57	62	75	81
The Netherlands, 1986	41	49	50	45
Luxembourg, 1986	42	45	52	45
Lorraine, 1986	52	64	71	86
Catalonia, 1988	12	10	16	N.A.

Table 5.33 shows that in the Benelux and Catalonia the efficiency of family allowances is rather low, mainly because the largest share of these transfers goes to households that are already secure. In Lorraine, however, the efficiency of family allowances is about twice as large as in the other countries, and less transfers flow to households that do not strictly need them in terms of a minimum income guarantee. This result is probably the expression of the selective family benefit systems in France, versus more universal schemes in the other countries. The low efficiency of family allowances (from the point of view of alleviating poverty) is of course mainly due to the fact that, in contrast to replacement income, it forms an addition to other incomes in the household (most often income from labour). Also, (as is true for most other transfers) these allowances do not have the elimination of poverty as their main aim. Nevertheless, given their rather moderate effectiveness and high inefficiency, it would seem that there is some scope for re-directing family allowances towards those households with children that are most in need.

Table 5.33
Efficiency and inefficiency of family allowances

	CSP			SPL			EC			Legal		
	(1)	(2)	(3)	(1)	(2)	(3)	(1)	(2)	(3)	(1)	(2)	(3)
Belgium, '85	25	11	64	20	11	70	18	10	72	5	7	88
The Netherlands, '86	6	3	91	10	4	86	19	6	75	7	3	90
Luxembourg, '86	17	7	75	8	5	87	18	5	77	3	3	94
Lorraine, '86	50	12	38	38	11	51	34	11	55	9	8	84
Catalonia, '88	36	18	45	35	19	47	17	4	78	n.a.	n.a.	n.a.

(1) part of aggregate family allowances flowing to poor households before family allowances, up to the level of the poverty line, but not in excess of the poverty line (= efficiency ratio).
(2) 'spill over' effect: part of aggregate family allowances flowing to households that are poor before family allowances but in excess of the poverty line.
(3) part of aggregate family allowances flowing to households already non-poor before family allowances.
(1) + (2) + (3) = 100.

5.10. Comparing adequacy of social transfers across sectors

Tables 5.34 to 5.37 provide an overview across the four sectors discussed, as well as across countries. Measuring effectiveness by the proportion of households actually receiving the particular kind of transfer and being poor without the transfer, that are lifted above the poverty line by the transfer, we observe that in all countries pensions are the most effective kind of transfer, followed, in this order, by sickness and invalidity allowances, unemployment allowances and family allowances. This pattern holds with few exceptions for the EC- and CSP-standards, but not for the SPL-standard. Using the SPL, with its relatively high poverty lines for the elderly, pensions are mostly not more effective than sickness and invalidity allowances, or, in the case of Belgium, are even considerably less effective. In Catalonia by all standards unemployment allowances are more effective than sickness or invalidity allowances.

Pensions seem to leave fewer beneficiary households in poverty than the other types of replacement income do. Again, this is only true for the EC and CSP-standards, but not using the SPL-standard. (Differences across types of transfer using the Legal-standard are very small). Unemployment allowances leave relatively many households in poverty.

Comparing across countries, we observe that all Dutch social security transfers are, with very few exceptions, more effective than their counterparts in other countries, and leave fewer households in poverty. The most important exception are family allowances, which by the EC-standard are less effective in the Netherlands than in Belgium and Lorraine. It may be recalled that the Dutch social security system as a whole was the most effective one only by the CSP-standard (cfr. tables 5.2, 5.7). This apparent contradiction is probably due to the fact that (the first) evaluation covered the population as a whole, including households that do not receive any social security transfers.

Catalonia has by all standards the least effective social security transfer systems, which leave rather many beneficiary households in poverty. The exception are the unemployment allowances, which do not perform worse in Catalonia than in Luxembourg and Lorraine.

Table 5.34

Indicators of the adequacy of four sectors of social security, for households actually receiving the particular type of transfer: percentage of households lifted above the poverty line; and percentage of households left in poverty; by the CSP-standard

	Pensions		Unemployment allowances		Sickn. or Inval. allowances		Family allowances	
	(1)	(2)	(1)	(2)	(1)	(2)	(1)	(2)
Belgium, 1985	69	28	50	34	58	24	42	17
Netherlands, 1986	90	8	64	22	76	15	52	4
Luxembourg, 1986	80	16	34	38	55	26	33	13
Lorraine, 1986	67	28	40	36	42	33	31	35
Catalonia, 1988	48	38	38	40	34	46	6	37

(1) number of households lifted above the poverty line, as a percentage of all households receiving the particular type of transfer and poor before this transfer.
(2) number of households in poverty (after transfers) as a percentage of all households receiving the particular type of transfer.

Table 5.35

Indicators of the adequacy of four sectors of social security, for households actually receiving the particular type of transfer: percentage of households lifted above the poverty line; and percentage of households left in poverty; by the SPL-standard

	Pensions		Unemployment allowances		Sickn. or Inval. allowances		Family allowances	
	(1)	(2)	(1)	(2)	(1)	(2)	(1)	(2)
Belgium, 1985	51	44	53	29	62	23	47	13
Netherlands, 1986	75	21	56	26	78	13	52	6
Luxembourg, 1986	69	22	40	22	70	15	45	5
Lorraine, 1986	60	34	40	25	47	26	42	21
Catalonia, 1988	34	48	36	43	34	48	6	40

(1) + (2) see table 5.34

Table 5.36
Indicators of the adequacy of four sectors of social security, for households
actually receiving the particular type of transfer: percentage of households lifted above
the poverty line; and percentage of households left in poverty; by the EC-standard

	Pensions		Unemployment allowances		Sickn. or Inval. allowances		Family allowances	
	(1)	(2)	(1)	(2)	(1)	(2)	(1)	(2)
Belgium, 1985	93	6	74	12	83	7	60	7
Netherlands, 1986	99	1	80	12	86	9	48	10
Luxembourg, 1986	91	7	48	20	72	14	39	9
Lorraine, 1986	88	9	48	17	58	13	55	13
Catalonia, 1988	67	19	59	22	51	26	11	17

(1) + (2) see table 5.34.

Table 5.37
Indicators of the adequacy of four sectors of social security, for households
actually receiving the particular type of transfer: percentage of households lifted above
the poverty line; and percentage of households left in poverty; by the Legal-standard

	Pensions		Unemployment allowances		Sickn. or Inval. allowances		Family allowances	
	(1)	(2)	(1)	(2)	(1)	(2)	(1)	(2)
Belgium, 1985	94	5	90	4	92	3	76	1
Netherlands, 1986	96	4	88	7	93	4	57	3
Luxembourg, 1986	92	6	80	6	83	7	50	2
Lorraine, 1986	96	3	82	3	62	8	76	2
Catalonia, 1988	-	-	-	-	-	-	-	-

(1) + (2) see table 5.34.

6 Poverty in panel perspective: Dynamic results

6.1. Introduction

Comparisons between the cross-sectional results for two subsequent years generally show that there are few significant changes across such relatively short periods. The impression of a stable situation could be misleading, if one would translate it from the macro-level to the micro-level. The result that the overall situation remains much the same from one year to the next does not imply that all or most households stay in the same position. In particular, a stable overall rate of poverty or insecurity of subsistence does not mean that the same households are poor in both years. Until very recently, this was a blind spot, at least in European poverty research, as panel data, which are needed to analyse this issue, were not available. The data that have become available, in the USA and more recently in some European countries, have shown that changes at the micro-level are unexpectedly large and frequent. They allow us to obtain a more refined knowledge, a more correct image and a better evaluation of poverty.

This part of the report presents some panel results on poverty for five countries in which two waves have been conducted: Belgium 1985-1988, The Netherlands 1985-1986, Luxemburg 1985-1986, Lorraine 1985-1986 and Ireland 1987-1989. Unfortunately, the time-gap between two waves is not the same for all countries: in The Netherlands, Lorraine and Luxembourg it is one year, in Ireland two years, and in Belgium three years. This obviously detracts somewhat from the comparability of the results.

The analysis concentrates on two points:
1. Poverty status of households across two waves (being poor in two waves, being non-poor in two waves, going in or out of poverty)
2. Poverty status of households across two waves by social characteristics of the head of household (in the first wave).

The panel results are somewhat limited in scope, because of the availability of only two waves, and because there was little time left for elaborate panel analyses. It has been the experience of all teams that setting up a panel data-base takes much more time and effort than a cross-sectional data-base. Nevertheless, they constitute one of the first comparative studies of transitions into and out of poverty in Europe.

The panel results (as all data in this report) are on the household level. Households were linked across waves if they had the same head in both years, or if the head had deceased and the partner had become head of household. This implies that certain wave-2 households that have split off from other wave-1 households, such as children who left their parent's home and women divorced from their husbands, are not included in the analysis. This is of course unfortunate, and together with the problem of defining longitudinal households it has led other researchers to analyzing mobility in poverty status on the individual level, where linking can be complete and unambigous. Due to technical problems, not all countries were yet able to produce results on the individual level. However, after only one or three years, the number of split-off households will be rather small, (1 to 3%) ([1]). Not all wave-1 households are included either, because some have left the population through death or emigration, and others are lost due to non-response. For these reasons the marginal figures in table A.18 in appendix, giving the number of insecure/secure households in each wave are sometimes sligthly different from those in table 4.1 in chapter 4 (number of insecure/secure at one moment in time).

The numbers of cases on which the panel analyses are based are as follows: Belgium: 3035; The Netherlands: 2712; Luxembourg: 1761; Lorraine, 607; Ireland, 787.

6.2. Longer-term poverty and poverty escape rates

The most interesting figure of the panel results is the proportion of households insecure of subsistence in the first wave, that are still so in the second year (and, of course, its complement, the proportion of these households that are not insecure any more). This is given in table 6.1. Interpretation of these figures is not alway easy. If the level of the poverty line has fallen between two waves, as has happened in some countries, this will itself produce some apparent mobility in poverty status even without there being any real change in any household's situation. If the poverty line has risen, this will probably reduce the number of households who have left poverty. Moreover, there are the differences in the period of time between waves.

Table 6.1
Proportion of all households insecure of subsistence
in first wave, that are still insecure in second wave

	CSP-standard	SPL-standard	EC-standard	Legal-standard
Ireland, 1987-1989	71,2	84,1	63,8	26,2
Belgium, 1985-1988	62,9	60,8	42,0	24,2
Netherlands, 1985-1986	47,3	69,7	40,6	30,6
Lorraine, 1985-1986	73,6	73,9	56,9	42,9
Luxembourg, 1985-1986	62,5	49,5	57,1	44,0

Nevertheless, it is clear from table 6.1 that there is *substantial mobility* from insecurity to security of subsistence. On the basis of the EC-standard, between 34% to almost 60%, depending on the country, of all households financially insecure in wave 1, are *not* so in wave 2. Using the legal standard, the mobility appears to be even more substantial. The more generous subjective standards produce results that indicate less change in status. If we exclude cases where the poverty rate in wave 2 diverges much from that in wave 1 ([2]), we find that generally 60% to 75% of households insecure in wave 1 remain in poverty. This is not true for The Netherlands, where the subjective standards are much lower.

These results seem to suggest an important methodological conclusion. It appears that in a given country, estimated mobility will be less if the poverty line is more generous. If it is more strict, a larger proportion of households below the poverty line at a certain moment will be able to cross it during a certain period. It seems likely that it is not the relative level of the standard itself that produces these differences. The lower transition rate in Ireland suggests that what is important is probably the percentile of the income distribution that is equal to the standard. Thus, the more households are below a certain standard, the smaller will be the proportion that will move out of poverty during a certain period. This hypothesis is confirmed by Duncan a.o. (1991), who find "a marked inverse relationship between the estimated incidence of poverty and escape rates" (p. 9).

This tendency obviously affects comparisons across countries. Thus, using the EC-standard, we find that less households leave the state of insecurity of subsistence in Ireland than in the other countries. But it is difficult to say whether this is the result of less extensive income mobility in Ireland or of the fact that there are more households below the EC-line in Ireland. Changes in poverty status also seem less frequent in Lorraine and Luxembourg, where the number of households below the EC-standard is nearer to that of Belgium and The Netherlands. However, it must be kept in mind that the time-gaps between the two waves are not the same. It seems probable that after three years as many or more households would have escaped poverty in Luxembourg and in Lorraine as have done in Belgium.

It is somewhat surprising that transitions are less frequent in Belgium, where three years have elapsed between the two waves, than in particular in The Netherlands, where there is only one year difference. Again, this might be interpreted in various ways. It is possible that changes in income in The Netherlands happen more frequently and are larger in any given year. It is also possible that there are two kinds of households below a poverty line at a certain moment: stayers, who remain in the same position for a very long time, and movers, who are poor for only a short period. In any case, the escape rate after three years is not simply the single year-escape rate to the power of three, unless there is complete homogeneity among the poor. Results for the United States have shown that there is in fact substantial heterogeneity among the poor (see Bane and Ellwood, 1986) as regards the length of poverty spells. Moreover, persons that have left poverty can of course fall back later. Nevertheless if the dynamics of poverty in two countries are similar, one would always expect that the longer the time-span, the more households have left poverty.

Of course, there are not only households that escape poverty, but also a certain number that *become* poor or insecure of the means of subsistence, that were not so in the first wave. Using the EC-standard, between 3,3% in Luxembourg and 8,8% in Ireland of all households that were financially secure in the first wave, have become insecure in the second wave. On the basis of the subjective standards, the number of these households is much larger, from 16% in Ireland, to less than 6% in Luxembourg. These results are of course only the complement of those discussed in the previous paragraphs, and the same remarks apply, mutatis mutandis, to them too.

Another way to look at these figures is to see what proportions of all households are insecure of the means of subsistence in *both waves*. Of course, these households cannot be equalled to the "permanent" poor in any sense of the word. Still, it would seem that these households are on average insecure or poor for a longer time than other households.

Table 6.2
Percentage of all households that are insecure of subsistence in both waves

	CSP-standard	SPL-standard	EC-standard	Legal-standard
Ireland, 1987-1989	22,3	31,2	10,2	1,7
Belgium, 1985-1988	13,5	14,9	2,4	0,6
Netherlands, 1985-1986	5,3	5,3	2,6	2,2
Lorraine, 1985-1986	19,3	19,1	6,1	2,0
Luxembourg, 1985-1986	9,4	9,8	4,4	2,8

Because of the mobility in poverty status, the figures in table 6.2 are much lower than the single-year poverty rates. Nevertheless, comparatively, previous conclusions are mostly confirmed. In fact the differences across countries are reinforced. Using the EC-standard, we find that Ireland has the largest proportion of households insecure in both waves, followed by Lorraine. In Belgium and The Netherlands this proportion is less than 3%. In contrast to the single-year results, Luxembourg has more "longer-term" poor than the other Benelux countries. On the basis of the subjective standards, the relative positions of Ireland and Lorraine are similar. But in The Netherlands, the number of households with incomes below the subjective standard is much smaller than in other countries, while in Belgium it is now larger than in Luxembourg (despite the longer time-gap in Belgium). This is at least partly an effect of differences in the relative level of the standard.

Of course, if, as has been argued above, the number of households that experience changes in poverty status depends partly on the level of the standard used, this is also true for the proportion of households poor in both waves. The comparisons must therefore be made with some caution.

However, even if the differences between countries could be wholly explained by the position of the standard within the income distribution, it would be wrong to regard them as only a statistical artefact. What one cannot do is conclude that there is less income mobility in Ireland. But, depending on the validity one is willing to grant to the various standards, one would still be justified in concluding that there is much more poverty of a more permanent kind in Ireland than in The Netherlands. In fact, it suggests that there are two types of gains in reducing inequality in the lower part of the income distribution: not only will there be at any given moment fewer households below any given poverty line, but in addition the average spell of poverty will probably be shorter.

6.3. The social distribution of the risk of longer-term poverty

What is interesting is not only to know how many households stay in poverty but in particular it is important to know which social categories have a high probability of experiencing longer-term poverty vs. short term poverty. In order to analyze mobility versus stability in poverty according to social categories the samples in the various countries are subdivided by social characteristics of the household or the head of household in the first wave. In many cases these characteristics may have changed in the second wave, but this is not taken account of in the present analysis. (Thus, the category "head of household at work" contains both households in which the head is still at work in the second wave, but also households in which the head has retired or become unemployed.) However, the effect of these changes on poverty, which is itself a social crucial one, is not shown in the present analysis.

For the present context it was found to be convenient to make a distinction between "longer-term poverty" (poverty in both waves) and "transient" or "short-term" poverty (poverty in only one of the two waves). Of course it should be realized that the concept "long-term" can hardly be used, because of the as yet limited duration (only two waves with mostly a short time-gap in between) of the panels in the concerned countries.

Results on "longer-term" poverty and on escape rates out of poverty by social category have been computed for the more interesting and relevant social categories. Because of the, sometimes large, fluctuations in the subjective standards, this has only been done for the EC-standard (see tables 6.3 to 6.6). For the reasons noted above (changes in the level of in particular the subjective poverty lines; dependence of the transition rate on the poverty rate itself) one must be cautious in drawing conclusions from these data. In addition, for some categories, the number of households poor at any time is rather small.

It appears that in general the panel results on "longer-term" poor confirm the cross-sectional results: categories of households that are at high risk of poverty at one moment in time are also at high risk of being in poverty in two consecutive waves. In many cases - but certainly not always - the differences are even reïnforced. This is an important conclusion, as it means that even though the poor at a certain moment may include many that are poor for only a short time, the results of cross-sectional studies are not *very* misleading as regards the *structure* of poverty, and provide good indicators of the categories of households that are at high risk of being in poverty, even in 'longer-term' poverty. Below we will only note where the social incidence of "longer-term" poverty deviates from that of poverty at one moment, and we will not repeat the conclusions reached in chapter 4 regarding the social structure of poverty.

It is noteworthy that in most countries *unemployed* heads of households have a relatively high risk of being in poverty in both waves, and a relatively low probability of escaping poverty, if they are poor at a given moment. This is somewhat surprising, as one would expect that this category of households would show the greatest mobility: some unemployed heads of households would have found work, others would be retired. This result suggests that unemployed heads of households who do not change employment status find it very difficult to escape poverty.

Table 6.3

Dynamics of poverty: "longer-term" poverty and escape rates, using the EC-standard by *employment status* of the head of household in the 1st wave

	Relative risk of poverty in 1st wave	% poor in both waves	Relative risk of poverty in both waves	% of poor in 1st wave escaping poverty
IRELAND, '87-'89				
head of household:				
- employed	73	7,4	73	37
- unemployed	366	44,2	433	34
- retired	57	3,0	29	67
- sick-disabled	89	9,5	93	55
BELGIUM, '85-'88				
head of household:				
- employed	35	0,4	17	80
- unemployed	505	14,1	588	51
- retired	121	2,9	121	58
- sick-disabled	140	2,7	113	66
NETHERLANDS, '85-'86				
head of household:				
- employed	69	1,8	72	59
- unemployed	295	12,6	504	33
- retired	67	0,0	0	100
- sick-disabled	216	4,6	184	67
LORRAINE, '85-'86				
head of household:				
- employed	83	3,7	61	58
- unemployed	(460)	(42,2)	(692)	(14)
- retired	62	4,2	69	36
- sick-disabled	(194)	(20,8)	(341)	(0)
LUXEMBOURG, '85-'86				
head of household:				
- employed	62	2,8	64	42
- unemployed	(838)	(49,5)	(1125)	(23)
- retired	134	6,0	136	42
- sick-disabled	(243)	(11,1)	(252)	(41)

Table 6.4
Dynamics of poverty: "longer-term" poverty and escape rates, using the EC-standard by *age* of the head of household in the 1st wave

	Relative risk of poverty in 1st wave	% poor in both waves	Relative risk of poverty in both waves	% of poor in 1st wave escaping poverty
IRELAND, '87-'89 Age head of household:				
- 16-24	188	25,0	245	17
- 25-49	129	14,6	143	29
- 50-64	103	8,5	83	48
- 65-74	43	2,7	26	60
- 75+	13	0,0	0	100
BELGIUM, '85-'88 Age head of household:				
- 16-24	65	1,6	67	57
- 25-49	100	2,3	96	60
- 50-64	61	1,7	71	51
- 65-74	121	2,7	113	61
- 75+	204	5,0	208	57
NETHERLANDS, '85-'88 Age head of household:				
- 16-24	235	7,2	276	53
- 25-49	109	3,3	132	53
- 50-64	84	1,0	40	81
- 65-74	47	0,0	0	100
- 75+	50	0,0	0	100
LORRAINE, '85-'86 Age head of household:				
- 16-24	257	3,8	63	86
- 25-49	99	6,4	105	40
- 50-64	86	5,0	82	46
- 65-74	78	5,5	90	34
- 75+	118	11,2	184	11
LUXEMBOURG, '85-'86 Age head of household:				
- 16-24	94	5,3	121	26
- 25-49	86	4,1	93	38
- 50-64	84	3,5	80	46
- 65-74	168	5,8	132	55
- 75+	127	6,5	148	35

Table 6.5
Dynamics of poverty: "longer-term" poverty and escape rates, using the EC-standard by *marital status* of the head of household in the 1st wave

	Relative risk of poverty in 1st wave	% poor in both waves	Relative risk of poverty in both waves	% of poor in 1st wave escaping poverty
IRELAND, '87-'89 head of household:				
- married	119	13,1	128	31
- single	78	5,8	57	54
- widowed	39	1,9	38	70
- divorced or separated	175	20,0	196	29
BELGIUM, '85-'88 head of household:				
- married	91	2,3	96	56
- single	81	6,7	29	85
- widowed	109	2,3	96	63
- divorced or separated	182	3,9	163	63
NETHERLANDS, '85-'88 head of household:				
- married	116	3,1	124	58
- single	92	1,7	68	71
- widowed	42	0,4	16	85
- divorced or separated	91	1,7	65	71
LORRAINE, '85-'86 head of household:				
- married	81	4,8	79	45
- single	165	5,0	82	72
- widowed	137	12,0	197	18
- divorced or separated	150	13,0	213	19
LUXEMBOURG, '85-'86 head of household:				
- married	100	4,9	111	36
- single	121	5,1	116	45
- widowed	107	1,6	36	75
- divorced or separated	88	4,5	102	34

Table 6.6
Dynamics of poverty: "longer-term" poverty and escape rates, using the EC-standard by *type of household* in the 1st wave

	Relative risk of poverty in 1st wave	% poor in both waves	Relative risk of poverty in both waves	% of poor in 1st wave escaping poverty
IRELAND, '87-'89				
- single elderly person	15	0,8	8	67
- single adult	81	4,8	47	63
- two elderly persons	46	4,9	48	33
- two adults	72	7,7	75	33
- two adults, 1 child	94	8,5	83	44
- two adults, 2 children	118	14,4	141	23
- two adults, 3 children	177	22,6	222	20
- one-parent households	354	34,9	342	39
BELGIUM, '85-'88				
- single elderly person	118	2,7	113	60
- single adult	33	0,0	0	100
- two elderly persons	175	5,0	208	50
- two adults	60	0,8	33	76
- two adults, 1 child	61	0,9	38	74
- two adults, 2 children	95	2,6	108	52
- two adults, 3 children	160	4,4	183	52
- one-parent households	274	9,2	383	41
NETHERLANDS, '85-'88				
- single elderly person	80	2,3	92	55
- single adult	188	3,8	152	68
- two elderly persons	244	0,8	32	95
- two adults	95	2,0	80	67
- two adults, 1 child	56	0,3	12	92
- two adults, 2 children	27	0,2	8	88
- two adults, 3 children	86	1,8	72	67
- one-parent households	231	6,7	258	62
LORRAINE, '85-'86				
- single elderly person	98	10,5	172	0
- single adult	222	14,3	234	40
- two elderly persons	52	2,8	46	50
- two adults	41	2,9	48	34
- two adults, 1 child	64	4,5	74	34
- two adults, 2 children	67	3,6	59	50
- two adults, 3 children	80	1,4	23	84
- one-parent households	186	0,0	0	100
LUXEMBOURG, '85-'86				
- single elderly person	117	3,5	80	61
- single adult	66	1,9	43	63
- two elderly persons	225	9,7	220	44
- two adults	44	2,2	50	35
- two adults, 1 child	55	3,1	70	26
- two adults, 2 children	122	5,3	120	44
- two adults, 3 children	193	10,9	248	27
- one-parent households	138	3,6	81	50

On the other hand, the rate of transition out of poverty of *retired* heads of households is considerable, and in Ireland and The Netherlands it is even above the sample average. This is not only true for the low EC-standard, but also for the more generous subjective standards. This result is a little surprising, as retirement is generally an irreversible condition. Looking at other categories of household, that empirically more or less coïncide with retired heads of households (head of household 65+ years, widowed heads of households, households composed of one or two elderly persons), the same patterns are observed. As might be expected, transition rates out of poverty are generally lower for the *very old, widows and widowers* and *single elderly persons* than for elderly heads of households below 75 years and for elderly couples. But even for these types of household, where one would expect few changes, there is considerable movement in and out of poverty. Only in Lorraine do less than 1 in 5 of poor households with these characteristics escape out of poverty.

By contrast, in Ireland *younger households*, and those with *two or more children* have a rather low probability of escaping poverty. This is especially true for households with three children or more, where the poverty rate is very high in the first place.

A category where one would expect much mobility across the poverty line are households with *very young heads* (< 25 years). However, only in Belgium and Lorraine do these households have a relatively high escape rate; in other countries, especially Ireland, they are more likely than the average poor household to remain in poverty. But the number of these households is in all countries too small to draw definite conclusions.

The last remark also applies to *divorced or separated* heads of households. In The Netherlands they appear to escape from poverty relatively easily, in Ireland relatively difficultly, in other countries the picture is mixed.

By the low EC-standard, in all countries *single* persons that are poor in the first wave, have a relatively high rate of transition out of poverty. By the higher subjective standards, this is mostly not true, though.

In Belgium, *one-parent families* are more likely to stay in poverty than the average poor households, by all standards, but the reverse is true for The Netherlands. For the other countries, the numbers in the sample are probably too small to get meaningfull results.

The general conclusion that can be drawn on the basis of these results seems to be that income mobility across the poverty line occurs frequently in *all* (or almost all) social categories. This implies that the general risk of "longer-term" poverty is much smaller than that of poverty at one moment, but that its social incidence is not much different. A more detailed and precise analysis of transitions into and out of poverty must await the availability of more waves, and in some cases, the use of larger samples.

Notes

(1)   Results for Belgium on the individual level were substantially the same; see the Belgian report.

(2)   These are: results with the SPL in Ireland, The Netherlands and Luxembourg, and with the CSP in Lorraine.

7 Summary and conclusions

7.1. Design and aims of the study

The aims of this study which was conducted within the context of the Second European Action Programme to Combat Poverty, were the following:
1) to establish in a comparative way the *number of poor households* in each country/region and to identify social groups at high risk of poverty;
2) to assess the *adequacy of social security*, in the sense of guaranteeing a minimum income;
3) to incorporate all results in a standardized *system of social indicators*;
4) to develop and evaluate *methods* of measurement of poverty;
5) to distinguish between temporary and more permanent poverty by means of the *panel method*.

The comparative *set of social indicators* would enable policymakers to monitor changes in the domains of poverty and social security. It aims at providing reliable and systematic information to the broad public, on the European level as well as in the member states, to stimulate political debate on these topics and to help formulating better policies in these domains.

The social indicators are based on surveys carried out on fairly large *representative samples of households* in seven countries: Belgium, the Netherlands, Luxembourg, France (Lorraine), Ireland, Spain (Catolonia) and Greece, using a standardized questionnaire.

In the first five countries two waves have been organised, using the panel method. This means that households being interviewed in the first wave are re-interviewed in the second wave.

Table 7.1
Overview of surveys

	First wave		Second wave	
	year	size of sample*	year	size of sample*
Belgium	1985	6471	1988	3779
The Netherlands	1985	3405	1986	4480
Luxembourg	1985	2013	1986	1793
Lorraine	1985	715	1986	2092
Ireland	1987	3294	1989	947
Catalonia	1988	2976		
Greece	1988	2958		

* Number of households in sample. Only households for which poverty-status has been established (which implies full income information) have been counted.

The questionnaires were mainly concerned with the socio-demographic characteristics of the household and its members (including labour market characteristics) and the various incomes received through earnings, social security and other sources.

From the beginning of the research work, the system of social indicators ensured a common comparative framework for analysis.

The system of social indicators is presented below:

PART A: **INDICATORS OF THE DISTRIBUTION OF EARINGS AND SOCIAL SECURITY BENEFITS (DESCRIPTIVE INDICATORS)**

I. **Distribution by household disposable income deciles**

  1. Distribution of disposable income over income deciles (and income inequality)
  2. Socio-demographic composition of income deciles
  3. Position of households receiving benefits in the income distribution
  4. Level of benefits over income deciles
  5. Distribution of income from labour and of social security benefits over deciles

II. **Distribution by household standardized income deciles**

PART B: **INDICATORS OF POVERTY AND THE ADEQUACY OF SOCIAL SECURITY (RESULT INDICATORS)**

I. **Indicators of poverty**

  1. Poverty lines (subjective standards, statistical standard, Legal-standard)
  2. Number of poor households
    - based on income standards (objective insecurity)
    - based on the appreciation of income (self-report insecurity)
  3. The social distribution of poverty
  4. Possession of life-style indicators among insecure/secure households

II. **Adequacy of social security**

  1. Number of poor households before and after social payments
  2. The poverty gap

PART C: **DYNAMIC RESULTS ON POVERTY: POVERTY IN PANEL PERSPECTIVE**

7.2. The distribution of income and social transfers

Overall income inequality

Income inequality is in this study measured by deciles (ranking all households by the level of their disposable income and dividing them into ten (deciles) equal parts). On the basis of these distributions Gini and Theil-coefficients (inequality indexes) can be calculated.

From table 7.2 it appears that three groups of countries can be distinguished: Greece with the most unequal income distribution; the intermediary countries being Ireland, Catalonia and Lorraine; and the Benelux countries with the lowest income inequality.

Table 7.2
Overall income inequality

	Gini	Theil
Greece, 1988	0,409	0,335
Ireland, 1987	0,379	0,233
Catalonia, 1988	0,339	0,189
Belgium, 1985	0,277	0,120
The Netherlands, 1986	0,292	0,138
Lorraine, 1986	0,319	0,144
Luxembourg, 1986	0,284	0,130

Socio-demographic structure

There are some significant differences between countries as regards socio-demographic structure. Household size is much higher in Catalonia and Ireland than in the other countries. In Ireland this is mainly due to the relatively large number of families with three children or more. Ireland and The Netherlands are characterized by a relatively low proportion of households headed by elderly persons.

Table 7.3
Socio-demographic characteristics

	Average size of households	Average number of children across all households	% of households with head 65 or over	% of households with no persons at work
Greece, 1988	3,08	0,83	19,9	23,3
Ireland, 1987	3,58	1,35	14,5	31,8
Catalonia, 1988	3,45	0,69*	17,4	21,3
Belgium, 1985	2,83	0,84	20,7	33,3
Netherlands, 1986	2,70	0,80	15,9	29,6
Lorraine, 1986	2,88	0,89	19,5	30,9
Luxembourg, 1986	2,73	0,67	21,9	28,7

* Only persons of 16 years or younger.

Partly due to the age-structure, partly to household formation, there are on average much more workers per household in Greece and Catalonia than in the other countries, and less households with no person at work, or with only one income provider. Considering Ireland's young population and large household size, there are relatively few workers per household.

The demographic characteristics of a household are strongly related to its position in the income distribution. In all countries the average size of households increases as income level rises. However, after taking into account the greater needs of larger households, by using standardized deciles, we find that there is virtually no relation between household size and the position in the equivalent income distribution. The distribution of dependent children is somewhat similar. We generally find that, across deciles of disposable income, the number of children averaged over *all* households, increases from the first until the fifth or sixth decile, and then levels off. Again, after taking needs into account by standardizing, we find that children are fairly evenly distributed over the deciles, or are even somewhat concentrated in the lower deciles. In particular in Ireland and The Netherlands a larger than proportionate number of children live in the bottom quintile of the economic welfare distribution.

In most countries, households with an elderly head are strongly concentrated in the bottom of the distribution of disposable income. The concentration is somewhat less, but generally still considerable, in the distribution of equivalent income. In Greece, however, relatively many elderly heads of households are in the middle and higher deciles, and in Ireland these households are much less than proportionally represented in the bottom quintile of equivalent income.

The number of income providers and workers is obviously an important determinant of the total income of which a household disposes. Not surprisingly, in all countries (except Greece) the proportion of households with only one income provider falls steadily as we move up the income distribution, both of equivalent and unstandardized income. In the lowest deciles, almost all households have only one income provider. Conversely, the average number of persons at work per family rises very strongly with decile number. Both patterns are a little less pronounced for the equivalent income distribution than for the unstandardized one. Also, Greece seems an exception to these patterns: the bottom deciles comprise many persons at work.

Number of benefiting households and level of social benefits

The number of households benefiting from social security in each country is the result of the demographic and socio-economic structure on the one hand and of the institutional arrangements as regards social security on the other hand.

In Greece and Catalonia, the number of households receiving earnings is much larger than in the other countries, which implies that in the southern group of countries there are probably fewer households for which social security is the only source of income.

Important differences can be observed as regards the various social security sectors. One third of all households are receiving pensions in Belgium, Ireland and Luxembourg. In Lorraine, Catalonia and in particular Greece this proportion is considerably higher; in the Netherlands it is much lower. Regarding unemployment allowances, Ireland is characterized by its large proportion of benefiting households. Within the Benelux, Belgium clearly has the highest proportion of households receiving an unemployment allowance. The incidence of social assistance is the highest in the Netherlands and the lowest in Belgium. A striking difference appears between the northern European countries and the southern ones as regards the number of households drawing family allowances. In the former countries, virtually all families with children are covered by a family allowance scheme. In the southern countries only limited schemes exist.

With regard to the level of social security benefits we observe that, depending on the country, replacement incomes are about 60% (the Netherlands and Lorraine) to less than 40% (Catalonia) of median income. Among replacement incomes pensions are generally highest, while social assistance provides the lowest amounts on average. Pensions are relatively high in the Netherlands and Lorraine and relatively low in Catalonia. Unemployment allowances seem relatively generous in the Netherlands and in Ireland. The level of sickness or invalidity allowances is most favourable in the Netherlands; they are on average low in Catalonia and Lorraine and very low in Greece.

Incidence of social security benefits by sector

In this section we discuss firstly the incidence of social security by sector in the income distribution (which households are receivers), next the level of the benefits, and thirdly the distribution of the aggregate transfers across deciles.

Contrary to households with earnings, the proportion of households with an income from pensions generally falls as we move up the scale of disposable household income. Nevertheless, in the highest deciles a large minority of all households have an income from pensions. The concentration of households with pensions in the bottom quintile is greatest in The Netherlands and Belgium, and least in Greece and Ireland. However, because most of the households with pensions are relatively small the distribution by equivalent income is much more favourable for these households. In Ireland, Lorraine and The Netherlands there is no concentration of households receiving pensions in the bottom quintile of equivalent income, and in the other countries it is much smaller than by disposable income.

While by unstandardized income households with *unemployment allowances* are in several countries distributed more or less evenly across all deciles, by equivalent income they are concentrated in the bottom quintile in most countries, especially in Ireland and The Netherlands. Probably because of the heterogeneity of this category, the distributions of households with *sickness or invalidity allowances* over disposable and equivalent income deciles show little pattern. Most households with *social assistance* are, unsurprisingly, in the bottom income groups.

Table 7.4
Percentage of households receiving certain kinds of income

	earnings	replacement income	pensions	unemploy-ment allowances	sickness or inva-lidity allowances	social assistance	family allowances
Greece, 1988	84,1	44,8	42,0	2,2	1,7	0,3	3,0
Ireland, 1987	61,5	58,9	34,0	21,6	12,3	1,2	45,0
Catalonia, 1988	94,3	40,3	30,1	4,7	8,0	2,9	6,8
Belgium, 1985	67,3	46,4	32,1	12,1	7,3	0,7	46,5
The Netherlands, 1986	71,2	39,7	21,5	6,8	9,5	7,6	41,7
Lorraine, 1986	73,0	42,8	29,4	9,0	10,6	1,0	35,2
Luxembourg, 1986	72,1	45,4	36,5	1,5	10,2	1,6	41,8

Table 7.5

Average amounts received of income from various sources, by households
actually benefiting, as a percentage of median total household income in each country

	earnings	replacement income	pensions	unemploy- ment allowances	sickness or inva- lidity allowances	social assistance	family allowances
				Source of income			
Greece, 1988	113	49	50	11	8	7	3
Ireland, 1987	133	50	46	41	42	23	7
Catalonia, 1988	106	38	36	35	30	11	3
Belgium, 1985	110	53	57	33	36	22	13
The Netherlands, 1986	112	60	68	42	53	19	8
Lorraine, 1986	104	57	68	23	22	5	15
Luxembourg, 1986	107	54	57	22	32	14	9

119

By unstandardized income, households benefiting from *family allowances* are found mostly in the upper half of the income distribution. But the distribution of these households across deciles of equivalent income is fairly even in Belgium and Luxembourg and shows a concentration in the bottom quintile in Ireland and The Netherlands. (In Greece and Catalonia there are very few family allowances.)

Households with a *replacement income* in general are found in fairly large numbers in all deciles of disposable income, but with a strong concentration in the bottom quintile, especially in the Benelux-countries and Catalonia. By deciles of equivalent income this concentration is generally much smaller, and very limited in Lorraine and Ireland.

In Catalonia and Greece, the distribution of households receiving any *social security* payment virtually equals that of replacement incomes. In the other countries, the proportion of households with social security payment is more or less the same in all deciles of disposable income. By deciles of equivalent income, the picture is somewhat different, though a large majority of all households in all deciles receive some income from social security.

Levels of the benefits

Though the average *pension* received rises with household disposable or standardized income decile number in all countries, it does not do so very strongly, compared with earnings. Even in the top deciles, the average pension received is generally below median household income or not much above it (except in Lorraine). The Netherlands has, in relative terms, the highest pensions in most deciles, while the opposite is true for Catalonia. The level of *other replacement incomes* shows little variation across deciles, or no consistent pattern. The average amount of *family allowances* is more or less constant across deciles of disposable and equivalent income, or increasing only very moderately with decile number.

By unstandardized income deciles the average amounts of *social security transfers as a whole* generally do not display a marked pattern. Only in Greece do the amounts produce a strongly rising curve. By equivalent income however, the amounts of social transfers are clearly at their highest level in the top deciles in Lorraine, Luxembourg and Catalonia as well as in Greece.

Distribution of aggregate benefits

By *un*standardized income, a larger than proportional share of aggregate *pensions* goes to the bottom deciles in Belgium, The Netherlands, Ireland and Catalonia. In Lorraine and Greece, on the other hand, aggregate pensions are concentrated in the top quintile. But by equivalent income, the distribution of aggregate pensions is in no country skewed towards households in the bottom half of the distribution. The bottom quintile of equivalent income does get a larger than proportional share of *unemployment allowances* in Ireland, The Netherlands, Belgium and Catalonia. The distribution across unstandardized deciles is generally more uniform.

Aggregate *sickness or invalidity allowances* are rather evenly distributed across the income distribution. *Social assistance* is concentrated mainly, but not exclusively, in the bottom quintile of disposable income and especially of equivalent income.

By unstandardized income, aggregate *family allowances* flow mainly to the upper half of the distribution. By equivalent income, however, the shares of family allowances are either more or less uniform across the distribution (Belgium and Luxembourg), or they are relatively large in the bottom deciles (Ireland and The Netherlands) or in the second quintile (Lorraine).

It is remarkable that, despite large differences between countries in economic, social and demographic conditions and institutional arrangements, we find everywhere that *social security transfers as a whole are widely distributed across income groups*. This does not imply that social security is hardly or not redistributive. It does imply that social security does not work solely, or even mainly, to relieve poverty. This is unsurprising, because of the various other aims and functions of social security.

7.3. The poverty lines

As has been noted in the introduction, the concept of poverty is ambiguous, and social research has not converged on a single valid poverty line. Instead, several approaches exist. In this project four poverty lines have been used. The *CSP*-method and the *SPL* belong both to the "*subjective*" approach to poverty measurement, in which the poverty line is derived from assessments of their own income by the households in the sample. The *EC*-method is a *relative* or statistical method, where the level of the poverty line is set at 50% of the average equivalent income for each country ([1]). The poverty line is thus defined in relation to the average level of economic welfare in each individual country, not in relation to the average level in the EC as a whole. Finally, the *legal* poverty line is equal to the guaranteed minimum income in each country.

The geometric means (a summary measure of the level) of the various standards for different types of households, in each country, are shown in figure 7.1.

The subjective poverty lines are in all countries much higher than both the EC-standard and the Legal-standard (except in The Netherlands). They indicate a social minimum. Not all households below it can be considered to be poor; rather they are living in "insecurity of the means of subsistence". The EC-standard is much lower in all countries. It indicates a "minimum minimorum"; households below it are really poor. The Legal-standard is generally even below the EC-standard, except in The Netherlands.

The EC-standard is in real terms at a rather low level in Greece and Ireland, and very high in Luxembourg. It reflects, of course, the average level of equivalent income in each country. Very broadly speaking the subjective standards follow a similar pattern, but with some important deviations, notably in The Netherlands (where they are relatively low) and in Catalonia (where the SPL is very high). There are also some considerable divergences between the subjective standards themselves.

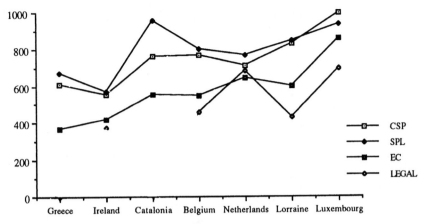

Figure 7.1: Geometric means of four poverty standards (minima in ECU) in seven countries (years see table 3.1).

Besides the differences in levels, there are also important differences in the equivalence scales. In particular, the EC-standard equivalence scale is much steeper than the equivalence scales which are implicit in the subjective standards and the Legal-standard. This is true for all countries, despite the variation across countries in the equivalence scales produced by the subjective and Legal-standards.

7.4. The extent of poverty

Table 7.6

Percentage of all households, whose means of subsistence are insecure

	CSP-standard	SPL-standard	EC-standard	Legal-standard
Greece, 1988	42,6	42,0	19,9	-
Ireland, 1987	29,6	31,6	17,2	8,1
Catalonia, 1988	31,3	37,3	15,1	-
Belgium, 1985	21,4	24,9	6,1	2,9
Netherlands, 1986	10,9	15,9	7,2	7,2
Lorraine, 1986	30,8	26,5	10,8	4,0
Luxembourg, 1986	14,5	12,5	7,6	5,0

One observes important differences depending on the poverty line used. The *Legal-standard* produces the lowest number of poor; the *subjective poverty lines* result in the highest poverty rates, while the *EC-standard* is in between these two. The *EC-standard* divides the countries in *two main groups*: on the one hand the Benelux and Lorraine with a relatively low poverty rate and on the other hand Greece, Ireland and Catalonia where the poverty rate is twice (or more) as high. Within the first group the poverty rate in Lorraine is higher than in the Benelux countries. The two subjective standards are ordering the countries in more or less the same way, although with notable differences, in particular for the Benelux countries. Surprisingly, 7-8% of all households find themselves below the Legal-standard in the Netherlands and Ireland.

In spite of the existence of social security systems in all countries, the poverty rate (EC-standard) is very high in the "poorer" countries (Greece, Catalonia, Ireland) and poverty still exists in the "richer" countries. Thus well-developed social security systems do not seem to be able to solve (financial) poverty completely. This conclusion is confirmed by using the more generous subjective poverty standards ("social acceptable minima" which measure insecurity of subsistence rather than poverty) as well as by using the more strict EC-standard. Considering the legal minimum, it is surprising that there seems to be a considerable number of households who have to live with an income beneath the legally guaranteed level in the countries concerned ([2]).

By way of comparison we give the poverty rates for all countries of the European Community in 1985, according to two other studies, which have used the same poverty line (Eurostat, 1990; O'Higgins and Jenkins, 1990). The Eurostat study uses household expenditure instead of household income, however.

Table 7.7
Poverty incidence in European countries (percentage of households and persons below the poverty line) according to three sources

	Eurostat (1985) [a]		O'Higgins (1985) [b]		Europass (1986) [c]
	% households	% households	% households	% households	% households
Belgium	6,3	7,1	6,3	7,2	6,1 (1985)
The Netherlands	6,9	9,6	5,3	7,4	7,2
Luxembourg	-	-	7,6	7,9	7,6
Denmark	8,0	7,9	14,7	14,7	-
F.R. of Germany	16,3	10,5	7,4	8,5	-
Italy	12,0	14,1	11,7	11,7	-
United Kingdom	14,1	14,6	9,8	12,0	-
France	18,0	19,1	14,5	17,5	-
Lorraine					10,8
Ireland	18,5	18,4	20,0	22,0	17,2 (1987)
Spain	20,3	20,9	20,0	20,0	-
Catalonia					15,1 (1988)
Greece	20,5	21,5	24,0	24,0	19,9 (1988)
Portugal	31,4	32,4	28,0	28,0	-
Total EC	14,1	15,5	12,1	13,9	-

[a] Eurostat, (1990).
  Poverty line: 50% of national average household expenditure per adult equivalent.
  Equivalence factors: first adult 1.00, other adult 0.7, child 0.5 (less than 14 years).
[b] O'Higgins, M. and Jenkins, S. (1990)
  Poverty line: 50% of national average equivalent disposable household income
  Equivalence factors: 1.00-0.7-0.5.
[c] Poverty line: 50% of average equivalent disposable household income
  Equivalence factors: 1.00-0.7-0.5.

The three studies are not wholly consistent. Nevertheless it is clear that the Benelux-countries have the lowest proportions of poor households and persons, while the poverty rate is relatively high in Ireland, Spain, Greece and Portugal. Thus, although only half of all EC-countries are represented in the "Europass"-project, these include some of the "richer", as well as some of the "poorest" countries ([3]).

7.5. The social structure of poverty

Poverty and insecurity of subsistence are clearly concentrated in certain social categories of the population. Tables 7.8 to 7.10 present the risk of poverty for some important social groups and allow us to discover social determinants of poverty.

In all countries (and by all standards), the poverty risk of a household is very high or highest if the household's head is *unemployed*; 50% to 70% of these households are in insecurity of subsistence. The number of households where the head is unemployed is however relatively small (1% - 5% of all households), except in Ireland (11%). In Greece poverty among households with one or more persons at work is almost as high as among households with no persons at work; this seems to indicate that the level of earnings is in very many cases insufficient. Among *retired* heads of households the risk of insecurity of subsistence is also high (except in Ireland, where it is below average), but it is less than among unemployed heads of households, and the average shortfall of income is smaller.

In all countries the risk of poverty or insecurity of subsistence is less if the *educational level* of the head of household is higher, or if his socio-professional status is better.

By the *age* of the head of household the risk of insecurity of subsistence often, but not always, follows a U-curve. In most countries it is high for very young households (head below 25 years), and relatively low for middle-aged heads of households. Generally the poverty-risk is higher than average again for the elderly, especially for the very old (75+). In Ireland, however, the poverty rate is at its highest level among middle-aged heads of households, and low among the elderly.

Looking at *household composition* we find high rates of poverty and insecurity of subsistence among single elderly (often very old or widowed persons), in the northern countries also among single persons of active age (many of them are either very young or divorced) and in some countries, notably Ireland, also among couples with three or more children. The highest rates of poverty or insecurity of subsistence are found in many countries among one-parent families (again, many of them divorced), but the number of these families is relatively small.

An important determinant of the risk of poverty and insecurity of subsistence is the *number of income providers* in the household. If a household has two or more income providers, the risk of poverty is low or very low (except in Greece). On the other hand, a single income, even if it is an earned income, seems to be in many cases insufficient to provide security of subsistence.

Table 7.8
Percentage of households insecure of subsistence in a number of social categories, CSP-standard

	BEL-GIUM 1985	NETHER-LANDS 1986	LUXEM-BOURG 1986	LOR-RAINE 1986	IRE-LAND 1987	CATA-LONIA 1988	GREECE 1988
all households	21.4	10.9	14.5	30.8	29.6	31.3	42.6
activity of head of household:							
employed	11.6	3.4	9.5	26.1	20.0	23.7	39.7
retired	29.8	16.4	15.0	29.1	18.1	40.3	46.5
unemployed	61.4	42.9	61.9	64.3	74.7	63.4	72.7
sick/disabled	38.0	28.6	40.0	46.9	61.1	63.4	-
only primary education	33.5	20.2	21.4	38.6	n.a.	40.4	55.7
widow/widower	33.0	23.4	19.1	42.0	23.5	47.0	57.1
divorced	30.3	16.9	13.9	25.4	53.4	33.6	51.4
Type of household:							
single elderly	36.7	22.8	25.7	41.9	27.0	46.2	55.9
two elderly	27.3	8.1	13.3	23.3	14.7	38.4	51.0
single active	29.9	23.0	20.8	29.7	44.4	27.9	45.1
single active, one child	51.7	3.3	47.0	38.1	45.6	42.9	45.5
two actives, three children	12.5	4.3	5.5	32.2	39.0	40.5	42.6

Table 7.9
Percentage of households insecure of subsistence in a number of social categories, SPL-standard

	BEL-GIUM 1985	NETHER-LANDS 1986	LUXEM-BOURG 1986	LOR-RAINE 1986	IRE-LAND 1987	CATA-LONIA 1988	GREECE 1988
all households	24.9	15.9	12.5	26.5	31.6	37.3	42.0
activity of head of household:							
employed	9.4	4.3	3.8	16.5	15.8	26.8	35.6
retired	47.2	29.0	16.5	35.9	35.2	58.6	54.2
unemployed	59.2	51.0	52.4	58.9	67.3	64.9	75.8
sick/disabled	34.6	28.4	25.1	31.2	57.0	61.0	-
only primary education	41.6	30.3	20.4	35.7	n.a.	49.3	54.6
widow/widower	55.2	42.6	31.7	54.4	52.0	64.0	59.7
divorced	34.4	32.8	12.4	34.5	58.6	44.3	49.1
Type of household:							
single elderly	67.7	47.8	46.0	72.6	70.2	85.9	70.5
two elderly	50.3	14.2	17.8	32.5	28.4	78.6	70.7
single active	40.6	38.6	19.2	43.7	52.5	39.9	35.8
single active, one child	54.0	33.9	47.0	52.4	67.7	52.4	44.1
two actives, three children	6.2	5.9	0.9	18.2	36.1	50.6	47.5

Table 7.10
Percentage of households insecure of subsistence in
a number of social categories, EC-standard

	BEL-GIUM 1985	NETHER-LANDS 1986	LUXEM-BOURG 1986	LOR-RAINE 1986	IRE-LAND 1987	CATA-LONIA 1988	GREECE 1988
all households	6.1	7.2	7.6	10.8	17.2	15.1	19.9
activity of head of household:							
employed	2.9	5.2	5.5	6.8	11.9	9.0	19.1
retired	6.6	2.4	7.4	9.3	7.9	22.1	21.7
unemployed	26.2	19.4	40.9	41.0	58.9	43.5	36.4
sick/disabled	10.7	10.0	19.6	22.9	24.4	40.7	-
only primary education	9.1	10.0	11.7	14.4	n.a.	21.8	28.7
widow/widower	4.6	2.3	5.3	15.4	6.6	27.3	22.0
divorced	9.1	8.5	11.6	11.7	33.1	21.2	27.0
Type of household:							
single elderly	5.0	1.6	7.1	19.3	3.0	29.3	24.1
two elderly	11.3	3.2	11.5	9.2	8.4	30.2	33.7
single active	5.8	8.5	7.0	12.5	20.3	10.1	7.4
single active, one child	7.5	3.3	25.6	9.5	19.3	23.8	30.3
two actives, three children	8.5	19.1	17.4	13.1	34.3	17.7	37.6

When the head of household has the *nationality* of a non-EC-country, the risk of poverty and insecurity of subsistence is higher than average.

These conclusions given so far hold good in general (with the exceptions noted). Nevertheless, there are important variations, both across standards, as well as across countries. The more generous subjective poverty lines identify more or less the same social categories in poverty as does the more severe EC-standard. The differences are mostly due to the much steeper equivalence scale of the EC-standard.

Across countries, we find that in the less wealthy countries (Ireland, Catalonia, Greece), similar categories of households are at relatively strong risk, but the absolute poverty rates are higher there. Especially in Greece, earnings are often insufficient. Generally, it seems that a number of socio-economic factors work in more or less the same direction in all countries, but the comparative analysis also shows that the countries of the EC are rather heterogeneous. This due not only to socio-economic and demographic differences, but also to important institutional and legal variations.

7.6. Deprivation and poverty

Poverty and insecurity of subsistence is not purely a financial problem, but it has its impact on the living standard (life style) of households. The deprivation of a household i.e. the extent to which it does not participate in the ordinary living patterns of community, can be measured by the non-possession of a certain number of items and in particular by the cumulation of these. In the context of this study especially the correlation between financial insecurity (poverty) and deprivation is important.

The possession of certain goods (but not all of them) appears to be fairly similar across countries (e.g. refrigerator, indoor toilet, bath/shower; table 7.11). The proportion of households not possessing any item is greater in Ireland than in any other country. Consequently Irish households are most at risk of being in deprivation (defined as not possessing three or more items), Dutch households are the least. The proportion of households in deprivation in Catalonia is barely higher than in Belgium and Luxembourg, which is in contrast to the results of the income standards.

Table 7.11
Percentage of all households who do not possess certain life-style indicators

	Belgium 1985	Netherlands 1986	Luxembourg 1985*	Lorraine 1986	Ireland 1987	Catalonia 1988
Refrigerator	2.4	1.0	2.4	n.a.	5.4	0.4
Indoor toilet	3.2	1.1	5.8	4.1	7.9	1.7
Bath/shower	9.4	n.a.	7.6	n.a.	9.8	2.4
Washing mach.	12.1	8.1	7.3	5.6	22.4	5.8
Dry dwelling	5.8	10.7	19.4	21.8	11.1	18.7
Colour TV	17.3	10.9	18.7	6.2	19.8	10.6
Car	27.5	30.0	27.7	24.5	42.4	31.1
Central heating	38.4	23.4	21.9	n.a.	48.0	71.4

* For Luxembourg, 1985 instead of 1986 results have been used, because the item "central heating" was lacking in the 1986 survey.

Figures in table 7.12 show also that in all countries households in financial insecurity and in poverty possess (participate) significantly less than secure households, but that nevertheless about two-thirds (or more) of all "poor" or insecure households are not deprived, according to this indicator.

Table 7.12
Percentage of households whose means of subsistence are secure/insecure, which do not possess three or more life-style indicators, out of eight*

	All households	CSP		SPL		EC		Legal	
		sec.	insec.	sec.	insec.	sec.	insec.	sec.	insec.
Belgium, 1985	15.2	10.4	33.1	7.8	37.3	14.0	32.3	14.4	42.3
Netherlands, 1986*	7.5	6.1	19.0	4.5	23.3	6.7	17.2	5.9	26.2
Luxembourg, 1985	14.8	10.9	37.2	8.8	34.6	13.0	37.3	12.4	49.3
Ireland, 1987	22.3	18.3	32.4	15.5	37.7	21.3	28.1	21.9	30.0
Catalonia, 1988	15.4	10.9	24.9	9.1	26.4	12.7	30.4	-	-

* in The Netherlands only seven indicators were used.

At least in the richer countries, almost all households have the basic amenities of an acceptable style of life. The "luxury" goods are less common, but non-possession of these does not constitute poverty. These results suggest that in these countries (but possibly not in Ireland) very few households are in absolute poverty, in the sense of lacking the basic amenities. The reason for this might well be that a permanent state of poverty is much less common than could be assumed on the basis of a single cross-sectional survey of income-positions.

7.7. Adequacy of social security

The issue of the adequacy of social security is central to this study. The question asked is: how many households would be non-poor or secure of the means of subsistence even without social transfers, how many are so only due to social transfers, and how many are poor or insecure despite the existence of social transfers? Table 7.13 gives these proportions for the various samples; in table 7.14 the more precise question is answered, how many households are lifted out of poverty or insecurity of subsistence, of those whose income without social security transfers would be below the poverty line.

Table 7.13
Percentage of households whose means are insecure/secure
of subsistence, before and after social transfers are granted

	CSP-standard				SPL-standard			
	(1)	(2)	(3)	Total	(1)	(2)	(3)	Total
Greece, 1988	42.9	14.5	42.6	100	45.8	12.2	42.0	100
Ireland, 1987	47.1	23.4	29.6	100	49.9	18.5	31.6	100
Catalonia, 1988	55.3	13.4	31.3	100	52.2	10.5	37.3	100
Belgium, 1985	48.5	30.1	21.4	100	50.9	24.6	24.9	100
Netherlands, 1986	62.9	26.2	10.9	100	61.3	22.8	15.9	100
Luxembourg, 1986	56.7	28.7	14.5	100	64.0	23.6	12.4	100
Lorraine, 1986	43.3	25.9	30.8	100	50.3	23.2	26.5	100
	EC-standard				Legal-standard			
	(1)	(2)	(3)	Total	(1)	(2)	(3)	Total
Greece, 1988	61.9	18.2	19.9	100	-	-	-	-
Ireland, 1987	53.8	29.0	17.2	100	57.5	34.4	8.1	100
Catalonia, 1988	69.2	15.7	15.1	100	-	-	-	-
Belgium, 1985	59.0	34.9	6.1	100	65.2	31.8	2.9	100
Netherlands, 1986	60.2	32.7	7.2	100	63.6	29.2	7.2	100
Lorraine, 1986	60.6	28.6	10.8	100	71.3	24.8	3.9	100
Luxembourg, 1986	61.1	31.4	7.6	100	68.3	26.7	5.0	100

(1) households secure before transfers
(2) households secure due to transfers
(3) households insecure after transfers

Table 7.14
Proportion of households, insecure before social security,
that are secure of subsistence due to social security transfers

	CSP-standard	SPL-standard	EC-standard	Legal-standard
Greece, 1988	25.4	22.5	47.8	-
Ireland, 1987	44.2	36.9	62.8	80.9
Catalonia, 1988	30.0	22.0	51.0	-
Belgium, 1985	58.4	49.6	85.1	91.3
Netherlands, 1986	70.1	58.9	82.0	80.2
Lorraine, 1986	45.7	46.7	72.5	86.4
Luxembourg, 1986	66.4	65.6	80.1	84.2

Using the latter indicator, the impact of social security is the strongest in the Benelux countries: by the EC-standard more than 80% of the (hypothetical) poor before social security are lifted out of poverty, by the more generous subjective standards the percentages vary between 50% and 70%. In Lorraine the proportions are a little lower. Ireland occupies an intermediary position. The effect of social security is the least, and in fact rather low, in Greece and Catalonia.

It appears that, despite very large financial resources and extensive administrative means, social security is not very successfull in relieving poverty and insecurity of the means of subsistence, except in the Benelux at a low level of minimum income. In Greece and Catalonia, social security is clearly inadequate, leaving a large part of the population in poverty or insecurity of the means of subsistence. (Even by the lowest standard, only half of those whose pre-transfer income is below the standard are lifted to or above this level by social security transfers.)

What are the reasons for this inadequacy? From a micro-perspective, some households are left in poverty, despite the existence of social security, either because the amount is not large enough, or because they do not receive social security transfers, due to lack of entitlement or non-take-up. From a macro-perspective, the proximate reasons for the inadequacy could be either the volume of aggregate social security transfers, relative to the aggregate needs (the poverty gap before social security) or the direction of the transfers, i.e. the extent to which they are targeted at the pre-transfer poor.

In all countries, the average pre-transfer income of those households that are non-poor only due to social transfers is about the same as that of households that are poor even after social security transfers are granted. The main difference between these categories of households is the much higher amount of transfers that the first kind of households receive, compared to the second kind (on average 2 to 4 times as large). This suggests that, in general, the most important reason why households are in poverty, or insecurity of subsistence, is that the transfers do not sufficiently cover the needs. On average, the post-transfer income of the poor falls between 20% (Benelux) and 35% (Greece) short of the poverty standard.

Table 7.15
The post-transfer poverty gap as a percentage of aggregate income of all households

	CSP-standard	SPL-standard	EC-standard	Legal-standard
Greece, 1988	n.a.	n.a.	n.a.	-
Ireland, 1987	5.0	4.5	2.7	1.7
Catalonia	5.3	7.0	1.8	-
Belgium, 1985	2.6	3.0	0.5	0.2
Netherlands, 1986*	1.0	1.6	0.9	1.0
Lorraine, 1986	5.4	4.0	1.4	0.4
Luxembourg, 1986	1.6	1.3	0.8	0.3

* figures calculated on the basis of average amounts.

Of the aggregate volume of social security transfers, the largest part (around 70-80%) goes to the pre-transfer poor or insecure; about a quarter is received by households that would be non-poor or secure of subsistence even without them. The resources of social security are employed *effectively* (in our use of the word) to the extent that he poverty gap is eliminated; and *efficiently* to the extent that the resources are targeted exclusively at the poverty gap, and do not flow to the pre-transfer non-poor, or to the pre-transfer poor in excess of what they strictly need to reach the level of the poverty-standard. These terms are of course abstractions from the reality of social policy. Social security is very effective in the Benelux countries (more than 85% of the poverty gap is eliminated), a little less in Lorraine and Ireland, and considerably less in Catalonia (no figures available for Greece). The remaining poverty gap after social transfers is (by the EC-standard) less than 1% of aggregate household income in the Benelux-countries, between 1% and 2% in Lorraine and Catalonia, almost 3% in Ireland, and it is at least as large in Greece (although no precise figure is available). All systems are rather inefficient in the sense that only part of the available means are in fact used to close the poverty gap. The Irish system is the most efficient one, where 54% is used to eliminate the poverty gap (EC-standard); in The Netherlands it is 50%, in the other countries around 40%.

These figures imply that there is in fact considerable redistribution of income, but also that it is not equalizing in the sense that only the bottom income groups would profit, and would all be lifted to the same minimum income level. These are of course conclusions at a high level of abstraction. In addition, it must be stressed that social security should not be evaluated exclusively in terms of a minimum income guarantee to all households; it has also other important aims.

To what extent can the differences in the extent of poverty that have been found across countries, be explained by the varying aggregate volumes of social security transfers?

Or must we also take into account the "needs" - the situation before social security transfers are granted - and the rules governing who gets what? One way to assess this issue is to perform a regression analysis across countries on various measures of adequacy, with the aggregate volume of social security transfers (as a proportion of aggregate household income) as the independent variable.

The results of such an exercise are reported in table 7.16. Because of the small number of cases, they must be interpreted with caution. It appears that the aggregate volume of transfers explains only a part of the variation in the extent of poverty. In the case of the poverty rate, a fairly large part is explained, in the case of the poverty gap, the R-square measure is much lower. If one takes "needs" into account by looking at the proportional reduction of the extent of poverty the correlations are quite high. (Even higher R-square's are obtained if "needs" are put into the regression equation as independent variables, instead of using proportional reduction measures.)

These correlations are considerably higher than those found by Mitchell (1991), who has used a fairly similar methodology, but a different sample of countries.

Table 7.16
Correlation of adequacy measures with the volume of aggregate
social security transfers, as a percentage of aggregate household income

Adequacy measure	Correlation (R2)	Total degrees of freedom
Post-transfer poverty rate	0.48	6
Post-transfer poverty gap	0.20	5
Proportional reduction of the poverty rate	0.83 *	6
Proportional reduction of the poverty gap	0.81 *	5

* significant at 5%-level.

Looking at the results country by country, we can characterize them in the following way:

- Catalonia and Greece: limited means, not very efficiently employed and therefore low effectiveness: relatively few households are lifted out of poverty by social security, many households stay in poverty or insecurity.
- Ireland has larger resources of which the employment is relatively efficient; but it has also very large needs. The poverty-eliminating effect of social security is therefore less than complete, and many households stay in poverty.
- Benelux and Lorraine: moderate needs and relatively ample means result in a high effectiveness and relatively few remaining poor or insecure households.

Comparing across sectors, we find that in all countries pensions seem to be the most effective in lifting beneficiary households out of poverty: in the Benelux more than 90% by the EC-standard. They are followed, in this order, by sickness or invalidity allowances, unemployment allowances and family allowances. Pensions also seem to leave relatively few beneficiary households in poverty, while unemployment allowances are for many households who receive them insufficient to escape poverty. These patterns hold in all countries, using the EC- and CSP-standards, though pensions perform relatively worse using the SPL-standard. All Dutch replacement income schemes, except family allowances, seem to work more effectively for beneficiary households than their counterparts do in the other countries. Catalonia, on the other hand, has by all standards the least effective social security systems, with the exception of unemployment allowances.

7.8. Poverty in panel perspective: dynamic results

Most countries (not Greece and Catalonia) have conducted two waves in the panel-survey (re-interviewing of the same sample). Unfortunately, the time-gap between the waves varies across countries between one and three years. Cross-sectional comparison between two waves has shown that there are few significant changes across such relatively short periods. The real value of the repetition of the surveys lies in the dynamic results, the so-called panel analyses, in which the same households are followed over time. The longitudinal study of households enables one to distinguish temporary and less temporary poverty. The stability of the cross-sectional results on poverty over time could easily mislead one into concluding that most of the poor at one moment belong to the permanent poor, and thus to an over-estimation of the problem of poverty.

The analysis concentrates on the poverty status of households across two waves. The most important results are:

1. By the more generous standards, around 60% to 75% of the poor households in wave one are in the same situation after an interval of one to three years. If the poverty-standard is more strict, the proportions vary between 40% and 64%.
2. The implication of this is that the number of households that are poor during at least one or several years is rather small in countries like the Benelux (by the strict EC-standard, down to less than 3%).
3. On the other hand, in the longitudinal perspective the differences between countries are more pronounced. In particular in Ireland, a smaller proportion of the poor at wave one have escaped poverty at wave two. One in ten of all households have incomes below the strict EC-standard in both years.
4. A methodological result is that the escape rate out of poverty is inversely related to the proportion of poor households in wave one, and therefore indirectly also to the level of the standard.

Table 7.17
Proportion of all households insecure of subsistence
in first wave, that are still insecure in second wave

	CSP-standard	SPL-standard	EC-standard	Legal-standard
Ireland, 1987-1989	71.2	84.1	63.8	26.2
Belgium, 1985-1988	62.9	60.8	42.0	24.2
Netherlands, 1985-1986	47.3	69.7	40.6	30.6
Lorraine, 1985-1986	73.6	73.9	56.9	42.9
Luxembourg, 1985-1986	62.5	49.5	57.1	44.0

Breaking down changes in poverty-status by characteristics of the household, the most important result is that income mobility across the poverty line occurs *frequently* in *all* social categories. Even among the kinds of household where one would expect few changes, like the very old, widows and widowers and single elderly persons, there is considerable movement into and out of poverty (though less than in the population at large). This implies that, although the overall risk of "longer-term" poverty is much smaller than the risk of being in poverty at a certain moment, its social distribution is not very different. In many cases the social structure of poverty appears to be the same, but more pronounced, in the longitudinal perspective: categories of households with a high relative risk of being in poverty at a certain moment have an even higher relative risk of being in poverty across two waves. This is, for instant, the case for unemployed heads of households. This is an important (though at the moment a somewhat preliminary) conclusion: it means that, even if the poor as identified at a certain moment may include many that are poor for only a short time, nevertheless the results of cross-sectional studies are not very misleading as regards the social structure of poverty, and provide good indicators of the categories of households that are at high risk of poverty, even of longer term poverty.

Table 7.18
Percentage of all households that are insecure of subsistence in both waves

	CSP-standard	SPL-standard	EC-standard	Legal-standard
Ireland, 1987-1989	22.3	31.2	10.2	1.7
Belgium, 1985-1988	13.5	14.9	2.4	0.6
Netherlands, 1985-1986	5.3	5.3	2.6	2.2
Lorraine, 1985-1986	19.3	19.1	6.1	2.0
Luxembourg, 1985-1986	9.4	9.8	4.4	2.8

7.9. Evaluation of poverty line methods

In this study four types of poverty line methods have been applied: subjective, statistical, legal and (to a limited extent) deprivation methods.

An important finding has been that the various poverty lines produce results that are in several respects rather dissimilar, even though one should not overlook the many important points on which they are in agreement with each other.

In the first place, the levels of the poverty lines vary considerably. Generally, the subjective methods produce the most generous poverty lines, while the legal method produces the lowest poverty lines. The statistical method, namely the "EC" poverty line, situates itself in between. Across countries, the subjective standards rise with increasing level of average income (as does, by definition, the EC-standard) but not smoothly.

Secondly, there is much variation in the "steepness" of the equivalence scales. The EC-standard has by far the steepest equivalence in all countries. Allthough the CSP- and SPL-methods produce equivalence scales that vary across countries, as well as relative to each other, they do seem to converge on a fairly narrow range.

Thirdly, mainly as a result of the variation in the level of the poverty lines, there are rather large differences in the estimated poverty rates (percentage of households in poverty). Generally, the subjective methods produce the highest estimates, and the legal poverty line the lowest ones. The EC-method and the subjective poverty lines identify the same groupes of high and low poverty countries, allthough within these groups there is some inconsistency.

Fourthly, and perhaps most importantly, the structure of poverty (i.e. the composition of the group of poor households and social categories at risk of poverty) depends on the poverty line used, in particular on the equivalence scale. Using the EC-line, which has a very steep equivalence scale, large families (generally headed by middle aged males at work) appear to be relatively more at risk of poverty than if the subjective methods are used, and the reverse is true for small households (often elderly, pensioners, female headed).

What conclusion follows from these findings?

Because poverty is an ambiguous, relative and gradual phenomenon, it is impossible to propose one single poverty line which is exact and undisputable. The choice of a poverty line is necessarily a conventional one and the number of poor depends on this choice, which may imply a strict or broad conception of poverty. The differences should therefore not be considered as just inconsistencies, but rather as the result of different ways of looking at the problem (or, perhaps, of looking at different aspects of the same problem). Therefore each poverty line must be judged on its own merits.

The advantage of the *subjective methods* is that they are socially the most realistic, being based on judgments by the population itself. On the other hand the levels of the subjective poverty line fluctuate across countries and across time. Furthermore the SPL and CSP-standards diverge within countries. These variations are at this moment difficult to interpret. One source of inconsistencies could be data quality: the precise formulation of the income evaluation questions, the identity of the respondent within the household and interviewer effects could have unknown effects. A second reason for the fluctuations could be that the model is too simple. In the Dutch report (Muffels a.o., 1989) it is shown that more sophisticated models produce more stable results across time. Finally, there are probably real, but unknown and unaccounted for factors influencing the appreciation of income.

The advantage of the *statistical methods* is that they are easy to construct, they are exact and they produce plausible results across countries as well as across time. Therefore they are suited to international comparisons. A problem is that they (and the equivalence scales) are completely arbitrary (why 50% of disposable equivalent household income and not 40% or 60%?) and therefore measure low income situations rather than poverty.

The *legal or political poverty lines* do not work in a comparative context. Though they may enjoy, depending on the political situation in a country, considerable credibility, it has become clear that their replicability is very low. In several countries no Legal-standard is defined, and in others it produces results, that are clearly implausible in a comparative context.

Deprivation standards might be useful in convincing the general public that poverty is a serious social problem, by revealing the actual living conditions of poor households. But at this moment the reliability, replicability and comparability of deprivation standards have not been tested to the degree that they can provide information to guide social policy. The choice of items remains a crucial and unresolved problem.

What are the implications of these results as regards the measurement of poverty in the European Community?

In the first place, it has been shown that the subjective standards work, at least in a national context, although their stability across countries and time is as yet unsatisfactory. Because the subjective standards are socially the most realistic ones, it seems worthwhile to continue research in this area.

However, from a (practical) policy-oriented point of view, the best choice at this moment appears to be a relative or statistical standard. But it should be kept in mind that they are based on a convention, and have no basis in any social reality. The choice of the level and the equivalence scale should be justified, in some degree, by reference to the results of other methods.

7.10. Concluding remarks

1. Compared to the reports on poverty in the first EC Programme to Combat Poverty, the research project presented in this report represents several *improvements*.

   a. In each participating country, data bases have been created, which make it possible to provide reliable information about poverty. This information includes data on disposable income of low-income groups, the sources of income, possession of some consumer durables and socio-economic and demographic characteristics of households.

   b. The long process which has resulted in this common and comparative research report has proved that it is possible to produce comparable (despite some remaining problems) results on income distribution and poverty, on the condition that comparable questionnaires have been developed, important concepts such as household and income have been defined in a comparable way and finally a common framework for analysis has been developed from the very first start of the project.

   c. A framework for the analysis of poverty and the effects of social security has been created in the form of a standardized system of social indicators.

   d. Several indicators of poverty have been applied in a comparable way.

These achievements are in keeping with the suggestions of the Commission in its report on the first EC Poverty Programme (1981; see also Roche, 1984). In future studies we must continue to work in these directions.

2. A very important development in poverty studies is to go beyond analysing poverty in cross-sectional perspective. The *panel* method allows to distinguish short-term from longer-term poverty. This is most important for social policymakers as it are especially the long-term or permanent poor towards whom they might want to direct resources.

First longitudinal results have been presented by the countries disposing of two waves. It has shown that there is considerable mobility within the group of poor as a whole as well as within particular social groups with a high poverty risk. More panel data and analysis are needed in order to detect which social conditions exactly produce longer-term poverty.

3. At the end of this research project a final question may be put forward: how can differences between the countries regarding the extent and distribution of poverty be explained? Explanations of differences between countries need to take into account the socio-economic and demographic conditions in each country as well as the functioning of the respective social security systems. An interesting observation is that the poverty rate is at a relatively low level in the Benelux-countries, where a national guaranteed minimum income exists since many years, alongside minimum amounts in the social insurance systems. Nevertheless, despite the existence of such a guaranteed minimum a number of households remain poor. A guaranteed minimum income seems to be a necessary, though not a sufficient condition to prevent poverty.

Within the scope of this research project, differences between countries as regards poverty have not been explained (nor could they have been). It will be a challenge of further research to fully interpret and exploit in depth the enormous bulk of information (indicators) made available by the various research groups and brought together in this final report.

Notes

(1) The statistical standard applied in this report is called "EC-standard" because an earlier version of this standard was used in the first EC poverty programme in 1981. The standard has been revised by O'Higgins and Jenkins (1988). They use the equivalence scale advised by the OECD (1982). It must be clear that what we call the "EC-standard" in no way refers to an official EC poverty line.

(2) In Lorraine and Luxembourg, the guaranteed minimum income was not yet in effect at the time of the survey.

(3) The discrepancies between the O'Higgins and Jenkins results and the Europass results for some countries are due to 1) different data sources (The Netherlands, Greece); 2) a slightly different definition of what a child is (persons between 16 and 25 in full time education are regarded as children in the Europass-project, not by O'Higgins and Jenkins); 3) the fact that in some cases, notably Ireland, the O'Higgins and Jenkins figures were based on very preliminary data. As far as Ireland is concerned the Europass figure should be regarded as definitive.

Appendices

Appendix A
Additional tables

Table A.1
Average amounts from different sources of income for beneficiary
households, in ECU, corrected by purchasing power parities

	BELGIUM		IRELAND		LORRAINE	
	1985	1988	1987	1989	1985	1986
I. Labour income	1280	1341	1246	1125	1319	1281
II. Income from social security	449	486	332	343	573	526
1. Replacement income	632	641	463	468	713	705
a. pensions	676	711	430	450	779	843
b. unemployment	394	361	384	399	307	283
c. sickness or invalidity	426	421	388	365	282	268
d. social assistance	262	222	215	156	0	65
2. Family allowances	153	160	65	78	211	189
Total household income	1299	1371	1168	1015	1387	1396

	NETHERLANDS		LUXEMBOURG		CATA-LONIA	GREECE
	1985	1986	1985	1986	1988	1988
I. Labour income	1289	1390	1799	1829	1429	904
II. Income from social security	461	462	608	618	449	372
1. Replacement income	728	744	922	925	504	391
a. pensions	805	837	921	972	474	410
b. unemployment	553	520	658	373	474	85
c. sickness or invalidity	627	652	716	545	396	67
d. social assistance	209	238	243	238	145	60
2. Family allowances	110	105	129	146	39	24
Total household income	1331	1406	1853	1896	1619	1013

Table A.2
Levels of social subsistence minima in monthly amounts
(in ECU, in prices of Jan. 1988) (ᵃ), Belgium, Ireland, Lorraine,
The Netherlands, Luxembourg, 1st and 2nd wave

BELGIUM	CSP 1985	CSP 1988	SPL 1985	SPL 1988	EC 1985	EC 1988	Legal 1985	Legal 1988
single elderly	509	540	639	549	313	333	336	364
single active	560	581	639	549	313	333	336	364
two elderly	662	727	797	757	530	567	465	484
one active, one elderly	769	769	797	757	530	567	465	484
two actives	806	810	797	757	530	567	465	484
two actives, one child	933	982	875	875	683	734	491	512
two actives, two children	1023	1081	935	989	838	903	588	602
two actives, three children	1051	1151	991	1091	996	1070	722	743
one active, one child	736	753	762	734	465	500	364	396
one active, two children	817	852	850	873		669	465	484
IRELAND	1987	1989	1987	1989	1987	1989	1987	1989
single elderly	296	312	402	428	238	248	211	213
single active	322	341	402	428	238	248	220	213
two elderly	510	539	544	576	405	421	351	358
one active, one elderly	489	517	544	576	405	421	400	358
two actives	649	687	544	576	405	421	428	358
two actives, one child	835	884	650	717	524	546	505	413
two actives, two children	858	889	738	783	643	670	581	466
two actives, three children	885	936	814	863	763	794	635	520
one active, one child	509	538	544	576	357	372	290	269
one active, two children	532	562	650	688	477	496	376	323
LORRAINE b	1985	1986	1985	1986	1985	1986	1985	1986
single elderly	432	478	737	685	326	341	288	275
single active	628	587	737	685	326	341	284	280
two elderly	560	723	821	816	555	579	415	401
one active, one elderly	756	832	821	816	555	579	414	406
two actives	952	840	821	816	555	579	422	409
two actives, one child	1093	1100	910	928	718	750	517	497
two actives, two children	1175	1195	1012	1033	881	920	588	577
two actives, three children	1234	1262	1138	1134	1044	1091	687	673
one active, one child	769	746	821	816	489	511	422	416
one active, two children	851	841	910	928	652	682	503	519

continuation of Table A.2

NETHERLANDS	CSP 1985	CSP 1986	SPL 1985	SPL 1986	EC 1985	EC 1986	Legal 1985	Legal 1986
single elderly	513	528	521	616	350	367	490	482
single active	583	570	521	616	350	367	479	478
two elderly	652	706	632	743	594	624	699	688
one active, one elderly	792	747	632	743	594	624	721	722
two actives	723	789	632	743	594	624	703	694
two actives, one child	825	836	708	830	769	808	753	745
two actives, two children	844	863	768	897	943	991	823	805
two actives, three children	858	882	817	953	1118	1174	904	874
one active, one child	616	617	632	743	524	551	707	684
one active, two children	635	644	708	830	699	734	767	755
LUXEMBOURG c	1985	1986	1985	1986	1985	1986	1985	1986
single elderly	573	637	828	747	445	474	520	519
single active	681	771	828	747	445	474	520	519
two elderly	870	845	1016	902	757	805	711	710
one active, one elderly	977	978	1016	902	757	805	711	710
two actives	1085	1112	1016	902	757	805	711	710
two actives, one child	1173	1249	1204	1007	981	1049	791	789
two actives, two children	1225	1330	1406	1089	1203	1281	871	869
two actives, three children	1262	1395	1632	1168	1427	1586	950	948
one active, one child	769	908	1016	902	682	745	600	599
one active, two children	821	1016	1204	1047	906	1088	680	678

[a] see appendix 3

[b] In Lorraine, the guaranteed minimum income (Revenu Minimum d'Insertion) was instituted on 1-1-'89. The amounts have been deflated to 1986 and 1985.

[c] In Luxembourg, the guaranteed minimum income (Revenue Minimum Garanti) went into effect on 26-7-'86. The 1985 amounts have been adjusted by the consumption price index.

Note: the list of household types is not exhaustive.

Table A.3
Percentage of households insecure of subsistence by activity
of head of household according to various standards

Activity of head of household	% of households in sample	CSP	SPL	EC	Legal
BELGIUM					
All households	100,0	21,4	24,9	6,1	2,9
employed	60,4	11,6	9,4	2,9	0,7
not employed	39,6	36,4	48,5	10,9	6,3
retired	29,1	29,8	47,2	6,6	5,2
unemployed	5,5	61,4	59,2	26,2	8,2
sick/disabled	3,2	38,0	34,6	10,7	5,4
other	1,9	62,6	61,3	33,1	19,4
IRELAND					
All households	100,0	29,6	31,6	17,2	8,1
employed	57,8	20,0	15,8	11,9	6,7
not employed	42,2	42,6	53,5	24,4	9,9
retired	14,5	18,1	35,2	7,9	4,1
unemployed	10,6	74,7	67,3	58,9	22,0
sick/disabled	6,0	61,1	57,0	24,4	8,7
other	14,1	33,9	61,4	13,0	6,6
LORRAINE					
All households	100,0	30,8	26,5	10,8	4,0
employed	61,5	26,1	16,5	6,8	1,7
not employed	38,5	38,2	42,5	17,1	7,4
retired	26,7	29,1	35,9	9,3	3,3
unemployed	4,0	64,3	58,9	41,0	20,1
sick/disabled	2,2	46,9	31,2	22,9	11,7
other	5,5	60,7	68,0	35,7	16,5
NETHERLANDS					
All households	100,0	10,9	15,9	7,2	7,2
employed	64,0	3,4	4,3	5,2	2,5
not employed	-	-	-	-	-
retired	19,2	16,4	29,0	2,4	8,8
unemployed	4,6	42,9	51,0	19,5	23,4
sick/disabled	6,5	28,6	28,4	10,0	9,9
other	4,5	33,2	70,2	36,1	45,7

continuation of Table A.3

Activity of head of household	% of households in sample	CSP	SPL	EC	Legal
LUXEMBOURG					
All households	100,0	14,5	12,5	7,6	5,0
employed	62,6	9,5	3,8	5,5	2,2
not employed	37,4	23,0	26,7	11,0	9,8
retired	17,6	15,0	16,5	7,4	4,0
unemployed	(0,7)	(61,9)	(52,4)	(40,9)	(31,2)
sick/disabled	5,6	40,0	25,1	19,6	17,1
other	13,5	24,4	39,4	10,5	13,2
CATALONIA					
All households	100,0	31,3	37,3	15,1	-
employed	68,2	23,7	26,8	9,0	-
not employed	31,2	47,9	60,0	28,5	-
retired	18,6	40,3	58,6	22,1	-
unemployed	4,4	63,4	64,9	43,5	-
sick/disabled	4,1	63,4	61,0	40,7	-
other	4,1	50,4	60,3	28,9	-
GREECE					
All households	100,0	42,6	42,0	19,9	-
employed	70,2	39,7	35,6	19,1	-
not employed	-	-	-	-	-
retired	23,6	46,5	54,2	21,7	-
unemployed	1,1	72,7	75,8	36,4	-
sick/disabled	-	-	-	17,0	-
other	4,7	53,3	60,0	-	-

Table A.4
Percentage of households insecure of subsistence by socio-professional status of head of household according to various standards

socio-professional status of head of household (employed only)	% of households in sample	CSP	SPL	EC	Legal
BELGIUM, 1985					
All households	100,0	21,4	24,9	6,1	2,9
un- or semi skilled manual worker	6,5	25,1	21,8	5,0	0,2
skilled manual worker	13,3	14,6	10,7	2,3	0,2
lower employee	21,2	8,3	7,1	1,2	0,1
higher employee (manager, liberal prof.)	8,2	1,5	0,9	0,4	0,2
small self-employed	10,2	13,4	10,8	6,7	3,2
farmer	0,7	21,3	21,3	17,0	4,3
IRELAND, 1987					
All households	100,0	29,6	31,6	17,2	8,1
un- or semi skilled manual worker	7,2	26,1	20,7	13,6	2,4
skilled manual worker	12,6	16,3	9,6	7,4	3,1
lower employee	13,1	13,6	9,7	5,3	2,5
higher employee (manager, liberal prof.)	12,9	5,6	4,6	3,2	2,5
farmer	12,0	42,6	38,5	32,0	22,1
LORRAINE, 1986					
All households	100,0	30,8	26,5	10,8	4,0
un- or semi skilled manual worker	9,0	42,8	35,4	16,7	2,3
skilled manual worker	21,2	33,3	15,5	4,4	1,5
lower employee	28,7	14,0	10,5	3,6	1,0
higher employee (manager, liberal prof.)	4,1	1,4	0,0	0,0	0,0
small self-employed	3,6	30,3	18,4	7,2	1,7
farmer	1,9	47,6	37,5	19,7	13,7
NETHERLANDS, 1986					
All households	100,0	10,9	15,9	7,2	7,2
un- or semi skilled manual worker	2,4	6,6	6,7	16,0	4,8
skilled manual worker	15,6	1,7	2,2	5,6	1,2
lower employee	11,1	2,6	4,7	4,2	1,4
higher employee (manager, liberal prof.)	25,7	2,7	2,9	3,1	1,8
small self-employed	2,3	12,8	15,7	13,7	10,8
farmer	1,3	25,4	23,7	23,7	24,6
LUXEMBOURG, 1986					
All households	100,0	14,5	12,5	7,6	5,0
un- or semi skilled manual worker	15,4	18,2	9,6	10,6	4,4
skilled manual worker	14,5	13,7	3,2	8,4	2,5
lower employee	20,2	1,8	0,4	0,7	-
higher employee (manager, liberal prof.)	7,6	3,5	2,6	2,6	2,6
small self-employed	3,3	6,9	2,5	4,5	2,5
farmer	1,6	16,4	6,3	7,7	1,8
CATALONIA, 1988					
All households	100,0	31,3	37,3	15,1	-
un- or semi skilled manual worker	12,1	38,7	40,9	17,1	-
skilled manual worker	21,8	28,2	32,6	9,7	-
lower employee	7,4	17,2	21,3	5,4	-
higher employee (manager, liberal prof.)	16,5	6,9	7,9	1,8	-
small self-employed	7,2	26,7	29,5	8,8	-
farmer	2,8	36,5	38,9	20,0	-
GREECE, 1988					
All households	100,0	42,6	42,0	19,9	-
un- or semi skilled manual worker	9,6	49,8	42,4	20,1	-
skilled manual worker	13,5	39,9	35,7	14,8	-
lower employee	9,5	31,2	23,6	8,0	-
higher employee (manager, liberal prof.)	11,7	15,4	14,2	6,7	-
small self-employed	6,8	33,3	31,3	14,6	-
farmer	19,6	56,6	53,4	36,5	-

Table A.5
Percentage of households insecure of subsistence by education
of head of household according to various standards

education of head of household	% of households in sample	CSP	SPL	EC	Legal
BELGIUM, 1985					
All households	100,0	21,4	24,9	6,1	2,9
primary education	28,7	33,5	41,6	9,1	4,5
secondary level-lower cycle (12-15)	24,4	22,4	23,9	5,7	2,3
secondary level-upper cycle (16-18)	24,0	13,4	13,7	4,4	2,0
non-universitary higher education	10,4	5,8	7,6	2,0	1,1
university	7,6	7,2	6,4	3,1	2,3
IRELAND, 1987					
All households	100,0	29,6	31,6	17,2	8,1
primary education	-	-	-	-	-
secondary level-lower cycle (12-15)	-	-	-	-	-
secondary level-upper cycle (16-18)	-	-	-	-	-
non-universitary higher education	-	-	-	-	-
university	-	-	-	-	-
LORRAINE, 1986					
All households	100,0	30,8	26,5	10,8	4,0
primary education	52,5	38,6	35,7	14,4	5,4
secondary level-lower cycle (12-15)	32,4	26,6	19,3	7,1	2,0
secondary level-upper cycle (16-18)	4,3	5,6	3,5	1,1	0,0
non-universitary higher education	0,5	(31,4)	(25,1)	(25,1)	(25,1)
university	8,0	6,3	4,7	3,1	3,1
NETHERLANDS, 1986					
All households	100,0	10,9	15,9	7,2	7,2
primary education	23,4	20,2	30,3	10,0	12,0
secondary level-lower cycle (12-15)	19,5	13,1	19,3	9,0	7,4
secondary level-upper cycle (16-18)	38,6	6,7	10,3	6,4	5,8
non-universitary higher education	12,4	5,6	5,8	2,9	3,9
university	5,0	4,5	5,0	3,2	4,1
LUXEMBOURG, 1986					
All households	100,0	14,5	12,5	7,6	5,0
primary education	45,0	21,4	20,4	11,7	8,1
secondary level-lower cycle (12-15)	-	-	-	-	-
secondary level-upper cycle (16-18)	-	-	-	-	-
non-universitary higher education	-	-	-	-	-
university	-	-	-	-	-
CATALONIA, 1988					
All households	100,0	31,3	37,3	15,1	-
primary education	44,7	40,4	47,9	21,8	-
secondary level-lower cycle (12-15)	21,9	32,1	37,2	10,9	-
secondary level-upper cycle (16-18)	13,2	18,5	24,1	6,6	-
non-universitary higher education	7,8	11,9	14,5	3,0	-
university	8,0	3,8	7,1	1,3	-
GREECE, 1988					
All households	100,0	42,6	42,0	19,9	-
primary education	57,1	55,7	54,6	28,7	-
secondary level-lower cycle (12-15)	8,9	38,9	40,3	17,6	-
secondary level-upper cycle (16-18)	24,1	25,7	25,2	7,0	-
non-universitary higher education	5,0	23,4	19,0	6,9	-
university	8,3	7,8	7,3	1,2	-

between brackets: based on less than 30 cases.

Table A.6
Percentage of households insecure of subsistence by marital status of head of household according to various standards

marital status of head of household	% of households in sample	CSP	SPL	EC	Legal
BELGIUM, 1985					
All households	100,0	21,4	24,9	6,1	2,9
married	73,7	17,8	17,6	5,8	1,9
unmarried	8,5	30,2	38,2	8,0	7,5
widow(er)	12,2	33,0	55,2	4,6	4,7
divorced/separated	5,6	30,3	34,4	9,1	5,6
IRELAND, 1987					
All households	100,0	29,6	31,6	17,2	8,1
married	69,1	29,4	24,7	19,0	8,0
unmarried	13,2	31,7	41,0	15,6	8,4
widow(er)	14,7	23,5	52,0	6,6	5,3
divorced/separated	3,0	53,4	58,6	33,1	21,5
LORRAINE, 1986					
All households	100,0	30,8	26,5	10,8	4,0
married	71,3	28,8	18,4	9,1	1,8
unmarried	10,6	35,1	45,3	16,1	11,7
widow(er)	11,8	42,0	54,4	15,4	9,6
divorced/separated	6,5	25,4	34,5	11,7	4,7
NETHERLANDS, 1986					
All households	100,0	10,9	15,9	7,2	7,2
married	68,3	7,1	7,5	7,2	4,2
unmarried	15,8	17,4	29,7	9,5	15,0
widow(er)	9,6	23,4	42,6	2,3	13,5
divorced/separated	6,1	16,9	32,8	8,5	11,5
LUXEMBOURG, 1986					
All households	100,0	14,5	12,5	7,6	5,0
married	66,4	11,5	5,3	7,6	2,8
unmarried	11,1	25,8	25,4	9,1	11,0
widow(er)	17,1	19,1	31,7	5,3	8,2
divorced/separated	5,5	13,9	12,4	11,6	10,2
CATALONIA, 1988					
All households	100,0	31,3	37,3	15,1	-
married	79,0	30,2	34,0	13,8	-
unmarried	7,3	23,4	34,9	10,1	-
widow(er)	8,8	47,0	64,0	27,3	-
divorced/separated	3,8	33,6	44,3	21,2	-
GREECE, 1988					
All households	100,0	42,6	42,0	19,9	-
married	77,7	41,5	39,8	20,8	-
unmarried	9,8	33,4	36,9	8,4	-
widow(er)	9,2	57,1	59,7	22,0	-
divorced/separated	3,8	51,4	49,1	27,0	-

Table A.7
Percentage of households insecure of subsistence by age
of head of household according to various standards

age of head of household	% of households in sample	CSP	SPL	EC	Legal
BELGIUM, 1985					
All households	100,0	21,4	24,9	6,1	2,9
16-24 years	3,2	32,4	40,1	11,6	9,2
25-49 years	49,1	16,4	12,9	6,0	1,5
50-64 years	26,8	22,2	23,2	4,3	2,4
65-74 years	12,8	25,9	46,1	6,9	5,3
75 years or more	7,9	38,0	65,1	9,2	6,9
IRELAND, 1987					
All households	100,0	29,6	31,6	17,2	8,1
16-24 years	2,0	42,5	38,6	31,4	11,4
25-49 years	49,0	31,2	26,8	21,8	8,6
50-64 years	25,9	35,2	32,0	16,4	9,2
65-74 years	15,7	20,7	40,3	8,4	6,2
75 years or more	7,4	13,9	43,8	4,1	3,4
LORRAINE, 1986					
All households	100,0	30,8	26,5	10,8	4,0
16-24 years	5,8	45,3	42,8	14,7	6,5
25-49 years	49,3	27,1	18,0	10,0	2,8
50-64 years	25,4	35,4	25,8	10,3	3,9
65-74 years	10,4	21,2	36,4	6,3	1,3
75 years or more	9,1	39,3	52,4	18,6	11,3
NETHERLANDS, 1986					
All households	100,0	10,9	15,9	7,2	7,2
16-24 years	5,3	20,3	40,9	19,5	24,5
25-49 years	57,6	6,8	9,7	8,6	5,0
50-64 years	21,3	16,3	17,1	4,0	7,8
65-74 years	10,4	14,4	25,6	2,4	7,5
75 years or more	5,5	16,7	34,7	2,5	11,2
LUXEMBOURG, 1986					
All households	100,0	14,5	12,5	7,6	5,0
16-24 years	3,2	32,3	26,7	17,6	12,4
25-49 years	48,7	10,4	4,5	6,9	3,1
50-64 years	26,2	17,6	10,7	7,5	5,4
65-74 years	13,4	18,0	30,4	7,6	6,7
75 years or more	8,5	16,3	29,3	7,8	9,5
CATALONIA, 1988					
All households	100,0	31,3	37,3	15,1	-
16-24 years	2,1	27,2	33,3	7,9	-
25-49 years	47,0	29,6	33,2	12,6	-
50-64 years	33,0	30,3	30,8	14,5	-
65-74 years	12,1	33,2	53,6	18,2	-
75 years or more	5,3	51,9	75,6	36,9	-
GREECE, 1988					
All households	100,0	42,6	42,0	19,9	-
16-24 years	3,4	46,5	50,0	10,9	-
25-49 years	44,1	35,7	32,9	17,9	-
50-64 years	33,2	47,7	39,5	18,1	-
65 years or more	20,0	48,4	63,7	29,0	-

Table A.8
Percentage of households insecure of subsistence by sex of head of household according to various standards

sex of head of household	% of households in sample	CSP	SPL	EC	Legal
BELGIUM, 1985					
All households	100,0	21,4	24,9	6,1	2,9
male	83,9	19,0	19,7	6,0	2,4
female	16,1	33,7	51,9	6,3	5,5
IRELAND, 1987					
All households	100,0	29,6	31,6	17,2	8,1
male	81,4	30,5	27,6	18,8	8,6
female	18,6	26,5	50,0	16,1	5,7
LORRAINE, 1986					
All households	100,0	30,8	26,5	10,8	4,0
male	82,8	28,0	20,0	9,0	2,3
female	17,2	44,3	57,4	19,1	11,6
NETHERLANDS, 1986					
All households	100,0	10,9	15,9	7,2	7,2
male	80,5	8,6	10,3	7,3	5,4
female	19,3	20,6	39,2	6,9	14,9
LUXEMBOURG, 1986					
All households	100,0	14,5	12,5	7,6	5,0
male	76,6	11,6	6,1	7,1	2,9
female	23,3	24,1	33,2	9,0	12,0
CATALONIA, 1988					
All households	100,0	31,3	37,3	15,1	-
male	84,1	29,6	33,7	13,6	-
female	15,4	40,6	56,2	23,4	-
GREECE, 1988					
All households	100,0	42,6	42,0	19,9	-
male	84,0	20,1	38,6	19,7	-
female	16,6	54,5	56,9	21,1	-

Table A.9
Percentage of households insecure of subsistence by nationality
of head of household according to various standards

nationality of head of household	% of households in sample	CSP	SPL	EC	Legal
BELGIUM, 1985					
All households	100,0	21,4	24,9	6,1	2,9
country	94,3	20,9	24,7	5,7	2,9
other EC-country	4,8	27,9	26,0	10,6	1,9
other	(0,9)	(41,7)	(38,3)	(21,7)	(8,3)
IRELAND, 1987					
All households	100,0	29,6	31,6	17,2	8,1
country	-	-	-	-	-
other EC-country	-	-	-	-	-
other	-	-	-	-	-
LORRAINE, 1986					
All households	100,0	30,8	26,5	10,8	4,0
country	92,9	29,0	25,6	10,1	4,1
other EC-country	4,5	46,7	30,5	11,3	1,0
other	2,5	66,9	52,6	34,4	0,9
NETHERLANDS, 1986					
All households	100,0	10,9	15,9	7,2	7,2
country	-	-	-	-	-
other EC-country	-	-	-	-	-
other	-	-	-	-	-
LUXEMBOURG, 1986					
All households	100,0	14,5	12,5	7,6	5,0
country	79,2	13,0	12,8	6,1	5,0
other EC-country	18,7	20,7	10,6	12,1	5,1
other	2,2	16,3	13,1	21,6	5,9
CATALONIA, 1988					
All households	100,0	31,3	37,3	15,1	-
Catalonia itself	55,6	26,4	34,0	11,8	-
other parts of Spain	41,6	38,3	41,7	19,6	-
other	1,6	20,8	27,1	10,4	-
GREECE, 1988					
All households	100,0	42,6	42,0	19,9	-
country	99,3	42,5	41,6	19,8	-
other EC-country	(0,4)	(46,2)	(46,2)	(30,8)	-
other	1,0	48,4	51,6	29,0	-

Table A.10
Percentage of households insecure of subsistence by type of household according to various standards

type of household (list is not exhaustive)	% of households in sample	CSP	SPL	EC	Legal
BELGIUM, 1985					
All households	100,0	21,4	24,9	6,1	2,9
single elderly	9,8	36,7	67,7	5,0	6,6
single active	7,2	29,9	40,6	5,8	7,3
two elderly	8,7	27,3	50,3	11,3	5,8
one active, one elderly	5,1	20,0	25,8	2,7	1,8
two actives	15,1	21,3	20,2	3,5	1,7
two actives, one child	14,0	18,4	14,7	5,0	1,3
two actives, two children	14,7	15,2	10,8	5,4	0,6
two actives, three children	6,0	11,4	6,2	8,5	0,5
one active, one child	1,3	51,7	54,0	7,5	3,4
one active, two children	1,1	24,6	26,1	13,0	4,3
IRELAND, 1987					
All households	100,0	29,6	31,6	17,2	8,1
single elderly	10,1	27,0	70,2	3,0	1,9
single active	6,5	44,4	52,5	20,3	10,9
two elderly	5,7	14,7	28,4	8,4	5,7
one active, one elderly	5,3	20,2	35,8	11,3	9,5
two actives	7,0	30,3	24,9	11,5	9,3
two actives, one child	7,7	35,4	23,7	17,1	8,9
two actives, two children	11,3	36,6	26,3	19,2	7,4
two actives, three children	18,4	39,0	36,1	34,3	10,9
one active, one child	(0,7)	(45,6)	(67,5)	(19,3)	(4,6)
one active, two children	1,6	59,6	68,1	61,0	23,3
LORRAINE, 1986					
All households	100,0	30,8	26,5	10,8	4,0
single elderly	8,5	41,9	72,6	19,3	14,5
single active	8,8	29,7	43,7	12,5	12,5
two elderly	8,3	23,3	32,5	9,2	2,5
one active, one elderly	4,9	26,8	26,8	7,0	0,0
two actives	14,6	23,0	15,0	4,2	2,8
two actives, one child	15,3	29,6	18,3	7,2	1,5
two actives, two children	15,2	26,7	13,8	7,0	1,8
two actives, three children	5,9	32,2	18,2	13,1	0,9
one active, one child	(1,4)	(38,1)	(52,4)	(9,5)	(0,0)
one active, two children	(0,8)	(41,2)	(41,2)	(23,5)	(0,0)
NETHERLANDS, 1986					
All households	100,0	10,9	15,9	7,2	7,2
single elderly	7,1	22,8	47,8	1,6	10,9
single active	14,7	23,0	38,6	8,5	16,5
two elderly	5,5	8,1	14,2	3,2	6,3
one active, one elderly	2,8	10,4	8,8	3,2	5,0
two actives	19,9	10,9	8,2	2,8	5,4
two actives, one child	10,0	5,4	5,4	4,5	2,5
two actives, two children	18,6	4,0	5,5	10,8	3,4
two actives, three children	7,3	4,3	5,9	19,1	4,7
one active, one child	1,3	3,3	33,9	3,3	11,7
one active, two children	1,1	8,0	30,0	14,0	14,3

type of household (list is not exhaustive)	% of households in sample	CSP	SPL	EC	Legal
LUXEMBOURG, 1986					
All households	100,0	14,5	12,5	7,6	5,0
single elderly	13,0	25,7	46,0	7,1	13,9
single active	8,8	20,8	19,2	7,0	7,0
two elderly	7,2	13,3	17,8	11,5	3,4
one active, one elderly	4,9	12,7	9,2	7,8	2,8
two actives	14,9	12,9	4,3	3,7	3,1
two actives, one child	11,1	12,6	4,6	5,2	2,1
two actives, two children	11,0	11,3	2,1	7,5	2,1
two actives, three children	4,5	5,5	0,9	17,4	4,0
one active, one child	(1,0)	(47,0)	(47,0)	(25,6)	(18,7)
one active, two children	(1,4)	(28,2)	(28,2)	(32,9)	(23,6)
CATALONIA, 1988					
All households	100,0	31,3	37,3	15,1	-
single elderly	3,5	46,2	85,9	29,3	-
single active	5,3	27,9	39,9	10,1	-
two elderly	5,3	38,4	78,6	30,2	-
one active, one elderly	3,9	45,3	53,9	17,1	-
two actives	11,3	21,8	30,1	8,6	-
two actives, one child	9,1	22,3	28,1	5,5	-
two actives, two children	10,1	37,2	46,1	14,5	-
two actives, three children	2,6	40,5	50,6	17,7	-
one active, one child	(0,7)	(42,9)	(52,4)	(23,8)	-
one active, two children	(0,4)	(36,4)	(72,7)	(18,2)	-
GREECE, 1988					
All households	100,0	42,6	42,0	19,9	-
single elderly	5,8	55,9	70,5	24,1	-
single active	5,6	45,1	35,8	7,4	-
two elderly	8,4	51,0	70,7	33,7	-
one active, one elderly	5,1	46,0	55,6	19,3	-
two actives	12,5	43,0	39,3	14,0	-
two actives, one child	8,2	37,6	32,9	10,3	-
two actives, two children	13,5	37,5	27,8	14,4	-
two actives, three children	4,8	42,6	47,5	37,6	-
one active, one child	1,1	45,5	44,1	30,3	-
one active, two children	1,1	33,3	36,4	24,2	-

between brackets: based on less than 30 cases.

Table A.11
Percentage of households insecure of subsistence by number of income providers and number of persons at work according to various standards

number of income providers / persons at work	% of households in sample	CSP	SPL	EC	Legal
BELGIUM, 1985					
All households	100,0	21,4	24,9	6,1	2,9
number of income providers					
0					
1	50,5	33,3	40,7	8,9	4,5
2	42,7	8,5	8,1	2,4	0,7
3 or more	5,8	2,9	1,1	0,8	0,8
number of persons at work					
0	33,3	40,7	55,8	11,8	7,0
1	35,5	19,0	15,7	4,7	1,1
2	27,9	3,7	2,8	1,6	0,7
3 or more	3,3	2,8	0,5	0,9	0,9
IRELAND, 1987					
All households	100,0	29,6	31,6	17,2	8,1
number of income providers					
0	5,7	61,7	61,6	52,0	37,3
1	52,7	39,5	45,1	22,7	9,1
2	28,4	16,2	14,3	6,9	3,4
3 or more	13,2	4,8	0,5	2,1	1,2
number of persons at work					
0	31,8	51,7	68,2	30,2	12,1
1	40,5	24,0	18,2	12,9	6,6
2	20,4	13,9	10,5	9,7	5,7
3 or more	7,3	7,9	5,4	5,3	5,0
LORRAINE, 1986					
All households	100,0	30,8	26,5	10,8	4,0
number of income providers					
0	4,6	74,4	84,9	43,0	26,6
1	46,5	40,5	39,1	13,9	5,0
2	41,6	15,9	9,6	4,4	1,0
3 or more	7,3	26,3	6,0	7,1	0,0
number of persons at work					
0	30,9	42,1	50,6	19,7	9,1
1	39,6	34,9	23,5	9,1	1,7
2	26,9	12,4	5,4	3,4	1,1
3 or more	2,6	22,8	4,8	4,9	0,0
NETHERLANDS, 1986					
All households	100,0	10,9	15,9	7,2	7,2
number of income providers					
0	0,6	80,8	80,8	73,1	80,8
1	53,5	14,9	23,5	9,2	9,1
2	34,6	2,9	3,6	2,5	2,4
3 or more	6,7	3,0	1,4	3,7	3,7
number of persons at work					
0	29,6	27,1	41,7	11,6	17,7
1	41,9	4,9	6,3	6,5	2,8
2	24,0	2,2	2,5	3,1	2,2
3 or more	2,8	3,2	2,4	3,2	4,0

continuation of Table A.11

number of income providers / persons at work	% of households in sample	CSP	SPL	EC	Legal
LUXEMBOURG, 1986					
All households	100,0	14,5	12,5	7,6	5,0
number of income providers					
0	(0,5)	(83,7)	(83,7)	(68,2)	(68,2)
1	55,9	20,7	19,5	9,5	7,3
2	34,4	6,8	3,0	4,5	1,7
3 or more	9,1	1,6	0,0	2,0	0,0
number of persons at work					
0	28,7	26,4	33,6	12,7	11,3
1	39,8	14,4	6,2	7,4	4,0
2	25,9	4,4	1,1	3,3	0,7
3 or more	5,7	1,6	0,0	2,3	0,0
CATALONIA, 1988					
All households	100,0	31,3	37,3	15,1	-
number of income providers					
0	(0,9)	(69,2)	(84,6)	(42,3)	-
1	37,6	48,1	60,5	24,7	-
2	37,9	23,3	28,4	10,1	-
3 or more	23,6	16,1	12,9	6,6	-
number of persons at work					
0	21,3	57,8	77,0	35,2	-
1	40,2	37,7	43,7	15,6	-
2	29,1	11,6	10,6	3,7	-
3 or more	9,4	5,0	2,1	2,5	-
GREECE, 1988					
All households	100,0	42,6	42,0	19,9	-
number of income providers					
0	3,8	66,0	70,3	26,4	-
1	41,4	47,5	48,3	18,9	-
2	40,1	36,4	35,9	18,7	-
3 or more	15,6	40,0	32,2	24,5	-
number of persons at work					
0	23,5	53,1	62,8	23,9	-
1	36,7	42,2	40,2	18,4	-
2	31,6	35,7	31,5	18,4	-
3 or more	8,9	40,8	28,6	21,5	-

* income providers: person with own income from earnings or from social security.

Table A.12
Percentage of households insecure of subsistence
by housing situation according to various standards

housing situation	% of households in sample	CSP	SPL	EC	Legal
BELGIUM, 1985					
All households	100,0	21,4	24,9	6,1	2,9
owner	61,3	17,3	20,6	19,8	4,6
tenant	34,4	27,6	31,7	31,0	8,5
IRELAND, 1987					
All households	100,0	29,6	31,6	17,2	8,1
owner	79,6	24,2	26,4	12,9	7,2
tenant	20,3	51,0	52,1	34,2	11,3
LORRAINE, 1986					
All households	100,0	30,8	26,5	10,8	4,0
owner	52,7	25,9	20,6	9,0	3,6
tenant	36,9	34,9	31,8	12,0	3,5
NETHERLANDS, 1986					
All households	100,0	10,9	15,9	7,2	7,2
owner	45,1	6,1	6,9	4,8	4,1
tenant	54,0	14,3	22,7	9,0	9,4
LUXEMBOURG, 1986					
All households	100,0	14,5	12,5	7,6	5,0
owner	65,4	11,1	9,8	5,4	4,0
tenant	27,2	22,9	17,7	13,1	7,6
CATALONIA, 1988					
All households	100,0	31,3	37,3	15,1	-
owner	-	-	-	-	-
tenant	-	-	-	-	-
GREECE, 1988					
All households	100,0	42,6	42,0	19,9	-
owner	72,7	42,5	42,1	21,5	-
tenant	23,6	39,3	37,1	13,2	-

Table A.13
The composition of the poor, by employment status of head of household

	BEL-GIUM 1985	NETHER-LANDS 1986	LUXEM-BURG 1986	LOR-RAINE 1986	IRE-LAND 1987	CATA-LONIA 1988	GREE-CE 1988
A. *EC-standard*							
Head of household							
at work	28,7	46,2	45,3	38,7	40,0	40,7	67,4
(farmers)	2,0	4,3	1,6	3,5	22,3	3,7	36,0
retired	31,5	6,4	17,1	23,0	6,7	27,2	25,7
unemployed	23,6	12,5	3,8	15,2	36,3	12,7	2,0
sick/disabled	5,6	9,0	14,4	4,7	8,5	11,1	-
other	10,3	22,6	18,7	18,2	8,4	7,9	4,0
All	99,8	96,7	99,3	99,7	99,8	99,4	99,1
B. *CSP-standard*							
Head of household							
at work	32,7	20,0	41,0	52,1	39,1	51,6	65,4
(farmer)	0,7	3,0	1,8	2,9	17,3	3,3	26,0
retired	40,5	28,9	18,2	25,2	8,9	24,0	25,8
unemployed	15,8	18,1	3,0	8,4	26,8	8,9	1,9
sick/disabled	5,7	17,1	15,5	3,4	12,4	8,3	-
other	5,6	13,7	22,7	10,8	12,7	6,6	5,9
All	100,2	97,7	100,4	99,8	99,8	99,4	98,9
C. *SPL-standard*							
Head of household							
at work	22,8	17,3	19,0	38,3	28,9	49,6	59,5
(farmer)	0,6	1,9	0,8	2,7	14,6	2,9	24,9
retired	55,2	35,0	23,2	36,2	16,2	29,2	30,5
unemployed	13,1	14,8	2,9	8,9	22,6	7,7	2,0
sick/disabled	4,5	11,6	11,2	2,6	14,6	6,7	-
other	4,7	19,9	42,6	14,1	19,4	6,6	6,7
All	100,2	98,6	99,0	100,0	100,0	99,2	98,7

Table A.14
The composition of the poor, by marital status of head of household

	BEL-GIUM 1985	NETHER-LANDS 1986	LUXEM-BURG 1986	LOR-RAINE 1986	IRE-LAND 1987	CATA-LONIA 1988	GREE-CE 1988
A. *EC-standard*							
Head of household							
married	70,0	68,3	66,4	60,1	76,3	72,2	81,2
unmarried	11,2	20,9	13,3	15,8	12,0	4,9	4,1
widowed	9,2	3,1	11,9	16,8	5,6	15,9	10,2
divorced or separated	8,4	7,2	8,4	7,0	5,8	5,3	5,2
All	98,8	99,4	100,0	99,8	99,7	98,3	100,7
B. *CSP-standard*							
Head of household							
married	61,3	44,5	52,7	66,7	68,6	76,2	75,7
unmarried	12,0	25,2	19,8	12,1	14,1	5,5	7,7
widowed	18,8	20,6	22,5	16,1	11,7	13,2	12,3
divorced or separated	7,9	9,5	5,3	5,4	5,4	4,1	4,6
All	100,4	99,8	100,2	100,2	99,9	99,0	100,3
C. *SPL-standard*							
Head of household							
married	52,1	32,3	28,2	49,5	54,0	72,0	73,6
unmarried	13,0	29,5	22,7	18,1	17,1	6,8	8,6
widowed	27,1	25,7	43,4	24,2	24,2	15,1	13,1
divorced or separated	7,7	12,6	5,5	8,5	5,6	4,5	4,4
All	99,9	100,3	99,5	100,3	100,9	98,5	99,8

Table A.15
The composition of the poor, by age of head of household

	BEL-GIUM 1985	NETHER-LANDS 1986	LUXEM-BURG 1986	LOR-RAINE 1986	IRE-LAND 1987	CATA-LONIA 1988	GREE-CE 1988
A. *EC-standard*							
Head of household							
16-24	6,1	14,4	7,4	7,9	3,7	1,1	1,9
25-49	48,3	68,8	44,2	45,7	62,1	39,2	39,7
50-64	18,9	11,8	25,9	24,2	24,7	31,7	30,2
65-74	14,5	3,5	13,4	6,1	7,7	14,6	29,2
75+	11,9	1,9	8,7	15,7	1,8	13,0	
All	99,7	100,4	99,6	99,5	99,9	99,5	100,9
B. *CSP-standard*							
Head of household							
16-24	4,8	9,9	7,1	8,5	2,9	1,8	3,7
25-49	37,6	35,9	34,9	43,4	51,6	44,5	37,0
50-64	27,8	31,9	31,8	29,2	30,8	32,0	37,2
65-74	15,5	13,7	16,6	7,2	11,0	12,8	22,7
75+	14,0	8,4	9,6	11,6	3,5	8,8	
All	99,8	99,8	100,1	99,9	99,7	99,8	100,6
C. *SPL-standard*							
Head of household							
16-24	5,2	14,4	7,4	9,4	3,7	1,9	1,9
25-49	25,4	68,8	44,2	33,5	62,1	41,8	39,7
50-64	25,0	11,8	25,9	24,7	24,7	27,3	30,2
65-74	23,7	3,5	13,4	14,3	7,7	17,4	29,2
75+	20,7	1,9	8,7	18,0	1,8	10,7	
All	99,9	100,4	99,6	99,9	99,9	99,1	100,0

Table A.16
The composition of the poor, by type of household

	BEL-GIUM 1985	NETHER-LANDS 1986	LUXEM-BURG 1986	LOR-RAINE 1986	IRE-LAND 1987	CATA-LONIA 1988	GREE-CE 1988
A. EC-standard							
Type of household [a]							
single elderly person	8,0	1,6	12,1	15,2	1,8	6,8	7,0
two elderly persons	16,1	2,4	10,9	7,1	2,8	10,6	14,2
one elderly + one adult [b]	2,3	1,2	5,0	3,2	3,5	4,4	5,0
one adult [b]	6,9	17,4	8,1	10,2	7,7	3,6	2,1
one parent households	3,9	2,7	9,4	3,0	6,4	1,6	3,0
two adults [b]	8,7	7,7	7,3	5,7	4,7	6,4	8,8
two adults [b] + one child	11,5	6,3	7,6	10,2	7,7	3,3	4,2
two adults [b] + two childr.	13,0	27,9	10,9	9,9	12,6	9,7	9,8
two adults [b] + three childr.	8,4	19,4	10,3	7,2	36,7	3,1	9,1
All	78,7	86,6	81,6	71,5	83,8	49,4	63,2
B. CSP-standard							
Type of household [a]							
single elderly person	16,8	14,9	23,0	11,6	9,2	5,2	7,6
two elderly persons	11,1	4,1	6,6	6,3	2,8	6,5	10,1
one elderly + one adult [b]	4,8	2,7	4,3	4,3	3,6	5,6	5,5
one adult [b]	10,1	31,0	12,6	8,5	9,8	4,7	5,9
one parent households	4,4	1,2	6,0	2,8	4,3	1,4	2,0
two adults [b]	15,0	19,9	13,3	10,9	7,2	7,9	12,6
two adults [b] + one child	12,0	5,0	9,7	14,7	9,2	6,5	7,2
two adults [b] + two childr.	10,4	6,8	8,6	13,2	14,0	12,0	11,9
two adults [b] + three childr.	3,2	2,9	1,7	6,2	24,2	3,4	4,8
All	87,8	88,4	85,7	78,3	84,3	53,2	67,7
C. SPL-standard							
Type of household [a]							
single elderly person	26,6	21,3	47,8	23,3	22,4	8,1	9,7
two elderly persons	17,6	4,9	10,3	10,2	5,1	11,2	14,1
one elderly + one adult [b]	5,3	1,6	3,6	5,0	6,0	5,6	6,8
one adult [b]	11,7	35,7	13,5	14,5	10,8	5,7	4,8
one parent households	4,0	4,9	6,9	4,0	5,0	1,8	2,1
two adults [b]	12,3	10,3	5,1	8,3	5,5	9,1	11,7
two adults [b] + one child	8,3	3,4	4,1	10,6	5,8	6,9	6,4
two adults [b] + two childr.	6,4	6,4	1,9	7,9	9,4	12,5	8,9
two adults [b] + three childr.	1,5	2,7	0,3	4,1	21,0	3,5	5,4
All	93,6	91,1	93,5	87,7	91,0	64,3	70,0

[a] List of household types is not exhaustive.

[b] Adult = non-elderly adult.

The composition of the poor, by number of
income providers and by number of persons at work

	BEL-GIUM 1985	NETHER-LANDS 1986	LUXEM-BURG 1986	LOR-RAINE 1986	IRE-LAND 1987	CATA-LONIA 1988	GREE-CE 1988
A. _EC-standard_							
Number of income providers							
0 or 1	73,7	74,5	74,4	78,2	86,8	64,0	44,3
2	16,8	12,0	20,4	17,0	11,4	25,4	37,7
3+	0,8	3,4	2,4	4,8	1,6	10,3	19,2
All	91,2	89,9	97,1	99,9	99,8	99,7	101,3
Number of persons at work							
0	64,4	47,7	48,0	56,4	55,8	49,7	28,2
1	27,4	37,8	38,8	33,4	30,4	41,5	33,9
2	7,8	11?6	13,0	9,7	13,8	8,7	38,8
All	99,6	97,1	99,7	99,4	100,0	99,9	101,0
B. _CSP-standard_							
Number of income providers							
0 or 1	78,6	77,6	82,7	72,3	82,2	59,8	52,0
2	17,0	9,2	16,1	21,5	15,5	28,2	34,3
3+	0,8	1,8	1,0	6,2	2,1	12,1	14,7
All	96,3	88,6	99,8	100,0	99,9	100,1	101,0
Number of persons at work							
0	63,3	73,6	52,3	42,2	55,5	39,3	29,3
1	31,5	18,8	39,5	44,9	32,8	48,4	36,4
2	5,3	5,7	8,5	12,8	11,5	12,3	35,0
All	100,1	98,1	100,3	99,9	99,9	100,0	100,7
C. _SPL-standard_							
Number of income providers							
0 or 1	82,5	82,1	80,6	83,4	86,3	63,0	54,0
2	13,9	7,8	8,3	15,1	12,9	28,9	34,3
3+	0,3	0,6	0,0	1,7	0,2	8,2	12,0
All	96,7	90,6	98,9	100,1	99,4	100,1	100,2
Number of persons at work							
0	74,6	77,6	77,2	59,0	68,6	44,0	35,1
1	22,4	16,6	19,7	35,1	23,3	47,1	35,1
2	3,2	4,2	2,3	6,0	8,0	8,8	29,8
All	100,2	98,4	99,2	100,1	100,0	99,9	100,0

Table A.18
Changes in poverty among households,
across two waves, according to four poverty lines*

BELGIUM 1985-1988

CSP		1985		
		SECURE	INSECURE	Total
1988	SECURE	85,8 (67,3)	37,1 (8,0)	75,3
	INSECURE	14,2 (11,2)	62,9 (13,5)	24,7
	Total	100,0 (78,5)	100,0 (21,5)	100,0

SPL		1985		
		SECURE	INSECURE	Total
1988	SECURE	89,2 (67,4)	39,2 (9,6)	77,0
	INSECURE	10,8 (8,1)	60,8 (14,9)	23,0
	Total	100,0 (75,6)	100,0 (24,4)	100,0

EC		1985		
		SECURE	INSECURE	Total
1988	SECURE	96,3 (90,9)	58,0 (3,3)	94,2
	INSECURE	3,7 (3,5)	42,0 (2,4)	5,8
	Total	100,0 (94,4)	100,0 (5,6)	100,0

Legal		1985		
		SECURE	INSECURE	Total
1988	SECURE	98,0 (95,4)	75,8 (2,0)	97,4
	INSECURE	2,0 (2,0)	24,2 (0,6)	2,6
	Total	100,0 (97,4)	100,0 (2,6)	100,0

* - Between brackets percentage of all households.
   - Only households with the same head, or with the same partner when the head has died, and known income in both waves, were selected.

THE NETHERLANDS 1985-1986*

CSP		1985		
		SECURE	INSECURE	Total
1986	SECURE	84,6	5,9	90,5
	INSECURE	4,2	5,3	9,5
	Total	88,8	11,2	100,0

SPL		1985		
		SECURE	INSECURE	Total
1986	SECURE	83,7	2,3	86,0
	INSECURE	8,7	5,3	14,0
	Total	92,4	7,6	100,0

EC		1985		
		SECURE	INSECURE	Total
1986	SECURE	90,2	3,9	94,1
	INSECURE	3,4	2,6	5,9
	Total	93,6	6,4	100,0

Legal		1985		
		SECURE	INSECURE	Total
1986	SECURE	89,0	5,0	94,0
	INSECURE	3,7	2,2	6,0
	Total	92,8	7,2	100,0

* percentage of all households.

LUXEMBOURG 1985-1986

CSP		1985		
		SECURE	INSECURE	Total
1986	SECURE	94,2 (80,0)	37,5 (5,6)	85,7
	INSECURE	5,8 (4,9)	62,5 (9,4)	14,3
	Total	100,0 (84,9)	100,0 (15,1)	100,0

SPL		1985		
		SECURE	INSECURE	Total
1986	SECURE	96,8 (77,6)	50,5 (10,0)	87,6
	INSECURE	3,2 (2,5)	49,5 (9,8)	12,4
	Total	100,0 (80,1)	100,0 (19,9)	100,0

EC		1985		
		SECURE	INSECURE	Total
1986	SECURE	96,7 (89,3)	42,9 (3,3)	92,6
	INSECURE	3,3 (3,0)	57,1 (4,4)	7,4
	Total	100,0 (92,3)	100,0 (7,7)	100,0

Legal		1985		
		SECURE	INSECURE	Total
1986	SECURE	97,8 (91,5)	56,0 (3,6)	95,1
	INSECURE	2,2 (2,1)	44,0 (2,8)	4,9
	Total	100,0 (93,5)	100,0 (6,5)	100,0

LORRAINE 1985-1986

CSP		1985		
		SECURE	INSECURE	Total
1986	SECURE	84,2 (62,1)	26,4 (6,9)	69,0
	INSECURE	15,8 (11,7)	73,6 (19,3)	31,0
	Total	100,0 (73,8)	100,0 (26,2)	100,0

SPL		1985		
		SECURE	INSECURE	Total
1986	SECURE	90,0 (66,7)	26,1 (6,8)	73,5
	INSECURE	10,0 (7,4)	73,9 (19,1)	26,5
	Total	100,0 (74,1)	100,0 (25,9)	100,0

EC		1985		
		SECURE	INSECURE	Total
1986	SECURE	95,4 (85,2)	43,1 (4,6)	89,8
	INSECURE	4,6 (4,1)	56,9 (6,1)	10,2
	Total	100,0 (89,3)	100,0 (10,7)	100,0

Legal		1985		
		SECURE	INSECURE	Total
1986	SECURE	99,3 (94,8)	57,1 (2,6)	97,4
	INSECURE	0,7 (0,6)	42,9 (2,0)	2,6
	Total	100,0 (95,4)	100,0 (4,6)	100,0

IRELAND 1987-1989*

CSP		1987		
		SECURE	INSECURE	Total
1989	SECURE	58,2	9,0	67,2
	INSECURE	10,5	22,3	32,8
	Total	68,7	31,3	100,0

SPL		1987		
		SECURE	INSECURE	Total
1989	SECURE	52,7	5,9	58,5
	INSECURE	10,2	31,2	41,5
	Total	62,9	37,1	100,0

EC		1987		
		SECURE	INSECURE	Total
1989	SECURE	76,6	5,8	82,3
	INSECURE	7,4	10,2	17,7
	Total	84,0	16,0	100,0

Legal		1987		
		SECURE	INSECURE	Total
1989	SECURE	90,9	4,8	95,7
	INSECURE	2,6	1,7	4,3
	Total	93,5	6,5	100,0

* Percentage of all households.

Appendix B
Applied procedures to convert cash amounts

In the national reports, on which this comparative report is based, cash amounts are expressed in the national currencies of the respective countries. In order to make these amounts comparable, two procedures were used. In some tables the amounts were recalculated as a percentage of the median monthly disposable household income, as measured in the surveys. In others the amounts were converted in ECU, employing purchasing power parities for private consumption (ppp). The first method makes it possible to compare the relative level of the amounts, the second to compare the absolute level (purchasing power).

The median incomes that were used can be found in table B.1.

Table B.1
Median income in national currency and in ECU

| | first wave | | second wave | |
	amounts converted in ECU	original amounts in national cur.	amounts converted in ECU	original amounts in national cur.
Belgium	1183.10	51.095 BEF	1273.52	55.000 BEF
Ireland	933.44	688 I£	833.88	640 I£
Lorraine	1194.54	7902 FF	1235.87	8611 FF
The Netherlands	1300.73	2979 FL	1240.48	2841 FL
Luxembourg	1649.39	64.000 LF	1710.22	66.500 LF
Catalonia	1345.64	140000 Pta	-	-
Greece	802.88	98917 Dr.	-	-

The second procedure may need some elucidation. The choice was made to use ppp, instead of currency exchange rates with ECU, as the latter do not take differences in price-level between countries into account. This means that the conversion into ECU, employing solely exchange rates, does not always allow an accurate international comparison of the spending power of incomes. This is illustrated in table B.2.

Table B.2
Level in ECU of median income on the basis of currency
exchange rates and on the basis of ppp for private consumption

	on the basis of currency exchange rates		on the basis of purchasing power parities	
	in ECU	index BEF = 100	in ECU	index BEF = 100
Belgium, 1985	1183	100	1183	100
Ireland, 1987	892	75	833	79
Lorraine, 1985	1245	105	1195	101
The Netherlands, 1985	1273	108	1301	110
Luxembourg, 1985	1493	126	1649	139
Catalonia, 1988	956	81	1346	114
Greece, 1988	535	45	803	68

The differences between the amounts in ECU based on exchange rates and those based on ppp have little meaning because they depend on the base-country of the ppp, which is an arbitrary choice. More important is how the levels of median incomes behave relative to each other. It can be noticed that, due to a relatively low price-level, the position of Catalonia is in fact better than the amounts obtained via exchange rates suggest. Because of the same reason the favourable position of Luxembourg becomes even more pronounced. Most countries change in the same direction, except for Lorraine. It should however be noticed that for Lorraine and Catalonia the ppp for resp. France and Spain were used because of a lack of data on the regional level.

Thus in this report amounts were converted in ECU according to following procedure. *Firstly*, to correct for price evolution between the moments at which the different surveys were carried out, all the amounts were converted into prices of january 1988. This date was chosen arbitrarily. The adjustment is based on the following index of consumer prices (table B.2) ([1]).

Secondly, the indexed amounts were converted into Belgian Frances (BEF) employing purchasing power parities for private consumption (ppp) for january 1988 ([2]). The following parities were used (table B.3).

Finally, the amounts in BEF were converted in ECU, employing the exchange rate BEF-ECU of january 1988 (43.1875).

The bypass via BEF is necessary because purchasing power parities between national currencies and ECU don't exist ([3]). The choise for BEF was arbitrary. Conversion into another currency would result in other absolute amounts but the rates between the amounts are independant of the reference country chosen.

Table B.3
Consumer price index, 1980 = 100, except where indicated

| | first wave | | second wave | | jan. '88 |
	month of survey	index of consumer prices	month of survey	index of consumer prices	index of consumer prices
Belgium	10/85	141.5	01/88	144.6	144.6
Ireland	08/87	191.8	03/89	112.0 [a]	193.3 - 108.4 [a]
Lorraine [b]	01/85	153.9	07/86	162.1	169.1
The Netherlands	10/85	123.2	10/86	123.2	122.2
Luxembourg	06/85	142.4	04/86	142.7	143.5
Catalonia [b]	10/88	218.1	-		208.9
Greece	10/88	437.6	-		390.3

[a] 1985 = 100

[b] For Lorraine and Catalonia the index-figures for France and Spain were used.

Table B.4
Purchasing power parities for private consumption, January 1988

	purchasing power parities for private consumption
Ireland	0.0172
Lorraine*	0.1683
The Netherlands	0.0526
Luxembourg	0.9054
Catalonia*	2.3074
Greece	2.5444

* For Lorraine and Greece the ppp for resp. France and Spain were used.

The procedure is summarised in following formula:

$$\text{amount in ECU} = \frac{\text{amount in national currencies* (index Jan. '88/index month of survey)}}{(\text{exchange rate BEF-ECU}) * (\text{purchasing power parity})}$$

The procedure leads to following coefficients by which the original amounts must be divided, to obtain the amounts in ECU.

Note that most cash amounts in the report are rounded. Mostly they will differ slightly from the original figures when recalculated back in the initial currencies.

Table B.5
Coefficients to convert original amounts into ECU

	first wave	second wave
Belgium (BEF-ECU)	43,188	43,188
Ireland (I£-ECU)	0,737	0,768
Lorraine (FF-ECU)	6,615	6,968
The Netherlands (FL-ECU)	2,290	2,290
Luxembourg (LF-ECU)	38,802	38,884
Catalonia (Pta-ECU)	104,039	-
Greece (Dr-ECU)	123,203	-

Notes

(1)   EUROSTAT, Eurostatistics, data for short-term economic analysis.

(2)   EUROSTAT, not published.

(3)   Purchasing power standard exchange rates on the level of private consumption weren't available at the moment of the editing of the report.

Appendix C
Some important concepts
used in the report

1. *Household*: a household is composed of all persons who live and eat together regularly and share a common household budget.
   In Belgium, Luxembourg, Ireland and Catalonia a household includes students, living away from home at rooms or boarding school students, but coming home for holidays. The Netherlands and Lorraine count students, not living in their parents home, as a separate household.

2. *Head of household*: if married or unmarried couple: the man (except in case of seriously incapacitated). In all other cases the person who the respondent mentions as the head of the household.
   In cases of doubt: the owner or tenant of the house (Luxembourg), the owner or tenant of the house or the oldest person (Catalonia), the owner or tenant of the house, the chief breadwinner or oldest person (the Netherlands), when there are several couples or parents, the oldest man (for a couple) or oldest parent (for a single) (Lorraine).

3. *Members in a household*:
   Adult: all persons above 15 years except for those in full time education. If living independently on their own or as part of a couple then they are anyway adult or elderly) (In Catalonia also persons of 16 to 25 years, independently of their activity and economic situation.
   Child: all persons under 15 years and those who are in full time education (except for those living independently on their own or as part of a couple); Students living away from home are considered as adults in The Netherlands and Lorraine. In Catalonia all persons younger than 16 years are children.
   Elderly: men: 65 or over
                 women: 60 or over
                 in Catalonia: all persons + 65 years

Retired: all elderly + any person early retired. Widows who never worked and do not receive a pension income are nevertheless retired; in Luxembourg, Lorraine, Ireland only persons who have in the past participated in the labour force can be retired.

Unemployed: Persons are defined as unemployed when (a) they have no work, (b) when they are in search of work and (c) when they are available for the labour market. All other non-employed (active) persons are treated under the category 'non-employed'.
Persons who are partly working, partly receiving an unemployment benefit are treated as employed.

Employed: Individuals are treated as "in employment" if they are working for at least one hour per week for payment or profit and if they consider themselves as employed. In Lorraine and Luxembourg persons working at least 9 hours a week are considered as employed. In Ireland, relatives working on family farms are included even if not in receipt of a regular wage.

4. *Total net disposable income of the household:* is the sum of all cash income (incomes in kind are excluded): from labour, capital and social security and other public and private allowances. All countries except for Lorraine, consider net income (after taxes) (due to the tax system in France it was not possible, for Lorraine, to calculate incomes after taxes).

- *income from labour:* net wages and salaries of the employed and earnings of the self-employed.
- *income from capital:* all countries have more or less detailed information on income from capital (interests from savings, income from immovable and movable property, life annuities), except for Belgium (first wave). The latter country only collected information on income from letting houses in the first wave. In the second wave data are available on interests from savings, income from movable and immovable (houses) property.
- *income from social security:* replacement income + family allowances.
   - replacement incomes: all countries measured the various replacement schemes existing in their country, being pensions, retirement, survival pensions, unemployment allowances, sickness and invalidity and social assistance. Only Lorraine did not ask for social assistance in their questionnaire. *In Catalonia social assistance is not included in replacement income.*
   - family allowances: all countries included child allowances. Luxembourg, Lorraine and Ireland have, besides child allowances, also included special family allowances schemes such as prenatal and birth premies, family supplement schemes, child benefits, ... these allowances have a social assistance character (means-tested) but as they are targeted for specific household situations they are classified under family allowances and not under social assistance.
- *public and private redistribution:* this item was questioned by the various countries differently.
BELGIUM: complementary pensions from private insurance, government study grants, alimony.

THE NETHERLANDS: alimony, private medical care insurance, study grants (government and private), inheritance, gifts, housing subsidies.

LUXEMBOURG and LORRAINE: alimony, private insurances, inheritance, study grants (government), special allowances (housing, Luxembourg: expensive life).

IRELAND: privated insurances, income transfers between households, educational grants and scholarships, reduction of rent, allowances for fuel, other welfare allowances (free milk, free domestic help, ...).

CATALONIA: private insurances, (annual) study grants, housing allowances, "indemnité d'expulsion".

5. *Educational level*
A five-fold classification has been computed by all countries covering (1) primary education, including those without education, (2) lower cycle (general, vocational and technical education, (3) higher cycle (general, vocational and technical education), (4) higher non-university education and (5) university. For a detailed knowledge on the national classification schemes we refer to the national questionnaires and the national reports.

6. *Socio-professional status*
A five-fold division has been computed by all countries covering (1) un- or semi-skilled manual workers, (2) skilled manual workers, (3) lower employees, (4) higher employees (managers, directors, free profession), 5) small self-employed and (6) Farmers.

For a detailed knowledge or the national classification schemes we refer to the national questionnaires and national reports.

More detailed descriptions of the operationalizations of concepts in each country are given in the following tables. These descriptions were not available for Greece.

	BELGIUM	THE NETHERLANDS	LUXEMBOURG
HOUSEHOLD	All persons who eat together and live from the same income, including children with their own income, who live with their parents; and students, dependent on the household, living elsewhere in rooms.	An individual living alone or a group of 2 or more persons living together and sharing a common household budget. Included are (1) children over 18, living in their parents home, earning their own income, if more than 50% of their income is part of the common budget and (2) children over 18, being students living in their parents home; (3) all children under 18. Excluded are children over 18, being students, not living in their parents home.	All persons living habitually in the same housing unit including children in boarding school, people in hospital, prison, people who are abroad for professional reasons, a subtenant who regularly eats with students living apart but coming regularly home. Are excluded: persons living only temporarily in the house, subtenants who live independently, prisonners.
HEAD OF THE HOUSEHOLD	If married or unmarried couple, the man. If single person with children, the man or woman. In all other cases, the person that by the respondent is considered as head of household.	If married couple, the husband. If single person with children, man or woman. In all other cases, the person that is considered as head of household. If there is any doubt then: . owner or tenant of the house . chief breadwinner . oldest person.	. Basic rule: an adult of more than 18 years old. . he/she who says he/she is the head (consensus in the household itself). couple: . married couple: husband . unmarried couple: . living together for more than one year: the man . less than one year: owner or tenant. . If the husband is incapaciated: the wife. If there is no couple: he/she who is the tenant or the owner.
MEMBERS IN A HOUSEHOLD Adult	All persons above 25 and under 60 (women) and 65 (men) and also all persons younger than 25 and working (or have worked) or receiving a replacement income.	Persons above 25 and under 60 (women) and 65 (men); all persons younger than 25 and having an economic activity (working or receiving an income); students living apart from their parents are adults.	Persons above 25 and under 60/65; persons under 25 working or receiving other income.

	BELGIUM	THE NETHERLANDS	LUXEMBOURG
Child	All persons under 25 in full-time education and not receiving any replacement income (economic dependently).	All persons under 25 in full-time education living with their parents and without an income.	Persons under 25 in full-time education without income. (included students living apart but coming home during weekends/holidays).
Elderly	Men: 65 years or over. women: 60 years or over.	Men: 65 years or over. women: 60 years or over.	Men: +65 women: +60.
Retired	All elderly + early retired. Widows who have never worked and not receiving a pension are considered as retired.	All elderly + early retired + widows (even if never worked).	All elderly + early retired (only when participated in labour force).
Employed	All persons working for at least one hour per week for payment.	All persons working for at least one hour for payment (not vacation jobs, ...).	All persons working at least 9 hours.
Unemployed	. All active persons not at work, in search of work and available for the labour market. . Part-time unemployed are included. . early retired/paid under employment schemes are treated as retired and their benefits as 'pension' incomes.	All (active) persons not at work in search of work and available for the labour market.	. All individuals not at work but in search of work and available for labour market.
INCOME	All incomes are asked net.	All incomes are asked net.	All incomes are asked net.
*1. Labour**	Wages and salaries of the employed (monthly). Earnings of the self-employed (monthly). Earnings from second job of	Wages and salaries . Income out of seasonal work (weekly, four-weekly or monthly). . Holiday allowances, 13th month bonuses, royalties (annual)	. Income from wages and salary (including: premium end of the year, 13th month, wages from extra jobs (also of pensioners with an extra job).

* between brackets period over which income was questionned.

173

	BELGIUM	THE NETHERLANDS	LUXEMBOURG
	employed or non-employed (monthly).	restitution. Earnings of the self-employed (annual) (+ Subsidy on investments (last year): + restitution of taxes (current year)).	. Earnings of self-employed . Income from a free profession
2. Capital	Income from letting houses, apartments etc. (monthly). In the second wave also movable capital was questionned (annual).	Movables cash interests, dividents etc. (gross, last 12 months) and immovables (income from houses).	. Income from immovables and movables property . Life-annuities . Interests from savings (current amount (monthly, three-monthly, annual).
3. Replacement *3.1. Unemployment payments*	Unemployment payments (monthly).	Unemployment payments, from 3 schemes: WW, WWV, RWW (insurance and assistance). (weekly, four-weekly, monthly).	Unemployment payments (current amount: monthly, three-monthly, annual).
3.2. Sickness or invalidity payments	Sickness or invalidity benefits (both for former employed and for the never employed), and benefits in case of occupational accidents and illnesses (monthly).	Disability benefits from 3 schemes: ABP, WAO, AAW. (sickness pay included in income from wages) (weekly, four-weekly, monthly).	Indemnities for occupational diseases. Indemnities for occupational accidents with life-long incapacity as consequence. Indemnities for incapacity, (temporarily) sickness (temporarily) and maternity. Indemnities for the disabled. Allowance for handicapped adult. Pensions for the incapaciated. (Current amount: monthly, three-monthly, annual).
3.3. Pensions	Pensions (retirement, survivors, early retirement, guaranteed minimum income for the elderly) (monthly). Complementary pensions (paid by former employer, collective insurance scheme, etc.).	Pensions. . Survivors pensions (AWW) and supplementary pensions (monthly). . Old age pensions: AOW and private pensions. life-insurance pay, early retirement benefits (Vut) (weekly and monthly).	. Legal pensions (old age and survival). . Allowances for those who do not benefit from a normal pension. (current amount: monthly, three-monthly, annual).

	BELGIUM	THE NETHERLANDS	LUXEMBOURG
3.4. Social assistance	Social assistance. allowances and assistance from the public centres for social welfare (monthly).	. Social assistance allowances (ABW) (weekly and monthly). . Lump Sum ABW-benefits (last year). . Lump Sum Benefit for Self Employed (special scheme ABW) (annual).	. National Solidarity Fund. . assistance from the social bureau. (current amount: monthly, three-monthly, annual).
4. Family allowances	Child allowances (monthly).	Child allowance (AKW) (eligible amount quarterly).	Child allowance. Family allowances (prenatal, birth, etc.) Special allowances for handicapped (current amount: monthly, three-monthly, annual).
5. Other public allowances *5.1. Education*	Scholarships, governments grants for studying children, secondary tertiary education (annual).	Study grants for children studying at secondary school (annual). Study grants for respondent himself (monthly or annual).	Study grants (current amount)
5.2. Housing		Housing subsidies scheme e.g. . rent subsidy (quarterly) . rent accustoming subsidy (annual). . bonus system on the purchase of a house (annual).	
5.3. Other	Indemnity for compulsory military service (monthly).	Restitution of paid taxes in advance (annual).	Supplementary allowances (allocation de vie chère, prime d'encavement, ...).
6. Private redistribution *6.1. Alimony*	Alimony for former spouse and children (monthly).	. Alimony for respondent (weekly, monthly, annual).	Alimony

	BELGIUM	THE NETHERLANDS	LUXEMBOURG
6.2. Private insurances for medical care, pensions, etc.	Complementary pensions from private insurance (monthly).	. Alimony for children (weekly, monthly, annual). Restitution private medical care insurance premiums (last year).	Private insurances
6.3. Private study grants	-	Study grants from employer or parents (monthly or annual).	
6.4. Private social assistance	-		Private social assistance
6.5. Inheritance, gifts	-	. Inheritance in cash from outside household (last 12 months). . Gifts in cash from outside household (last 12 months).	Inheritance
6.6. Other	-		Games, lotteries (monthly or latest received amount).
SOCIAL SECURITY INCOME (replacement income + family allowance)			
TOTAL NET DISPOSABLE HOUSEHOLD INCOME	Sum of all cash income from labour, capital, social security and other public and private allowances.	Summation of incomes of all householdmembers mentioned above, in monthly amounts.	Sum of all incomes from labour, capital social security and other public and private income sources.

	LORRAINE	IRELAND	CATALONIA
HOUSEHOLD	All persons living in the same housing unit related to a non-married or married couple. Included are persons renting a part of the house provided they share the same kitchen and bathroom plus all persons temporarily absent e.g. people in hospital, prison, children in boarding school, people working abroad for a period, people doing military service. Excluded: Students living apart near the university.	Person or group of persons who live together regularly and from whom food is provided by the same person (or rota of persons). Includes those normally living with the household even if temporarily away (students, boarding school students).	Individuals living alone or with more persons and sharing the same house and budget, including students living apart from parents, persons in military service, in hospital or in prison.
HEAD OF THE HOUSEHOLD	'referee': adult of more than 18 years old. . the man in a couple. . if several couples, the oldest man of the active or the oldest man of the inactive. . if one parent and children: the parent . if several parents and children: the oldest parent of the active parents or the oldest of the inactive.	In general a person or spouse of person who either owns the accommodation, is responsible for the rent or is entitled to the accommodation because of employment or others. In other cases, self-classification to identify the 'main provider'.	When a couple, the man; when a one-parent family, the parent; in all other cases the one mentioned by the respondent, in case of doubt the owner or tenant or the oldest person when serious disabled, the wife.
MEMBERS IN A HOUSEHOLD *Adult*	All persons who are not defined as 'child' or as 'elderly'.	All men aged 25-64 and women 25-59 and those under 25 who are employed or entitled to unemployment benefit.	All persons above 16 years independently of their activity and economic situation.

	LORRAINE	IRELAND	CATALONIA
Child	All persons under 16 years and all persons above 15 years and in full time education. Students living independently are considered as adults.	All persons under 25 and in full-time education.	All persons under 16 years.
Elderly	Men: 65 years or over women: 60 years or over.	Men: 65 years or over women: 60 years or over. (although entitlement to pensions begins at 65 or 66 for both men and women).	All persons above 65 years.
Retired	All retired and early retired from a professional activity independant from receiving a pension or not.	All elderly and early retired but only when participated in labour force in past.	All elderly, all early retired and all widows even if they had no professional activity in the past.
Employed	All persons working for at least 9 hours a week.	Individuals are treated as 'in employment' if working at least one hour per week for payment. Relatives working or family farms are included even if not paid regularly.	All persons working at least one hour.
Unemployed	. All persons not working and declaring to be in search of work weather effectively looking for work or not at moment of questionnaire.	. All persons not at work but in search of work and available for labour market.	All not employed persons in search of work.
INCOME	All incomes are after social contribution but before taxes (a).	All incomes are asked net.	All incomes are asked net.
1. Labour (b)	. Wages and salaries of the employed (plus bonus paid by employer). . Earnings of the self-employed . Occasional earnings (holiday work, ...) (current amount,	Income from wages/salary for employed in both main and subsidiary job(s) (most recent weekly or monthly amount). Sufficient information has been	Wages and salaries plus overwork (monthly, net), plus bonus (annual: net). Earnings from the self-employed (annual).

(a) For Lorraine the amount of income questionned over a certain period of time (weekly, monthly, three-monthly) has been subject of recalculation according to following procedure: currently received income x number of times.

(b) between brackets period over which income was questionned.

	LORRAINE	IRELAND	CATALONIA
	monthly, three-monthly, annual,...).	collected to allow a 12-month income estimate to be constructed (however not used in this study). Earnings of the self-employed (last year amounts), earnings of farmers (outputs and costs asked for by a detailed seperate questionnaire).	
2. *Capital*	. Income from dividents, obligations. .... . Income from savings . Income from immovables (current amount: monthly, three-monthly, annual,...)	Rental income from land or property; interests and dividents; annuities (amount received over past year or specification of period currently receiving).	Immovables and movables (annual).
3. *Replacement* 3.1. *Unemployment payments*	Unemployment payments . unemployment from the national scheme ASSEDIC . unemployment benefits paid by employer ('primes de licenciement') (current amount: monthly, three-monthly, annual).	Unemployment benefits and unemployment assistance (current amount: weekly or monthly).	Unemployment benefits (unemployment insurance and assistance (from central government and other government levels (generalitat, diputació, municipalité) (monthly).
3.2. *Sickness or invalidity payments*	. Invalidity pensions . Allowances for the disabled. . Benefits for sickness, maternity and accidents. (current amount: monthly, three-monthly, annual).	Disability benefit, invalidity pension, injury and disablement benefit. Disabled persons's allowance maintenance (most recent weekly or monthly amount).	Allowances for sickness, invalidity, accidents (monthly).
3.3. *Pensions*	. Pensions for the employed. . Pensions for the self-employed. . Pensions for farmers. . War pensions; guaranteed minimum pension. (current amount: monthly, three-monthly, annual).	Old age pensions. Social welfare retirement pension Widow's pension (contributory and non-contributory) (most recent weekly or monthly amount). Occupational and other private pensions and annuities.	Retirement, Survivor's pension, orphan's pension (monthly).

	LORRAINE	IRELAND	CATALONIA
3.4. Social assistance	Public assistance (only in 1986 questionnaire).	Supplementary welfare allowances (most recent weekly or monthly amount).	Periodical allowances (public and private), allowances from Diputació and Generalitat, FAS (Fonds Assistance Sociale - Vieillesse; Fonds Assistance Social - Handicap - Sickness) Allowances for handicapped persons (miners) (monthly).
4. Family allowances	. Child allowances . Allowance for special eduction (for disabled children). . Family support allowance (for orphans). . Allowances after birth. . Allowances for one parent families. . Family Supplement. . Allowances for parents interrupting their job temporally. (current amount: monthly, three-monthly, annual, ...).	Child benefit, Family Income Supplement, birth grants, maternity allowance. Orphan's pensions / allowances, allowance for unmarried mothers, deserted wife's benefit and allowance, prisoners wife allowances, single women's allowance. (current amount: weekly, monthly, three-monthly, ...). Most of these allowances have a social assistance character but are classified under family allowances and not under 'social assistance'.	Child allowances (monthly). Allowances for large families (monthly).
5. Other public allowances 5.1. Education	Bursaries and scholarships (+ special allowances)	Educational grants and scholarships.	Scholarships and grants (bourse d'étude).
5.2. Housing	. personal support for housing (A.P.L.). . social housing allowances . family housing allowance (current amount: monthly, three-monthly, annual).	Rent reductions.	
5.3. Other	Allowance in case of military service.	Residual category.	
6. Private redistribution 6.1. Alimony	Alimony	A general question was asked on transfers from other households	

	LORRAINE	IRELAND	CATALONIA
		(which would include alimony).	
6.2. Private insurances for medical care, pensions, etc.	Private insurances (medical care, pensions).	Private pension schemes, sick pay from employer, Trade union sick pay, private income continuances.	
6.3. Private study grants	-	Insurance for paying out educational fees or expenses.	
6.4. Private social assistance	Private social assistance (only in 1986 questionnaire).	Assistance from private charity.	
6.5. Inheritance, gifts	Income from inheritance, games, lotteries.		
6.6. Other			
SOCIAL SECURITY INCOME (replacement income + family allowance)			
TOTAL NET DISPOSABLE HOUSEHOLD INCOME	Sum of labour, capital, social security and other public and private income sources. (Amount calculated on annual basis and expressed monthly).	Sum of all incomes from labour, capital, social security and other public and private income sources.	Sum of all cash income from labour, capital, social security and other public and private income sources.

Appendix D
Poverty line methods

D.1. Estimation of the CSP socio-vital minima

The purpose of the socio-vital minima (s-v m.) is to determine by induction the income which is considered necessary to live decently.

For this the replies to three questions are to be used:

1. "How great do you think the minimum net income of a household like yours should be at least to make ends meet?" This question enabled us to determine the income considered necessary.
2. "With your current monthly income, everything included, can you get by: with great difficulty, with difficulty, with some difficulty, fairly easily, easily, very easily, for your household?" This scale with six levels enabled us to define the level of the households subjective security of subsistence.
3. The question pertaining to the household disposable income. A household is composed of all persons who live and eat together regularly and share a common household budget. The total net disposable income of the household is the sum of all common incomes: from labour capital, social security and the private and public allowances.

Standard procedure

The answers to these questions are used as follows:

- Only households answering *"with some difficulty"* on question 2 are taken into consideration.
- For each household, the so-called "minimum income" is established. The minimum income is equal to either the income considered necessary, or the disposable income of

the household, whichever is the smallest amount.
- The average minimum-income is computed per type of household. Type of household is defined by the number of active persons, the number of aged persons and the number of children in the household. (For definitions of active, aged and child, please refer appendix B). Each unique combination of these numbers constitutes one type of household. Each type is labelled by a three-digit code, the digits representing respectively the number of active persons, the number of aged persons and the number of children. In the Belgian sample, about 80 different household-types were found.
- Cases with extreme values on minimum income, that is outside two times the standard deviation from the mean for their type of household, are excluded, and a new average minimum income per household type is computed.
- If the average is computed over at least 30 households of a certain type, then this average is considered a valid estimate of the CSP-minimum income for that type of household. In this way a CSP-minimum could be calculated for the 8 basic, most common, types of household in the Belgian sample.
- In order to be able to determine CSP-minima for the other, less frequently occurring, types of household, minimum costs for additional persons of each kind (e.g. third active person, third aged person, fourth child) are calculated, using the minima for the basic types of household. The estimate of these costs are made by subtracting the minimum of a certain type of household from the minimum of a type that has one person more. For instance the cost of a fourth child is computed as: minimum for a couple with three children minus the minimum for a couple with two children. How in practice this can be done depends on the types of household for which minima can be computed directly. This in turn depends on the size of the sample, its distribution over the various types of household, and the degree of subjective insecurity of subsistence. The following table shows, as an example, how the estimates were made for the Belgian 1985-sample.

Minimum cost Estimate for: (sort of person)	Calculated as the differences between the minima for household-type (A) and household-type (B)
a. third and following active person(s)	(A): active couple (B): single active
b. third and following aged person's); any aged person living with two or more active persons	(A): aged couple (B): single aged
c. first child, living with one or two active persons	(A): active couple with one child (B): active couple without children
d. second child, living with one or two active persons	(A): active couple with two children (B): active couple with one child
e. third and following children, living with one or two active persons; any child living with three or more active persons	(A): active couple with three children (B): active couple with two children

There is some room for variation in the computation of these estimates. One should take care that they are, as far as possible, reasonable and consistent with each other.

- Now, to establish the minimum for any type of household, for which the minimum could not be directly computed, one works as follows. First, one reduces the household-type to one of the basic types by subtracting, in this order, one or more children, one or more aged persons, and/or one or more active persons. For instance, the household-type with three active, one aged persons and three children is "reduced" to the basic type with two active persons. Then, starting with the minimum for the basic type, one adds the appropriated amounts for (in this order) the additional active persons, the additional aged persons, and the additional children.
- To each household in the sample the minimum for its households type is awarded.

Estimation of the CSP-socio-vital minima with smaller samples

The procedure for the implementation of the CSP-method described above, proved to be not feasible in certain samples. The minimum number of thirty cases per household type, over which the minima should be calculated, was not always attainable, either because the sample size is not large enough, or because the percentage of households making ends meet "with some difficulty" is too small. For this kind of situation a procedure is developed, using regression, that is as far as possible analogous to the standard procedure. This procedure is as follows:

1. Select households scoring 3 ('with some difficulty') on the Subjective Scale of Subsistence ('How do you manage to make ends meet ?') (but see below if this step diminishes the number of usable households too much).
2. Select households with a non-complex composition, that is households of the types mentioned in table 3.2.
3. Compute the Minimum Income (MI), being equal to either the household disposable income or the necessary income, whichever is the smallest amount.
4. Estimate the following regression equation:

   (1) $MI = a + b1.NACT + b2.NELD + b3.LOGNCHILD + e$

   in which: MI: Minimum Income, computed in step 3
   NACT: Number of adult persons of active age
   NELD: Number of elderly persons
   LOGNCHILD: Natural logarithm of the number of children plus one ($LOG(NCHILD + 1)$)
   a, b1, b2, b3: coefficients to be estimated
   e: statistical error

   The definitions of 'adult of active age', 'elderly' and 'child' are as above.
5. Exclude cases, whose standardized residuals for equation 1 are below -2.0 or above 2.0.
6. Again estimate equation 1.
7. Using the estimates for the coefficients, obtained in step 6, compute the socio-vital minima (SVM) for each household with equation 2:

   (2) $SVM = a + b1.NACT + b2.NELD + b3.LOGNCHILD.$

This procedure has been tested on the Belgian sample and has been found to produce estimates for the minima, that are within a margin of 3% from those computed with the normal method.

It is possible that the procedure just described does not work satisfactorily, the estimates being implausible, inconsistent or unreliable, because the number of cases is too low. The restriction to households scoring 3 on the Subjective Scale of Subsistence relaxed can then be. Households with score 2 ('difficulty') or 4 ('fairly easily') may be included. (Households with scores further away from 3 should be included only if really necessary.) These added groups should be represented in the regression equation by dummy variables, equal to one for the group in question and to zero for others. In this way one controls for the differences in welfare between households. The equation to be estimated then becomes:

(3) $MI = a + b1.NACT + b2.NELD + b3.LOGNCHILD + b4.SSS4 + b5.SSS2 + e$

in which: SSS4: dummy-variable, 1 if $SSS = 4$, 0 otherwise
              SSS2: dummy-variable, 1 if $SSS = 2$, 0 otherwise.

In all other respects the procedure remains the same. Equation (2) can still be used to compute the minima. The extension to even more score-groups is straightforward.

In the Belgian sample, the extension in this way of the number of households over which the minima are computed, did not alter the estimates significantly.

D.2. Estimation of the SPL

Measurement of y_{min}

Measurement of a respondent's minimum income takes place by asking the minimum income question (MIQ).

A problem is the income concept the respondent has in mind. For policy purposes it appears rather obvious that after tax family income is the appropriate concept. If the respondent has learned exactly what his or her after tax family income is before the MIQ is posed, the answer to the MIQ can be assumed to represent the appropriate income concept.

If this condition is not fulfilled (it may for example be very cumbersome to add up all the income components during the interview), it is important to learn which income concept the respondent has in mind. The way to do this is to ask what the respondent has in mind. The way to do this is to ask the respondent, just before the MIQ, what he or she thinks that the actual tax family income is. This question can be asked in two different ways. One way is to ask the respondent to state the money amount he or she thinks his or her after-tax family income is equal to. In this case the correction is exceedingly easy:
Let y_r be the after tax family income the respondent believes he or she has. Let y_a be the actual after tax family income calculated on the basis of the detailed income questions in the questionnaire. Then we adjust y_{min} by multiplying it by $y_a/y2$.
A second way is to ask for the income bracket in which the respondent thinks his or her after tax family income will fall. Given this response, one can use the following approach

186

to correct $\ln y_{min}$.
We postulate the following relation between the income y* underlying the answer to the income question in brackets and the income components yi (i=1, ..., n) recorded in the questionnaire:

$$(3.1) \quad y^* = (\sum_{i=1}^{n} \alpha_i y_i) . e^u$$

where the a_i 's are unknown parameters and u is a normally distributed error term with zero mean and variance s_u. The respondent's answer falls in the i-th bracket if y* is between the upper and lower bound of this bracket. We expect the a_i to lie in the unit interval. The lower a parameter a_i is, the more the respondent "forgets" the i-th income component in answering the income question in brackets.

We assume that if the respondent would have been aware of the actual value of his households income as measured by the sum of the income components, the resulting value for ymin would have been higher, by the same percentage as by which Sy_i exceeds Sa_iy_i. Thus we adjust the measured value of ymin for each respondent as follows:

$$y^*_{min} = y_{min} (\sum_{i=1}^{n} y_i / \sum_{i=1}^{n} \alpha_i y_i)$$

where y_{min} is the adjusted value.

Construction of poverty lines

For the comparative report, only a basic model is used.
The equation remaining is then

$$(a) \quad \ln y_{min,n} = \alpha_0 + \alpha_1 (1-\alpha)_2 \ln fs_n + \psi (1-\alpha_2) \ln fs_n \ln y_n + \alpha_2 \ln y_n + u_n .$$

where $\ln y_{min,n}$ is the value of $\ln y_{min}$ for family n, fs_n is the size of family n, Y_n is its after tax income, u_n is an error term capturing all omitted factors. An interaction term $\ln fs_n \ln y_n$ has been introduced, to allow that the cost of an increase in family size varies with income (as a percentage). If coëfficiënt y is negative, the percentage increase in Y_{min} for an additional family member is smaller at higher income levels.
This equation can be estimated by ordinary least squares.
If y is not significantly different from zero (at the 5%-level, say) it is suggested that one sets y = 0 and reestimate (a) with this restriction imposed.
The poverty line for each household can then be computed as follows:

$$SPL = \exp \left[\frac{\alpha_0 + \alpha_1 (1-\alpha_2)\ln fs}{(1-\alpha_2)(1-\psi \ln fs)} \right]$$

D.3. Calculation of EC.Poverty Line

The EC poverty line used here is equal to the one described as Method 1, Scale C, 50% level, by O'Higgins and Jenkins.
For this method one must have a microdata set with information on a cross-section of households, where A is the number of adults and C the number of children in each household.
For each household, equivalent disposable income (E) is the households disposable income (Y) divided by the equivalence factor for that household (F), where $F = 1 + 0.7$ $(A - 1) + 0.5C$; basis C.

For the sample as a whole, AEDII (i.e. average equivalent disposable income) is then simply the average value of E, i.e. E/N, where N is the number of households in the sample.
The poverty line (P) for a single person is then 50% of AEDII.
Poverty lines for households with more than 1 person are derived by multiplying the single person poverty line by the equivalence factor (F) for a household of that size. (E.g. for a household with two adults and one child, multiply P by 2.2.).

D.4. Calculation of the legal standards

The legal standards are computed as follows:

BELGIUM: Guaranteed Income for the Elderly ("Gewaarborgd Inkomen voor Bejaarden") or Right to a Subsistence Minimum ("Recht op Bestaansminimum") plus guaranteed child allowances.

THE NETHERLANDS: The legal standard is computed as follows:
+ minimum benefits in social assistance ("Algemene Bijstands Wet")
+ holiday allowances for beneficiaries of ABW
+ additional benefits for households which have to live on one minimum income ("eenmatige uitkering", "uitkering voor meerderjarige minima", "eenmalige tegemoetkoming in stookkosten").
+ child allowances
- reduction for single households living with others in the same dwelling ("voordeurdelers")

LUXEMBOURG: Guaranteed minimum income ("revenu minimum guaranti"), as laid down by the law of 26-7-'86, adjusted for the consumption price index of april 1985.

IRELAND: Amounts as in the Supplementary Welfare System.

LORRAINE: Guaranteed minimum income ("Revenu Minimum d'Insertion RMI), deflated byh the consumption price index.

Appendix E
Detailed list of maquette
tables

PART A: Descriptive indicators

I. Indicators of the distribution of income and social transfers.

TABLE 1.a.: Distribution of monthly disposable household income by income deciles, in ECU, in prices of Jan. 1988, Belgium, Ireland, Lorraine, The Netherlands, Luxembourg, Catalonia and Greece, 1st and 2nd wave.

TABLE 1.b.: Cumulative percentage of total disposable household income by income deciles, Belgium, Ireland, Lorraine, The Netherlands, Luxembourg, Catalonia and Greece, 1st and 2nd wave.

TABLE 1.c.: Income inequality, Belgium, Ireland, Lorraine, The Netherlands, Luxembourg, Catalonia and Greece, 1st and 2nd wave.

TABLE 2.a.: Socio-demographic composition of the income deciles: average size of household, Belgium, Ireland, Lorraine, The Netherlands, Luxembourg, Catalonia and Greece, 1st and 2nd wave.

TABLE 2.b.: Socio-demographic composition of the income deciles: average number of children per household, Belgium, Ireland, Lorraine, The Netherlands, Luxembourg, Catalonia and Greece, 1st and 2nd wave.

TABLE 2.c.: Socio-demographic composition of the income deciles: % elderly heads of households, Belgium, Ireland, Lorraine, The Netherlands, Luxembourg, Catalonia and Greece, 1st and 2nd wave.

TABLE 2.d.: Socio-demographic composition of the income deciles: % of households in each decile with one income provider, Belgium, Ireland, Lorraine, The Netherlands, Luxembourg, Catalonia and Greece, 1st and 2nd wave.

TABLE 2.e.: Socio-demographic composition of the income deciles: average number of employed per household, Belgium, Ireland, Lorraine, The Netherlands, Luxembourg, Catalonia and Greece, 1st and 2nd wave.

TABLE 3.a.: Percentage of households with income from labour by total income deciles; Belgium, Ireland, Lorraine, The Netherlands, Luxembourg, Catalonia and Greece, 1st and 2nd wave.

189

TABLE 18e: Catalonia, 1988. Incomes and poverty-gaps or income surplus, before/after social assistance, recipient households only, amounts in ECU, in prices of January 1988.

TABLE 19a: The Netherlands, 1986. Incomes and poverty-gaps or income surplus, before/after pensions, recipient households only, amounts in ECU, in prices of January 1988.

TABLE 19b: The Netherlands, 1986. Incomes and poverty-gaps or income surplus, before/after unemployment allowances, recipient households only, amounts in ECU, in prices of January 1988.

TABLE 19c: The Netherlands, 1986. Incomes and poverty-gaps or income surplus, before/after sickness or invalidity allowances, recipient households only, amounts in ECU, in prices of January 1988.

TABLE 19d: The Netherlands, 1986. Incomes and poverty-gaps or income surplus, before/after family allowances, recipient households only, amounts in ECU, in prices of January 1988.

TABLE 19e: The Netherlands, 1986. Incomes and poverty-gaps or income surplus, before/after social assistance, recipient households only, amounts in ECU, in prices of January 1988.

PART D: Panel.

TABLE 13: Changes in poverty among households, across two waves, according to four poverty lines.

TABLE 14: Changes in poverty-status among households across two waves, broken down by some social characteristics in the first wave, according to four standards.

These tables are contained in the full report, which is available on request at:

The Centre for Social Policy

University of Antwerp (UFSIA)
Prinsstraat 13
B-2000 Antwerp
Belgium

tel. ++ 33-3 220 43 31
fax ++ 33-3 220 43 25

References

Abel-Smith, B. (1984), 'The study and definition of poverty: values and social aims' in Sarpellon, G. (ed.), *Understanding Poverty*, Milano, pp. 68-86.

Bane, M.J. and Ellwood, D. (1986), 'Slipping into and out of poverty: the dynamics of spells', *The Journal of Human Resources*, vol. 21, no. 1, pp. 1- 23.

Beckerman, W. (1979), *Poverty and the Impact of Income Maintenance Programmes*, Geneva.

Berghman, J., Muffels, R., De Vries, A. and Vriens, M. (1989), *Armoede, bestaansonzekerheid en relatieve deprivatie. Rapport 1988*, Tilburg.

Buhmann, B., Rainwater, L., Schmauss, G. and Smeeding, T. (1988), 'Equivalence scales, well-being inequality and poverty: sensitivity estimates across ten countries using the Luxemburg Income Study (LIS) database', *Review of Income and Wealth*, vol. 34, no. 2, pp. 113-142.

Callan, T., Nolan, B. a.o. (1989), *Poverty, income and welfare in Ireland*, Research paper no. 146, ESRI, Dublin.

Commission of the European Communities (1981), *Final report of the first programme of pilot schemes and studies to combat poverty*, Brussels.

Deaton, A. and Muellbauer, J. (1980), *Economics and consumer behavior*, Cambridge.

Deleeck, H., De Lathouwer, L. and Van den Bosch, K. (1988), *Social Indicators of Social Security. A comparative analysis of five countries*, Centre for Social Policy, Antwerp.

Deleeck, H. (1989), 'The adequacy of the Social Security System in Belgium, 1976-1985', *Journal of Social Policy*, vol. 18, no. 1.

Desai, M. and Shah, A. (1988), 'An econometric approach to the measurement of poverty', *Oxford Economic Papers*, vol. 40, pp. 505-522.

De Vos, K. and Hagenaars, A. (1988), *A comparison between the poverty concepts of Sen and Townsend*, Erasmus University, Rotterdam.

De Vries, A. (1986), *Armoede onderzocht. Effecten van sociale zekerheid, onderzoek, theorie, methode, deel 3*, Tilburg.

Dickes, P. (1988), 'L'impact des groupes de revenu sur les mesures de bien-être subjectif', *Cahiers Economiques de Nancy*, no. 20, p. 49-71.

Duncan, G., Gustafson, B. a.o. (1991), *Poverty and Social Assistance Dynamics in Eight Countries*, Paper for the conference "Poverty and Public Policy", Paris.

Duncan, G. (1983), 'The Implications of Changing Family Composition for the Dynamic Analysis of Family Economic Well-Being' in Atkinson, A. and Cowell, F. (eds.), *Panel Data on Incomes*, ICERD, London.

Eurostat (1990), *La Pauvreté en Chiffres l'Europe au début des années 80*, Luxembourg.

Foster, J. (1984), 'On Economic Poverty; A Survey of aggregate measures', *Advances in Econometrics*, vol. 3, pp. 215-251.

Gailly, B. and Hausman, P. (1984), 'Des désavantages relatifs à une mesure objective de la pauvreté' in Sarpellon, G. (ed.), *Understanding Poverty*, Milano, pp. 192-216.

Goedhart, T., Halberstadt, V., Kapteyn, A. and Van Praag, B. (1977), 'The poverty line: Concept and measurement', *The Journal of Human Resources*, vol. 12, no. 4, pp. 503-520.

Hagenaars, A. (1986), *The Perception of Poverty*, Amsterdam.

Hagenaars, A. (1987), 'A class of poverty indices', *International Economic Review*, vol. 28, pp. 299-231.

Hagenaars, A. and De Vos, K. (1988), 'The Definition and Measurement of Poverty', *The Journal of Human Resources*, vol. 23, no. 2, pp. 211-221.

Hauser, R. (1984), 'Some Problems in defining a poverty line for comparative studies' in Sarpellon, G. (ed.), *Understanding Poverty*, Milano.

Haveman, R. (1990), 'Poverty Statistics in the European Community: Assesment and recommendations' in Teekens, R. and Van Praag, B. (eds.), *Analysing Poverty in the European Community*, Eurostat News Special Edition, Luxembourg, pp. 459-467.

Jeandidier, B., Bigotte, M.-L. and Kerger, A. (1988), 'La mise en oeuvre, sur le terrain, de la notion de groupe de revenu en Lorraine et au Grand-Duché de Luxembourg', *Cahiers Economiques de Nancy*, no. 20, pp. 5-36.

Mack, J. and Lansley, S. (1985), *Poor Britain*, London.

Mayer, S. and Jencks, C. (1989), 'Poverty and the Distribution of Material Hardship', *The Journal of Human Resources*, vol. 24, no. 1, pp. 88-113.

Mitchell, D. (1991), *Income Transfers in Ten Welfare States*, Aldershot.

Muffels, R., De Vries, A. a.o. (1989), *Poverty in the Netherlands, first report of an international comparative study*, Tilburg.

O.E.C.D. (1976), *Public Expenditure on Income Maintenance Programmes.* Studies in Resource Allocation, Paris.

O.E.C.D. (1982), *The OECD list of social indicators*, Paris.

O'Higgins, M. and Jenkins, S. (1990), 'Poverty in the EC: estimates for 1975, 1980, 1985' in Teekens, R. and Van Praag, B. (eds.), *Analysing Poverty in the European Community*, Eurostat News Special Edition, Luxembourg, pp. 187-212.

Orshansky, M. (1969), 'How poverty is measured', *Monthly Labor Review*, pp. 37-41.

Ray, J.-C. (1989), 'Analyse fine des configurations de ménages dans l'E.S.E.M.L. 85. Vers un usage de la notion de groupe de revenu pour l'étude de la cohabitation', *Cahiers Economiques de Nancy*, no. 22, pp. 159-184.

Rein, M. (1970), 'Problems in the Definition and Measurement of Poverty' in Townsend, P. (ed.), *The Concept of Poverty*, London.

Roche, J. D. (1984), 'Methodological and data problems in inter-country comparisons of poverty in the European Community: an examination of possible problems to solutions' in Sarpellon, G. (ed.), *Understanding Poverty*, Milano.

Rowntree, Seebohm, B. and Lavers, G. (1951), *Poverty and the Welfare State: A third survey of York*, London.

Sarpellon, G. (1984), *Understanding Poverty*, Milano.

Sen, A. (1976), 'Poverty: an ordinal approach to measurement', *Econometrica*, vol. 44, pp. 219-231.

Townsend, P. (1979), *Poverty in the U.K.*, London.

Van Praag, B., Goedhart, Th. and Kapteyn, A. (1980), 'The poverty line - a pilot survey in Europe', *The Review of Economics and Statistics*, vol. 62, pp. 461-465.

Van Praag, B., Hagenaars, A. and Van Weeren, J. (1980), *Poverty in Europe*, Report to the Commission of the EC, University of Leyden.

Van Praag, B., Hagenaars, A. and Van Weeren, J. (1982), 'Poverty in Europe', *The Review of Income and Wealth*, vol. 28, pp. 345-359.

Whiteford, P. (1985), *A family's needs: equivalence scales, poverty and social security*, Research Paper nr. 27, DSS, Melbourne.

XXX (1974), *Five Thousand American Families - Patterns of Economic Progress*, vol. 1, Ann Arbor, Michigan.